Wedding Dress Across Cultures

Dress, Body, Culture

Series Editor **Joanne B. Eicher,** *Regents' Professor, University of Minnesota*

Books in this provocative series seek to articulate the connections between culture and dress which is defined here in its broadest possible sense as any modification or supplement to the body. Interdisciplinary in approach, the series highlights the dialogue between identity and dress, cosmetics, coiffure, and body alterations as manifested in practices as varied as plastic surgery, tattooing, and ritual scarification. The series aims, in particular, to analyze the meaning of dress in relation to popular culture and gender issues and will include works grounded in anthropology, sociology, history, art history, literature, and folklore.

ISSN: 1360-466X

Previously published titles in the Series

Helen Bradley Foster, *"New Raiments of Self": African American Clothing in the Antebellum South*

Claudine Griggs, *S/he: Changing Sex and Changing Clothes*

Michaele Thurgood Haynes, *Dressing Up Debutantes: Pageantry and Glitz in Texas*

Anne Brydon and Sandra Niessen, *Consuming Fashion: Adorning the Transnational Body*

Dani Cavallaro and Alexandra Warwick, *Fashioning the Frame: Boundaries, Dress and the Body*

Judith Perani and Norma H. Wolff, *Cloth, Dress and Art Patronage in Africa*

Linda B. Arthur, *Religion, Dress and the Body*

Paul Jobling, *Fashion Spreads: Word and Image in Fashion Photography*

Fadwa El-Guindi, *Veil: Modesty, Privacy and Resistance*

Thomas S. Abler, *Hinterland Warriors and Military Dress: European Empires and Exotic Uniforms*

Linda Welters, *Folk Dress in Europe and Anatolia: Beliefs about Protection and Fertility*

Kim K. P. Johnson and Sharron J. Lennon, *Appearance and Power*

Barbara Burman, *The Culture of Sewing*

Annette Lynch, *Dress, Gender and Cultural Change*

Antonia Young, *Women Who Become Men*

David Muggleton, *Inside Subculture: The Postmodern Meaning of Style*

Nicola White, *Reconstructing Italian Fashion: America and the Development of the Italian Fashion Industry*

Brian J. McVeigh, *Wearing Ideology: The Uniformity of Self-Presentation in Japan*

Shaun Cole, *Don We Now Our Gay Apparel: Gay Men's Dress in the Twentieth Century*

Kate Ince, *Orlan: Millennial Female*

Nicola White and Ian Griffiths, *The Fashion Business: Theory, Practice, Image*

Ali Guy, Eileen Green and Maura Banim, *Through the Wardrobe: Women's Relationships with their Clothes*

Linda B. Arthur, *Undressing Religion: Commitment and Conversion from a Cross-Cultural Perspective*

William J. F. Keenan, *Dressed to Impress: Looking the Part*

Joanne Entwistle and Elizabeth Wilson, *Body Dressing*

Leigh Summers, *Bound to Please: A History of the Victorian Corset*

Paul Hodkinson, *Goth: Identity, Style and Subculture*

Michael Carter, *Fashion Classics from Carlyle to Barthes*

Sandra Niessen, Ann Marie Leshkowich and Carla Jones, *Re-Orienting Fashion: The Globalization of Asian Dress*

Kim K. P. Johnson, Susan J. Torntore and Joanne B. Eicher, *Fashion Foundations: Early Writings on Fashion and Dress*

Wedding Dress Across Cultures

Edited by

Helen Bradley Foster
and
Donald Clay Johnson

Oxford • New York

First published in 2003 by
Berg
Editorial offices:
1st Floor, Angel Court, 81 St Clements Street, Oxford, OX4 1AW, UK
838 Broadway, Third Floor, New York, NY 10003-4812, USA

Berg is an imprint of Oxford International Publishers Ltd.

Library of Congress Cataloging-in-Publication Data
Wedding dress across cultures / edited by Helen Bradley Foster and
Donald Clay Johnson.
       p. cm. – (Dress, body, culture)
Includes bibliographical references and index.
    ISBN 1-85973-742-0 – ISBN 1-85973-747-1 (paper)
   1. Wedding costume–Cross-cultural studies. I. Foster, Helen Bradley.
II. Johnson, Donald Clay, 1940– III. Series.

   GT1752.W43 2003
   392.5′4—dc21

                2003010060

British Library Cataloguing-in-Publication Data
A catalogue record for this book is available from the British Library.

ISBN   1 85973 742 0 (Cloth)
       1 85973 747 1 (Paper)

Typeset by JS Typesetting Ltd, Wellingborough, Northants.
Printed in the United Kingdom by Biddles Ltd, Guildford and King's Lynn.

www.bergpublishers.com

Contents

List of Illustrations   vii

Contributors   ix

Introduction   1
Helen Bradley Foster and *Donald Clay Johnson*

1   Something Plain and Simple? Unpacking
Custom-made Wedding Dresses from Western
Canada (1950–1995)   5
Kathryn Church

2   Satin Dresses and Caribou Kamiks: Negotiation
of Tradition in Northern Alaskan Iñupiaq
Weddings   23
Cyd Martin

3   Packaged in Japan: Elite Weddings in Osaka   39
Masami Suga

4   Korean Wedding Dress from the Chosun Dynasty
(1392–1910) to the Present   53
Na Young Hong

5   Marriage and Dowry Customs of the Rabari of
Kutch: Evolving Traditions   67
Eiluned Edwards

6   Pragmatism and Enigmas: the Panetar and
Gharcholu Saris in Gujarati Weddings   85
Donald Clay Johnson

7   Swazi Bridal Attire: Culture, Traditions and
Customs   93
Lombusa S. Khoza and *Laura Kidd*

Contents

8   Gender, Identity and Moroccan Weddings: The
    Adornment of the Ait Khabbash Berber Bride
    and Groom   105
    Cynthia Becker

9   An Athenian Wedding, Year 2000   123
    Helen Bradley Foster

10 An Historic Perspective of English and Soviet
    Bridalwear between 1917 and 1960   141
    Janice Mee and Irina Safronova

11 He Gave her Sandals and She Gave Him a
    Tunic: Cloth and Weddings in the Andes   157
    Lynn A. Meisch

12 Slavic Wedding Customs on Two Continents   173
    Patricia Williams

13 Always Remembering the Motherland: Tai Dam
    Wedding Textiles and Dress   191
    Elyse Demaray and *Melody Keim-Shenk*

14 The American Groom wore a Celtic Kilt: Theme
    Weddings as Carnivalesque Events   207
    Theresa M. Winge and *Joanne B. Eicher*

Index   219

List of Illustrations

1.1 1958: eleven tiers of five-inch lace sewn onto a ballerina-length skirt, classic 1950s. 7

1.2 1975: the author's wedding suit in ivory gabardine, an early feminist statement. 11

1.3 1995: Lorraine's last wedding dress in ivory satin à la Princess Grace of Monaco. 12

2.1 Wedding in Valdez, Alaska, ca 1909. 30

2.2 Wedding in Wainwright, Alaska, 1921, ship's officer in fur clothing officiating. 31

2.3 Wedding in Anaktuvak Pass, Alaska, 1999, Harriet and Earl Williams. 32

2.4 Wedding in Anchorage, Alaska, 1999, Francine Hopson-Rochon and Frank Rochon. 33

4.1 The groom going to the bride's house for the wedding ceremony during the Chosun dynasty. 55

4.2 Traditional wedding ceremony during the Chosun dynasty. 56

4.3 The groom wears *samokwandae* and the bride wears *whalot* in the twentieth century. 60

4.4 The bride wears a white veil and a *hanbok* in a western-style wedding in 1930. 64

5.1 Vagadia Rabari (migratory group). 68

5.2 Dhebaria Rabari wedding, 1997. 69

5.3 A dowry instalment of a Vagadian Rabaran, ca 1955. 75

5.4 Vagadia Rabaran wearing one of her dowry veilcloths. 78

7.1 A Swazi woman in traditional bridal attire. 96

7.2 The outline of the *ligcebesha* necklace with one style of "love letter" pendant. 97

7.3 One modern style variation of *sidziya*. 100

7.4 A typical print-cloth *lihiya*. 101

8.1 A group of women surround the bride while she is dressed and henna applied to her hands. 108

8.2 A fully dressed Ait Khabbash bride. 109

8.3 The groom's family fills a tray with silver bracelets, an amber necklace, a red silk cloth and green and red tassels and presents this to the bride. 112

8.4 A groom covers his face with a women's red silk belt and white turban. 116

9.1 The priest leads the couple in the "Dance of Isaiah." 125

9.2 Commercial bridal shop, Pyrgos (Eleia), 2001. 127

9.3 Wedding dress of Katerina and Miltos. 130

9.4 Wedding dress of Miltos's maternal grandparents, Panayotis and Ephrosyni Apostolopoulos, Lidoriki, 1930. 131

10.1 Models of wedding dresses (1916). 144

10.2 Dresses for brides (1924). 147

10.3 Festive dresses (1939). 149

10.4 Festive dresses (1941). 153

11.1 The church marriage of the Inca Sayri Topa and his sister Beatris in Cuzco, Peru, AD 1558. 159

11.2 The sacrament of matrimony in the early colonial era, with the groom's dress showing considerable Spanish influence. 163

11.3 An Otavalo wedding in 1935 with the bride in *chola* dress and the groom wearing a checked *ikat* poncho. 166

11.4 Luz Quizhpe and Jaime de la Torre at their wedding reception in Ilumán (Otavalo valley), Imbabura, Ecuador, June 1998. 168

12.1 Removing the bride's floral headdress, 1992. 178

12.2 Village matrons "capping" the bride, 1992. 179

12.3 Bridesmaid removing the bride's veil, 1964, Chicago area. 185

12.4 Tying the apron, 1964, Chicago area. 186

13.1 Components of "traditional" Tai Dam women's dress in Northwest Vietnam prior to 1954. 193

13.2 Sisters Sack and Chap Baccam with a "dragon tail" or *maa koon* at a New Year's celebration in Des Moines, Iowa, January 2001. 196

13.3 A wedding blanket or *faa* made in the United States using fabric from Laos for the center panel. 198

13.4 An example of the embroidered black scarf or *piav* made by the bride and given to her mother-in-law and other female relatives. 199

Contributors

Cynthia Becker is Assistant Professor of Art History at the University of St. Thomas. Her research on Berber arts in Morocco explores the interrelationship between identity, gender, and ethnicity. Other research interests include the influence of the trans-Saharan slave trade on arts and culture in Morocco, with particular focus on the Afro-Islamic aesthetics and ceremonial practices of the Gnawa.

Kathryn Church is Research Associate for the Ryerson-RBC Foundation Institute for Disability Studies Research and Education at Ryerson University, Toronto, Canada. Her work attempts to make invisible histories visible through the use of autobiographical research methods and alternative forms of representation including first-person narratives. From 1999 to 2001, Church was guest curator of the award-winning exhibit entitled "Fabrications: Stitching Ourselves Together" installed in seven Canadian museums.

Elyse Demaray studied Tai Dam textiles and dress as a part of her M.S. coursework in the Textiles and Clothing department at Iowa State University. Her interests center on how people establish identity and create symbolic meanings through textiles and dress in other countries as well as in the United States. Prior to her degree in textiles and clothing (2001) she received a PhD in English and Women's Studies at Indiana University (1996).

Joanne B. Eicher, Regents' Professor at the University of Minnesota, has expertise on dress as nonverbal communication, especially African and Asian, with fieldwork on dress and textiles of the Kalabari people of Nigeria. Her current research focuses on dress of Hmong and Somali immigrants and refugees in Minnesota. She co-authored *The Visible Self: Global Perspectives on Dress* (2000), edited *Dress and Ethnicity* (1995), co-edited *Beads and Beadmakers*, (1998) and *Dress and Identity* (1995), serves as "Dress, Body, Culture" Series Editor for Berg Publishers, and, wrote the introduction to *National Geographic Fashion* (2001).

Eiluned Edwards is a research fellow in Textiles and Dress at PRASADA (Practice, Research and Advancement in South Asian Design and Architecture) at De Montfort University, Leicester, England. She has done extensive field research on the textiles of Kutch and Gujarat and has worked closely with a number of communities including the nomadic Rabaris, Vankars and Khatris. Her current research, funded by the British Academy, focuses on the commoditization of dowry embroidery and the significance of cloth in India.

Helen Bradley Foster received her PhD from the Department of Folklore and Folklife, University of Pennsylvania. She teaches at the University of Minnesota and the College of Visual Arts, St. Paul. Foster has authored *"New Raiments of Self": African American Clothing in the Antebellum South* (1994) and articles on African American, American, and Greek material culture.

Na Young Hong is Associate Professor of Clothing and Textiles at Ewha Womans University, Seoul, Korea. She teaches and does research on the history of Korean costume and Asian folk dress. Her special research interests are Chinese influences on traditional Korean costume, historical changes of Korean costume design, and the westernization of Asian dress.

Donald Clay Johnson is the Curator of the Ames Library of South Asia of the University of Minnesota. He actively lectures on the history of Indian textiles. In 2000 he published *Agile Hands and Creative Minds: A Bibliography of the Textile Traditions of Afghanistan, Bangladesh, Bhutan, India, Nepal, Pakistan, and Sri Lanka.*

Melody Keim-Shenk earned a Master's degree in Textiles and Clothing from Iowa State University in 2001. Her current research interests focus on tourist art, alternative trading organizations (ATOs), cultural change and identity. She worked for many years with Ten Thousand Villages, an ATO that markets handicrafts in the US and Canada from over 30 countries around the world.

Lombuso S. Khoza was a lecturer at the University of Swaziland and has Master Degrees from the University of California-Davis and Leeds University, UK. She currently is a PhD student at Southern Illinois University, Carbondale, Illinois.

Laura Kidd is an Associate Professor in the Fashion Design & Merchandising Program at Southern Illinois University at Carbondale. She received her PhD from Iowa State University and her teaching and research interests include western and ethnic costume, fashion design and construction. She is a contributor to Scribner's *Encyclopedia of Modern Asia*.

Cyd Martin is a cultural anthropologist and Chief of the Office of American Indian Trust Responsibilities for the Intermountain Region of the National Park Service. She received her PhD from the University of Alaska, Fairbanks in 2001; her dissertation research focused on the negotiation of identity and tradition through contemporary Iñupiaq clothing in northern Alaska.

Janice Mee is the Programme Leader for Contour Fashion at De Montfort University, Leicester, England, and actively lectured and published on lingerie with specialities on the corset and the bra. With Michael Purdy she produced *Modelling on the Dress Stand* (1987) and subsequently published it as a book. She has organized exhibitions on numerous aspects of fashion.

Lynn A. Meisch has conducted fieldwork in Colombia, Ecuador, Peru and Bolivia since 1973, and published on *artesanías*, traditional Andean textiles, costume and ethnicity, globalization, gender and tourism, the indigenous rights movement, and the prevention of intractable interethnic violence in Ecuador. She received her PhD from Stanford University in 1997 and is currently an Associate Professor of Anthropology at Saint Mary's College of California.

Irina Nikolaevna Safronova graduated from the St. Petersburg State Art and Industrial Academy and is the Head of the Department of Costume Design of the St. Petersburg State University of Technology and Design. She designs theatrical costumes. She and Janice Mee organized the exhibition "Princess for a Day?" which compared English and Soviet wedding dress, 1917–1990.

Masami Suga is originally from Osaka, Japan. She conducted research on a Hmong sewer for her M.A., published a chapter on the Japanese royal wedding, and earned a PhD from the Design, Housing, and Apparel Department of the University of Minnesota.

Patricia Williams, a Professor at the University of Wisconsin–Stevens Point, conducted research in the Czech Republic and Slovakia in 1992 and 1995 and received her PhD from Leeds University. Her teaching and research interests include symbolism in architecture and textiles, non-Western material culture and immigrant culture in the United States. Williams' recent work has appeared in *Folk Dress in Europe and Anatolia* and in *Dress*.

Theresa M. Winge is completing a PhD on subcultural dress in the Design, Housing, and Apparel Department of the University of Minnesota. She also did advanced academic study on urban subcultures and in chaos theory. She uses her diverse educational and practical experience, along with an interest in sustainable design, to produce one-of-a-kind fashions for presentation in juried fashion exhibitions, both on runways and in galleries.

Introduction

This book highlights the specific and varying status of wedding dress practices across the globe, covering five continents: Africa, Asia, Europe, North America and South America. The impressive diversity of contexts emphasizes the logic and rationale behind the choice of wedding attire in a range of local settings. Although great variety appears among the social groups discussed, the essays also identify many common themes and concerns.

Dress serves as one of the most important markers of cultural identity (Barnes and Eicher, 1992). The term "dress" as used in this volume means more than clothing; it also encompasses modifications of the body (hair, skin, nails, etc.) and body supplements (enclosures, attachments and hand-held objects) (Eicher and Roach-Higgins, 1992). Perhaps the most visible and telling of dress modes are wedding garments, the choice of which makes a statement by showing comparative prestige, wealth or perceived status. Part of cultural tradition, it changes only in modest increments. In a larger sense, wedding dress forms a complex set of interlocking relationships that tie a society together as it unites a couple in marriage.

The essays show that while this particular form of dress is under threat through modern, global communication and loss of certain traditions, it simultaneously proves to be highly adaptable and deeply cherished. The authors use dress as the means by which to explore the interaction between two people and the societal mores imposed on the couple by the retention of older customs that often intertwine with the adaptation of newer fashions from other cultures. The contributors' different approaches reflect the diverse disciplinary training and methodologies that encompass anthropology, apparel design, art history, folklore, history, and women's studies. These various disciplines enrich the work with their enhanced viewpoints and document that no single academic approach can claim wedding attire as its exclusive purview. In spite of their intellectual approach, the authors avoid academic jargon and foreign words that are not directly related to dress, making the topic available to a wide reading audience.

The book discusses the dress of both the bride and the groom; but the essays show that in many societies, the bride's dress links more closely to cultural tradition than does the groom's. One reason for this appears to be women's long established link to the production of cloth and clothing. Further accounting for this, of course, are women's roles as childbearers which thus keep families and the larger community developing. The obvious fact that women's roles change most after marriage also helps explain the prominence of the bride's dress.

Although the essays discuss a variety of cultural uses and meanings for bridalwear, they also demonstrate intriguing commonalties. For instance, many societies require the bride to wear aprotropaic items. The Berber bride of Morocco is in public at her wedding, but her body is totally covered to prevent effects of the evil eye (Cynthia Becker). The bridal head veil, that also provides protection from the evil eye, is a common object of dress in many traditions; in Russia, another way for the bride to avoid contamination is for her to wear gloves to avoid touching anything that may contain evil. The comparison of wedding attire during the first half of the twentieth century in England and the former Soviet Union documents commonalties on either side of the Iron Curtain (Janice Mee and Irina Safronova).

Symbolism of color in the bride's wedding dress seems almost universal. In Europe and North America, white, symbolizing "purity," remains the preferred color, a reflection of the pervasive power of English Victorian society to impose its value system throughout many parts of the world. Color, however, also may be used to mark the bride's new status. For instance, among the Gujarati of India, the reverse color proportions of red and white from the sari of the natal family to that of the sari given by the groom's family documents the transition into married life (Donald Clay Johnson).

Each of these studies confirms that although the term 'tradition' assumes customs are static, they are, in fact, constantly evolving to reflect the changing goals and values of a society. Use of "tradition" simply signals a notion of what the societal norms were at an earlier time and the use of the word represents the attempt to honor the spirit of those norms rather than a strict retention of the actual style of dress worn in the past. Society in Swaziland, southern Africa, for example, did not receive notable outside cultural influences until its independence in 1968 and, thus, its wedding attire remains focused upon traditional dress (Khoza Lobbuso and Laura K. Kidd). Although the white, western wedding gown received widespread adoption around the world during the twentieth century, the essays on Korea (Na Young Hong) and on the Iñupiaq of Alaska (Cyd Martin) each discuss a return to earlier, pre-Victorian wedding dress as the new millenium approached. In a similar manner, residual elements of much earlier Inca wedding traditions have been revived during a time of rapid cultural change and receive attention in the chapter on wedding dress in Bolivia, Ecuador and Peru (Lynn A. Meisch). In Greece, where much of the urban population retains strong ties to its rural origins, many wedding customs conserve rural elements and thus its values (Helen Bradley Foster).

In numerous societies, the wedding couple still dress in attire that originated in a remote past in order to meet cultural hopes and expectations, but these older dress styles frequently have no relationship to contemporary daily fashion. This grasp of the past, nevertheless, sometimes allows the bride or the groom opportunities to alter, enhance, or to suppress portions of their seemingly "traditional" dress. The motivation for these actions, in part, may reflect current societal values or the individuals' personal tastes; but the choice of what the wedding couple wears follows the spirit of their cultural traditions and worldview. From this vantage point, in Osaka, Japan, modern packaging of weddings fits into the larger theoretical perspective of the Japanese desire to analyze, to compartmentalize, and to produce a unified whole from numerous sub-parts (Masami Suga). Further exploration of the ongoing evolution is presented in two essays that document the changes that intercontinental immigrations to the United States have had on wedding dress customs for the Tai Dam from Vietnam to Des Moines, Iowa (Elyse Damaray and Melody Keim-Shenk) and the Czechs and Slovaks from eastern Europe to Chicago, Illinois (Patricia Williams).

The contrast between what the bride wishes to wear and what the greater community will accept receives insightful discussion in two chapters. Exploration is made of what is considered appropriate bridal attire in rural, western Canada during the last half of the twentieth century (Kathryn Church) and the effects of the edict of the ruling Rabadi council of Gujarat, India, that prohibited embroidered dowry pieces is discussed (Eilund Edwards). These two studies sharply contrast with the absolute freedom of expression allowed to American couples who develop theme weddings, a recent phenomenon, in which both bride and groom exhibit profound distance from societal norms (Theresa Winge and Joanne B. Eicher).

Of late, an increased interest in wedding dress has been coming to the fore. In her 1999 book, for example, Chrys Ingraham deals with western culture's continuing obsession with the white wedding dress. As well as its prominence in western culture, many of our authors still find this style in remote places, but they also discuss current changing nuances in wedding attire wherein white is being replaced by what is considered to be more traditional to the cultures examined. While not dealing specifically with dress, Wendy Leeds-Hurwitz draws from case studies to explore and analyse inter-faith weddings and what customs will be retained or negotiated between the couple (2002). In contrast, our book concentrates on wedding dress in several faiths, but each author writes about a defined group in which the couple shares the same religious beliefs. Another example of the current interest in wedding dress is on permanent display at the Seattle Art Museum, where a Masai bride's dress from Kenya was assembled by Kakuta Hamissi. Included in the exhibition is detailed explanation of how the women of the bride's community assembled her outfit. These recent examples merely touch upon what is available on the topic, but they clearly demonstrate that wedding dress has become an important popular and intellectual focus as we seek to understand other peoples of our world.

The genesis for this book, in fact, derived from the keynote panel of the 1999 Ars Textrina Conference, held at the University of Minnesota. The papers dealt with wedding dress in Osaka, Japan (Masami Suga); in Gujarat, India (Donald Clay Johnson); in Morocco (Lotus Stack) and in the United States (Colleen Kahn). Expanded versions of the first two papers appear in this volume. Following the conference, Joanne Eicher, General Editor of Berg's 'Dress, Body, Culture' series, asked Johnson and Foster to co-edit a book on wedding dress around the world – one that would present another slant on the topic.

The chapters in this volume introduce complex sets of symbolic values found in all weddings. Every essay describes, discusses and analyses the specific wedding dress found in disparate social groups. In their collectivity, however, they point out not only the differences but the commonalties in wedding dress customs inherent to this universal rite of passage.

References

Barnes, Ruth and Joanne B. Eicher, (1992), "Introduction," in *Dress and Gender: Making and Meaning in Cultural Contexts,* Oxford: Berg, pp. 1–7.

Eicher, Joanne B. and Mary Ellen Roach-Higgins (1992), "Definition and Classification of Dress: Implications for Analysis of Gender Roles," in Ruth Barnes and Joanne B. Eicher (eds), *Dress and Gender: Making and Meaning,* Oxford: Berg, pp. 8–22.

Ingraham, Chrys (1999), *White Weddings: Romancing Heterosexuality in Popular Culture,* Routledge: New York and London.

Leeds-Hurwitz, Wendy (2002), *Wedding as Text: Communicating Cultural Identity Through Ritual,* New Jersey and London: Lawrence Erlbaum Associates.

1

Something Plain and Simple? Unpacking Custom-made Wedding Dresses from Western Canada (1950–1995)

Kathryn Church

From 1950 to 1995, my mother, Lorraine, constructed wedding dresses for twenty-two women living in rural Alberta, Canada. I retrieved the dresses from their owners for an exhibit entitled *Fabrications: stitching ourselves together* (Church, online; Church, 1997; Church and Martindale, 1999; Church, 2002), which was also a sociological analysis of them.[1] The meanings of these garments to the women who designed and wore them reveal the values and beliefs of the culture that literally gave them shape.

Entry Points

I came to the study of wedding dresses as a daughter. The *Fabrications* project was my way of bridging the gap that distance, time and education had put between my mother and me. I used it to come to terms, intellectually and emotionally, with her skilled domestic labor, and the place this labor did or did not make for her in the world. As the exhibit developed, I became increasingly aware of the actual objects that Mom had created – her reality. One by one, out of boxes, trunks and closets, the wedding dresses came home to her. Each had its own story and impact. I remember Mom's tears, for example, upon rediscovering forty hand-covered buttons that march down the back of the first wedding dress she ever sewed – buttons made with curiosity and optimism by the hands of an inexperienced, young woman.

Two of the women for whom my mother made bridal dresses lived with her before she herself married. Two others worked with my father, ten years apart and in different offices. A woman who initially came to Mom for a brides-maid's dress returned the following year for a wedding dress. Twenty years later, before this same woman died of cancer, her daughter sought out my mother for the same reason.

Mom made wedding dresses for two sets of sisters who grew up in her neighbourhood, including the red-haired, freckle-faced best friend of my childhood. Other brides were members of our church or babysitters. Two women considered our house their second home; one actually lived with my parents for a time. My three brothers faithfully brought prospective wives to be outfitted; the eldest brought two brides about fifteen years apart. One bride was a family friend who married my cousin; another bride was a transient younger cousin who came at the urging of my grandmother.

But the memories evoked are not solely of people. The dresses also connect me to the house in which I grew up, the streets I roamed with amazing physical freedom as a girl, the small town that was the centre of my world, and the landscape itself: its endless sky and daunting extremes of weather.

Situating the dresses

A strange place it was, that place where the world began. A place of incredible happenings, splendours and revelations, despairs like multitudinous pits of isolated hells . . . A place of jubilation and mourning, horrible and beautiful.
It was, in fact, a small prairie town . . .

Margaret Laurence, *Where the World Began*, 1976

The first three dresses in the *Fabrications* exhibit belong to my grandmother (1928), my mother (1951) and myself (1975). Made by her mother and thus part of our sewing lineage, Grandma had a bright turquoise flapper dress. It is one of only three dresses in the exhibit that feature colors: the other two feature, respectively, a soft blue print, and solid bright yellow. Mom's dress has a full circle skirt made of elegant white lace. Two other 1950s dresses and one from the 1990s share a similar mid-calf, "ballroom" length (Figure 1.1). The rest are full-length formals. Mine is an ivory-colored three-piece suit; its original hemline later shortened to street-length. There are several other ivory or off-white dresses in the collection but the shifts in hue are subtle. Thus, for the most part, the exhibit visitor sees clusters of mannequins dressed in long

Figure 1.1 1958: eleven tiers of five-inch lace sewn onto a ballerina-length net
skirt, classic 1950s. Photograph: Gail Handley.

white(ish) gowns.[2] Although the accompanying text panels point to a rich
array of stories, the dresses themselves are stylistically uncomplicated. Why
do they look this way? The answer takes me back home.

Alberta is one of Canada's three western, prairie provinces. My town,
Lacombe, is located midway between the provincial capital of Edmonton and
its more southerly rival, the stampede city of Calgary. Boasting a current

population of 8,500, Lacombe, a farming community now relies increasingly on its oil and gas resources. Historical home of the Blackfoot and the Cree Indians, the first Europeans to arrive were male fur traders, trappers and bull train drivers. The latter piloted their carts along a wagon trail that opened the way for pioneers who came to bring the land into production.

The first white settler, Ed Barnett, received land in 1883 because of his service to the Northwestern Mounted Police. Ed's sister-in-law was the first white woman in the area, the only one to come out prior to the completion of the Calgary and Edmonton Trail.[3] These early settlers, most from eastern Ontario and the United States, were joined by a flood of others arriving after the completion of the railway in 1891. All were drawn by the promise of land. In 1896, when "Barnett's Siding" officially became a village, it was renamed in honor of the "great and fearless" Father Albert Lacombe, a Jesuit missionary who worked for peace on the Alberta frontier. The town was in the heart of his mission field (Lacombe and District Chamber of Commerce, 1982: 1–5, 13–25).

According to G. Laird, commerce and evangelism were the two founding activities of Europeans in Canada (1998: 3–18). In that sense, the history I have just recounted mirrors a more general pattern. At the same time, he identifies Alberta as the cultural heart of the country's "right wing revolution." Governed for decades by former Baptist clergy, the province was the birthplace of Social Credit, a movement and a political party that "took its message and style straight from biblical teachings of imminent apocalypse" (Laird, 1998: 42). More recently, it fostered the emergence of the Reform Party with its commitment to private property and family values: procreation, stay-at-home mothers, heterosexuality, and the nuclear family. Years after the passing of its pioneer generations, Alberta's political and social leaders continue to pursue a frontier fantasy: "happy white folks breeding, toiling, and building civilization in the face of sin, savagery and urban corruption" (Laird, 1998: 107).

The brides my mother dressed were shaped by this milieu. Married young, they currently range in age from their mid-thirties to their early seventies. Raising children has been and continues to be a primary occupation, even among the grandmothers. To that they have added other jobs: farming, nursing, teaching, secretarial work, and advertising. One woman established and ran dance studios while raising goats in her spare time; another drove rig trucks. One woman ran a beauty salon; another decorated cakes at the local grocery store. Three of the wedding dresses my mother sewed were for second marriages. Six of the brides she sent down the aisle later separated from their husbands or were divorced; two were widowed.

The lives of these women span significant social, economic and technological change. The Depression, World War II, and post-war suburban development influenced the early brides who aspired to model family relationships in keeping with the popular American television show, "Leave It to Beaver." A later group grew up exposed to the ideals of the 1960s: flower children, hippies, Woodstock, folksingers, equality, peace, harmony, sex, drugs, and, rock and roll. The 1970s brides remember extravagant big sleeves and bell-bottoms. Through this decade and the 1980s they felt the impact of Women's Liberation, the Pill and controversies over keeping one's maiden name after marriage. The 1990s ushered in a small group of second-time brides.

Sensitivity to Context

One of the chief considerations for a bride in the selection of her dress is the audience she anticipates, real or imagined (Friese, 1997). My mother's brides were certainly sensitive in this way. Expressing a general sentiment, one of them noted she was "very aware of other people's expectations about how I should look. I felt I had to take that into consideration." Said another, "I was very conscious of wanting to look nice for other people, of choosing styles to please other people."[4]

Asked whether their mothers had in any way influenced the look or style of the dress, the brides invariably said "no." The mothers of these women deliberately took a hands-off approach to their daughters' weddings. In spite of that, with their dresses, the brides attempted to present their mothers with womanly images of themselves that were locally appropriate. One bride recalled: "I am an only daughter and I felt my mother's expectations keenly." Another pointed out that her mother, now deceased, "got to see me in a long white wedding dress that wasn't too showy. I think she was happy about that."

Beginning in the 1970s a number of the brides fantasized about getting married in blue jeans. They resisted the impulse, however, because of an important second audience: family members. Again, it was a question of other people's happiness. Said one bride: "I would have been married in boots and faded blue jeans but I didn't have the guts to do that. I wanted acceptance from my grandparents. I walked a fine line between what I wanted for myself and what I wanted for them." Another was at odds with her family's understanding of women's roles. Still, she felt bound to her father and brothers in such a way that she could not risk using her wedding dress to declare her disagreement, "I wasn't going to choose anything provocative because I was concerned how my family would see me. My dad's philosophy was that a woman's place was to do the washing, ironing, the dishes, and cleaning. That was our job. That is why we were created. According to that standard I was already deviant."

Often entwined with feeling about the family, the church was a major concern. Churches were among the first institutions to be established in prairie towns. In a varied array of denominations, their buildings continue to dot the landscape. Religion was a factor in the choices that a number of brides made about their weddings and their dresses. "We were married on a Friday," remembered one woman, "so that the church could be cleaned and ready for the Sabbath. That was out of respect for God's day and those who have to prepare for it."

If the bride's beliefs were congruent with church doctrine and practice, all was well, but if she questioned or was in conflict with them, things were more difficult. Having been in this position myself, I had great empathy for a bride who explained that, "Coming alive sexually meant coming into conflict with religion in my life. The church must have been in my thoughts in a big way. If there had been no connection there, my choices would have been different." How did this translate into the style of her dress? "You just didn't dress with cleavage. It would have been frowned upon," she explained.

Prairie towns retain a healthy respect for conservatism. As a second-time bride noted, "You are always worried about what other people will think instead of doing what you want." While claiming that people should live their own lives, she was "scared of what people would think of me choosing a traditional white dress. I was really worried at the time." In order to transgress traditional expectations about the wedding dress, then, the bride needed to keep in mind a different audience, presumably another group of women. My ivory suit was not far off the norm but even that tiny break with tradition was possible only with my exposure to a university-based feminist community (Figure 1.2).

The pressure to conform to local standards was most obvious in bridal deliberations over color. "In my day," recounted one bride, "because of the purity, virginity thing, traditional white was IT." Other ways of signaling that you were not a virgin included the absence of a church wedding or the decision not to wear a veil. "Now, people don't really distinguish like that. Back then there was no option," commented another. As a result of significant changes in color coding over the past few decades, more recent brides did have more choices. They could, for example, afford to be more interested in aesthetics (i.e. looking better in off-white) than in the opinions of the neighbours (Figure 1.3).

For the most part, however, my mother's brides held to relatively narrow conventions. "I didn't consider anything but white," said one, voicing the general opinion of the group. "I could have picked ivory but anything else would have been a problem. My mother is very traditional and she would have had a fit!" Another bride simply sensed that her mother "would have been upset if I had gone with a color." A third knew she would have looked nicer

Figure 1.2 1975: the author's wedding suit in ivory gabardine, an early feminist statement. Photograph: Gail Handley.

in off-white but did not choose it. For her, white was so synonymous with wedding dresses that other options never crossed her mind.

Practices of Revealing and Concealing

Sociologist Chrys Ingraham positions her book as "one of the first in-depth examinations of weddings in American culture" (1999: 3). *White Weddings*

Figure 1.3 1995: Lorraine's last wedding dress in ivory satin à la Princess Grace of Monaco. Photograph: Gail Handley.

is a materialist feminist analysis of the "wedding industrial complex" that addresses issues of commodification, accumulation and labor as well as secondary and tertiary markets. The wedding, she argues, is "one of heteosexuality's key organizing rituals" (14). "This romance with wedding culture works ideologically to naturalize the regulation of sexuality through the institution of marriage, providing images or representations of reality that mask the historical and material conditions of life (14). Ingraham pursues the "hetero-sexual imaginary" through wedding-related print, film and television materials in an attempt to trace its consequences for gender, race, class, and sexuality in American culture.

Without a doubt, the forces that Ingraham traces so carefully had an impact on my mother's brides. I would argue, however, that even though these women selected traditional white dress, because they deliberately stepped out of mainstream relations of dress production, they were far from passive recipients of ideological regulation. Mixing and matching pieces from graded patterns or inspired by pictures in magazines, they worked closely with my mother to design their dream dress.[5] In the process, they actively negotiated with the "heterosexual imaginary," taking on major issues of body and self-presentation through conscious practices of revealing and concealing.

In a study conducted in mid-western American bridal salons, Susanne Friese found that prospective brides chose a particular dress because when they put it on they felt suddenly transformed – as if by magic (1997). My mother's brides felt this way too but having been deeply involved in dress construction, they understood the structure of that magic. They favored features that flattered their bodies. "I didn't want the dress to just look good, I wanted it to look GREAT!" exclaimed one. Or, as another put it, "I wanted something that would be attractive on me for the one day in my life when people would look at me more than ever before." The choice of styles reflected this concern, not just for themselves but for all of the women in their wedding party. "I picked a style that enhances the figure of a lot of people," recalled one. "Whether you are fat or slim, big busted or small busted it makes you look good."

For my mother's brides, "attractive" is a code word for slender. "I have a small waist and am a tiny person," asserted one. "If a woman has a nice slender waistline and she can wear something slender and wonderful, why not?" Why not, indeed? Brides who were confident about their weight chose styles that celebrated slim bodies. "I wanted a style that showed off my waist," stated one, echoing the sentiments of several others. "I wanted that waistline cinched in, very well-fitted." Another bride felt her body would have sustained any style that she chose. She picked one that emphasized her breasts. A third insisted on a sweetheart neckline, giving her wedding guests a glimpse of ripe cleavage in a dress that otherwise suggested nun-like chastity.

Some women retained the traditional color codes in order to reveal aspects of their sexual history. A first-time bride told me she would have felt uncom-fortably hypocritical in white. She chose off-white specifically because she was not a virgin. "I consciously thought that through," she explained. "It had to do with having lived with men before my marriage. That spoiled the whiteness option. White was out." In a similar manner, a second-time bride saw white as inappropriate, "I did not want for one minute anyone to think I wasn't aware of my past," she declared firmly. "To use white is a little bold. I wanted a traditional dress in off-white to indicate that I have a past."

In choosing the style and color of their dresses, however, relevation was only part of what the brides had to consider. Concealment was also important. A pointed example: several brides deliberately retained traditional color codes to send a false signal about themselves. They used their knowledge of family, church and community expectations to give their sexuality some privacy. "If I had thought about cream there would have been questions raised as to why," explained one. "What are you trying to tell us? I wasn't about to share my private life with anybody." Her white dress hid a self she believed others would have judged inappropriate. "I was trying to portray the goodie-goodie girl who went to church and youth group. I was still buying into all of that. I wasn't celebrating who I really was. I should have let my hair go all over the place. I regret that."

Women who thought of themselves as overweight avoided full skirts, binding waists and ornamentation. Instead, they chose Empire waists and A-line skirts made up in soft fabrics. Body weight remains a concern for many of these women. Being slim is seen as inherent to femininity. "Back then I needed all the help I could get with my weight. Now I'm happy to say the dress is really big on me," one declared triumphantly. Thus, using the dress as a marker, these women continue a dialogue with the bodies that they inhabited before they were altered by age and/or childbirth.

The element of disguise was at work on other body parts and features as well. One bride chose a high neck with a fair amount of detail because she was very "small on top" and wanted to distract people from her (absence of) bosom. Several brides perceived themselves as unusually short. Long dresses were particularly important to them as, unbroken from collar to floor, they conveyed an impression of height. A bride who was far from elderly still thought of herself that way, at least by the standards of rural communities at the time. To compensate, the bright dress she helped to construct suggested youth.

Getting it Right

The revealing/concealing I have just described is an integral part of being female in rural Canada. Expert in these practices, my mother's brides used them to create a look highly appropriate to their prairie place. The two primary qualities of this look are: (1) modest sexuality, and, (2) low-maintenance femininity.

Modest Sexuality

C. Luchetti's fascinating 1996 account of courtship, love and marriage on the American frontier from 1715 to 1915 documents two centuries of physical mobility that led to fractured family structures, cultural values, courting habits, and patterns of domesticity. In their westward migration, women broke free of parental discipline, church hegemony and mid-Victorian moralism. They increased their independence through women's suffrage, newly available contraceptive devices and fast, inexpensive divorce. As they did so, there was a loosening of fashion, a setting aside of skirts and bonnets for "pants, hats and pistols" (1996: 54). Although these shifts took place several generations ago, in the era of my foremothers, they live on as a significant part of my own heritage.

This shift is a significant part of my own heritage and of the brides whom my mother dressed. As contemporary western women, we value informal, comfortable clothing. These qualities were a major part of what my mother's brides achieved through their design experiments with her. In spite of that, none of us escaped the moralistic forces of our own day in the way suggested by Luchetti's description of our adventuring foremothers. As is already obvious, an unresolved anxiety about women's bodies and sexual purity is threaded through the activities of creating bridal dress.

Twenty-five years after her wedding, one bride wondered why she had not shown off her "lovely figure" a little more. "Why wouldn't I have gone with something more form-fitting? That was when I looked my best. I couldn't have been mature about the way I looked at my body. There were all of these inhibitions, the insecurity about your body." For another bride, that insecurity was so deep it verged on self-loathing and it continued into her mature years. "The dress was supposed to be low in the back," she told me. "I had Lorraine change it. I didn't want something open. I don't like showing too much, and I didn't want something tight-fitting. I am so self-conscious of my body, always have been."

A standard of female modesty was deeply internalized by my mother's brides. They wanted to be attractive but needed to be subtle about their bodies, especially about their sexuality. "I chose a plain style because I didn't want to draw attention to my body," noted one. "I wanted femininity but not a sexual femininity. I may have thought to present my body in a way that was complimentary rather than sensual, or sensual through very conservative means."

Balancing these qualities is a big part of being a proper woman in central Alberta. As one bride explained, it was important to look nice but also to blend in. "To me that's what a woman is about. I am not one of those people who says, hey, look at me! You want to say you are there but you don't need to shout it. Sometimes less is more." The implicit instruction, as one bride put it, was to "Cover up! Cover up!" Otherwise, you risked gaining a reputation for bad taste or loose morals. Becoming a wife and the new relationship to a husband are also part of this dynamic. "What I've got belongs to him," one bride declared, "and doesn't need to be displayed to the whole wedding. I am his bride as of today. I want him to be proud of me and not embarrassed that I am showing too much chest or too much leg, to be seen to be flaunting it."

Low-Maintenance Femininity

By "low-maintenance femininity" I mean the brisk, no-fuss, no-nonsense style that characterizes the identity share by many western women. It is most visible in my mother's brides' insistence on wedding dresses that were plain and simple: no ruffles, frills, fullness, layers, poofs, ribbons, beading or fancy stuff. This theme emerged quickly and remained strong in my interviews with these women. For a variety of reasons, some brides had only a short time to prepare. "We kept the dress simple," said one, "because there wasn't a great deal of time before the wedding and I have too many kids for anything complex!" But that wasn't the primary reason: most of the brides simply saw themselves as plain and simple women.

By "simple," however, the brides did not mean simplistic. One woman carefully pointed out the difference between "peasant," which was acceptable and "bumpkin," which was not. "I was going for a more causal look," she explained. "I didn't want it really formal because that wouldn't fit into our rural setting. I didn't want a train because there is too much dirt on the farm. At the same time, it wasn't in vogue to be too rural." This bride and others like her were attempting to create a kind of sophistication appropriate to their surroundings. They wanted an elegance of style befitting open spaces and an informal western lifestyle.

Many achieved these blends by focusing on fabric. At a time when all of her peers were using satin and brocade, for example, one bride chose a non-traditional crepe. To her, this informality was more in keeping with the spirit of her whole wedding. Another chose a plain fabric that had a lovely texture and richness. For these women, elegance was skin deep, a matter of touch as well as cut and fit. One bride summed it up for me: "The styling was simple so that I could accentuate the type and quality of fabric. Mine was real bridal satin; my bridesmaids were cut velvet. Some people are taken by elaborate style. I like the style simple and will pay top dollar for high quality fabric." Other brides concurred. As a group, they appreciated and were attuned to subtlety.

In keeping with their settler heritage, Mom's brides came from families that believed in hard work, self-sufficiency and the value of a dollar. Keeping the dress simple also reduced its cost. One told me proudly that her fabric cost twenty dollars while the lace, a big splurge, was another twenty. "A forty dollar dress!" she exclaimed. "I hope you are impressed." And I was. Just as I was impressed with myself when Mom and I paid twenty-three dollars for the gabardine to make my wedding outfit and then splurged on a broad-brimmed hat that cost seven dollars. A thirty-dollar suit![6]

Expensive weddings were simply not congruent with small-town culture. "To be able to say that I had a ten-thousand dollar wedding would be just ludicrous," declared one bride. "To be able to say that I had a pretty wedding with my friends and we had a good time and that I did that all very inexpensively is more like it! It is not that I am cheap. To have something left over to give to my family or friends or to have for a rainy day, is more important than to have a big show for today and then pay for it."

The older women were conditioned by knowledge of scarcity in hard times. Born in the Depression, one remembered that, "You made do with what you had and you used it several times. We didn't have running water for years. You used water to have a bath; you might reheat it and use it for scrubbing the floor." Just prior to their weddings, a number of the more recent brides were putting themselves through post-secondary job training. They were working with modest expectations on small budgets, covering a lot of the wedding expenses themselves. "We weren't big spenders," one bride explained. "We weren't thinking borrow and pay it back. We didn't want things to get out of hand cost-wise." Good wives were expected to be good money managers, a point made by another bride who was practicing to be frugal: "I wanted to save as much on everything as I could. You are just starting off in a new marriage and getting to know the guy. Mine was a plain western kind of man. I was a typical new bride trying to appeal to a new husband."

Narratives of the Self

One of the most startling revelations of C. Ingraham's recent study appears in the epilogue where she confesses the internal struggles that made writing her book a "wrenching experience"

> Watching video after video of wedding stories, there were times when I would feel my emotions and my intellect split apart. Tears would be streaming down my face as I empathized with the characters in a movie while, at the same time, I would be taking notes critiquing the heterosexual imaginary (1999: 169–70).

This "splitting" points to the most significant finding of my own study: wedding dresses remain active and powerful in the lives of women because they operate at the level of identity and sense of self.

Post-modern theorists have argued that, far from disappearing with use, consumer goods have symbolic properties that create desired identities. In other words, when you purchase a product, you simultaneously create a particular sense of self (Friese, 1997). Sociologist Susanne Friese takes up this notion in a pioneering study of brides in the American midwest (1997). She argues that the process of selecting a ready-made wedding dress is critical to the prospective bride's social movement through pre-wedding "limbo" into the circle of married women. The dress facilitates this rite of passage. Searching the bridal stores to select "the perfect dress" helps her gain access to, and become familiar with, the bridal role and then adapt it to her personal concept. The customizing of ready-made bridal dresses is a means by which women gain some sense of producing their own consumption experience. "Traditions related to the dress are often reinterpreted," Friese claims, "to allow for personal convictions taking control over institutional prescribed ways" (1997: 56).

My mother's brides illustrate this seemingly contradictory notion of production of identity by consumption. In a period of life transition, creating a dress was a major vehicle for self-expression. As I have pointed out, each worked from a repertoire defined by key audiences in a socio-cultural milieu specific to place. The possibilities and limitations were collectively shared and reinforced. And yet, each woman emerged from the dressmaking process with the sense of having produced a representation unique to her character or personality. The action of defining the dress created an intense sense of identification with it.

To illustrate, one bride recounted: "For nearly a year prior to the wedding I mulled over ideas for the dress. I brought to bear on it all the artistic expressions I had developed to that point. By the wedding day, I knew that dress inside and out in a way I never would have known a ready-made. I value the uniqueness of this dress as well as the ways it reflected my experience and maturity. It was who I had become." For some brides, feelings such as these were sustained for decades. As another bride noted: "This was a special dress made to fit me alone. It suited me so well as a person that I still have strong ownership for it. I would have a difficult time passing it along."

Brides marrying for a second time made particularly strong links between self and dress. They used the garment as a vehicle to rework identities that had been lost or damaged with an initial marriage breakdown. Said one: "The dress reflected the decision I had made to be comfortable with certain things about myself and my life. It said: 'This is me. This is who I am.'" It was an expression of individuality, of becoming a person. Another woman reinforced these words by describing her dress as "the new me, the woman I have become, a woman who is elegant and self-confident. I have grown so much that I don't want to hide behind anybody anymore." Thus, the dresses marked changes in these women and their relationships that they hoped would be permanent.

For other brides, their dresses were points of reference against which to make visible their evolving selves. "I do not see myself as quite as childish and plain as I looked in that dress," noted one, somewhat embarrassed. "I wish that I had been a little more worldly, searched beyond just my own ideas and thinking. I regret having been that way at such a time. I was making a lifetime commitment but was so childlike in style of dress." A second agreed, "When I look at the dress now I see youth and inexperience and a very narrow focus. I had only been in Lacombe; I hadn't gone anywhere else."

A third bride perceived her wedding dress as a transitional object, something that expressed who she was for many years but it was an object insufficient to communicate who she has since become. "I was searching for an idea of who I was separate from other people. The dress was pivotal to that." The dress ironically delivered on that promise in a way that the bride found unsettling, "I had the weirdest wedding day," she recalled. "It just seemed like nobody talked to me. I just remember being all dressed up and everybody was talking to each other and I was sort of stuck. The dress was definitely a separator."

After their big days, most of my mother's brides carefully cleaned and stored their dresses. "I cried when I put the dress away because I can't wear it again," confessed one. "More than your labor, your heart goes into it." As storehouses of body/self memories, the brides kept the dresses safe. In cases where the marriage ended, the dress became vulnerable. One had been thrown away, post-divorce, while another was recovered dirty and neglected. These tended to be isolated cases, however, as even divorced women kept the dresses for their historical value. This was not necessarily an easy thing to do. "It is hard now to know what to do with it," declared one bride. "There is so much meaning in it that I don't want to get rid of it but I don't want it around where I see it every day. It reminds me of the struggle I was going through."

Conclusion

In this essay, I focused on a small number of brides whose wedding dresses were made by my mother, Lorraine, between 1950 and 1995. By concealing certain body parts and aspects of self while revealing others, these women created dresses conspicuous for their simplicity. Their look emphasizes modest sexuality and low maintenance femininity. These are the distinguishing qualities of a cultural repertoire that is collectively shared by woman in small town and rural Alberta. Each bride, however, "discovered" this repertoire independently, and became committed to it as an expression of her unique self. Each also negotiated with the repertoire and potentially destabilized it. That process was limited by the degree to which, through family, church and community connections, she was embedded in a highly conservative (entrepreneurial–evangelical) social context.

Notes

1. Since opening at the Red Deer and District Museum, Alberta, *Fabrications* had a six-city tour of Canada (1998–2001). Stops included the Canadian Museum of Civilization in Hull, Quebec; the Glenbow Museum in Calgary, Alberta; the Nova Scotia Museum of Industry in Stellarton, Nova Scotia; the Welland Canal Centre in St. Catharines, Ontario; the Thunder Bay Art Gallery in Thunder Bay, Ontario.

2. *Fabrications* is not organized chronologically or in terms of changing dress styles but as a biography of my mother and her work as a dressmaker. Clusters of dresses appear in association with different phases of her life and key relationships to women in the local community.

3. Since the early 1960s, my parents have lived at 5210 C&E Trail on the original wagon route between Calgary and Edmonton. When I lived there, Lacombe was a town of roughly 3,000 people.

4. All of the quotes in this essay are taken directly from transcripts of interviews that I conducted with my mother's brides either in person or by phone in 1997–98. The argument that I make here is based on in-depth analysis of those transcripts, along with participant observation during the development and implementation of the *Fabrications* exhibit.

5. Like the brides themselves, I was surprised at how quickly my mother put the dresses together. Most brides remembered that it was about three to six weeks from first fitting to final alternations. However, the design process often involved visits to dress shops and fabric stores, a highly social process for both parties. This meant that my mother was involved with the bride for several months prior to her wedding.

6. Most of the wedding dresses in my mother's collection were made for less than $100 Canadian, and some, as I have said, for as little as $20 to $30. Brides chose good quality but not overly expensive fabrics, and kept embellishment to a minimum, but their major savings were in the labor costs. In five decades of sewing, by her own decision, Mom rarely charged more than $20 for a dress. Many were gifts.

References

Church, Kathryn (2002), "The Hard Road Home: Towards a Polyphonic Narrative of the mother/daughter relationship", in Bochner, A. and Ellis, C. (eds) *Recomposing Ethnography: Autoethnography, Literature, and Aesthetics*, Alta Mira.

Church, Kathryn (online), "Fabrications: Stitching Ourselves Together", http: // womenspace.ca/Fabrications/

Church, Kathryn and Martindale, W. (1999), "Shall We Dance? Looking Back Over a Community-Museum Collaboration," in *Muse* (Canadian Museums Association) 17:3, 43–50.

Church, Kathryn (1998), "The Dressmaker," in *Elm Street*, Summer, 54–62.

Friese, S. (1997), "A Consumer Good in the Ritual Process: The Case of the Wedding Dress," *Journal of Ritual Studies* 11: 2, 51–62.

Ingraham, C. (1999), *White Weddings: Romancing Heterosexuality in Popular Culture*, New York and London: Routledge.

Lacombe and District Chamber of Commerce (1982), *Lacombe: The First Century*. Available from the Lacombe and District Chamber of Commerce, PO Box 1026, Lacombe, Alberta TOC 1S0

Laird, G. (1998), *Slumming It at the Rodeo: The Cultural Roots of Canada's Right-Wing Revolution*, Vancouver & Toronto: Douglas and McIntyre.

Laurence, M. (1989), "A Strange Place It Was", in Frances, D., *Images of the West: Changing perceptions of the Prairies, 1690–1960*, Saskatoon: Western Producer Books, p. 210.

Luchetti, C. (1996), *"I Do!" Courtship, Love and Marriage on the American Frontier; A Glimpse at American's Romantic Past Through Photographs, Diaries and Journals, 1715–1915*, New York: Crown Trade Paperbacks.

2

Satin Dresses and Caribou Kamiks: Negotiation of Tradition in Northern Alaskan Iñupiaq Weddings

Cyd Martin

The newly emergent "tradition" of wearing updated forms of Iñupiaq *atikluks* (parka-style dresses or jackets) for weddings represents a creative synthesis of materials and values drawn from indigenous and introduced cultural milieus. Iñupiaq people are asserting claims to tradition and ethnicity by constructing wedding *atikluks* that blend a nineteenth-century Iñupiaq clothing innovation with the specialty fabrics of standard American wedding attire. These lace and satin garments are creative and strategic statements that simultaneously position northern Alaskan Iñupiaq people as authentically traditional and undeniably modern.

Many Iñupiat recently choose to have what they term "traditional Iñupiaq" weddings, where participants wear Iñupiaq-style dress instead of typical Western wedding attire. The ceremonies and clothing worn at these "traditional" weddings are not derived from long standing Iñupiaq practices, however. Instead, they are a new phenomenon springing as much from Euroamerican influences as from indigenous historical or prehistorical traditions. Regardless of the ceremonies' lineage, Iñupiaq people claim them as "traditional." The increasing popularity of such ceremonies during the past decade illustrates the growing strength of indigenous rights, the desire for self-determination and the increasing political benefits of an "authentic" and "traditional" demeanor.

Clothing, a venerable expression of the Iñupiaq relationship to the environment, is an important icon of Iñupiaq identity in modern contexts. In choosing to have "traditional" weddings, Iñupiaq people are constructing tradition to affirm their position in Alaskan society and are using dress to mediate the ever-shifting boundary between tradition and modernity. Although these weddings are termed "traditional," they are firmly embedded in the social and political environment of contemporary Alaska. In this essay, I consider the cultural, historical and social conditions that have coalesced to shape the current practice.[1]

Historical, Cultural and Environmental Overview

Both the environment of northern Alaska and its animal populations were important factors in the formation of Iñupiaq culture.[2] Beginning at least 1,000 years ago the ancestors of the Iñupiat developed sophisticated strategies for utilizing the resources of the north. The harvest of large marine mammals and seasonally available caribou herds required the cooperation of many people; in the face of this necessity, Iñupiaq social structure maximized the concept of extended family. Kinship, fictive or actual, linked people and facilitated the cooperation necessary for the greater good of the community.

Iñupiat people recognize kinship bilaterally, providing the individual with a wide array of kin on whom to depend. Individuals belong to an extended kin group in addition to their nuclear family, and non-blood relationships are also recognized, widening the sphere of kinship relations.[3] In the past, extended family members were interdependent and provided assistance in times of stress. Individuals knew that relatives would not refuse them food, clothing or shelter (Burch, 1975: 198). The extended family system still operates in contemporary villages. Nuclear family homes are often clustered in kin-related groupings and many essential tasks are shared, including women sewing, preparing food and caring for children, and men sharing equipment and helping with hunting related tasks.

The environment-influenced, family-based social structure embodies core Iñupiaq cultural values: respect for animals, family loyalty, sharing, cooperation, and the subsistence partnership between husband and wife. The role of subsistence in contemporary Iñupiaq life cannot be overemphasized. Iñupiaq village routines and, in fact, the lives of many Iñupiaq city dwellers, revolve around subsistence activities. In most communities work and school are suspended to allow people to participate in hunting, fishing or other seasonal activities. Throughout the year people will also trap or fish after work or on weekends if there is a chance of catching something. Subsistence foods are shared with family, community and beyond. Meat from a whale caught by residents from coastal villages such as Kaktovik or Barrow easily makes its way to relatives in other villages and urban areas.

Iñupiaq Weddings Prior to Euroamerican Contact

In precontact and continuing into historical times one primary goal of Iñupiaq marriage was to extend the bonds of cooperation. Marriage was an economic necessity. The man provided meat and fish for food and raw materials for clothing and the woman in turn fashioned the materials into the tailored clothing that permitted the man to hunt and to fish. Together, the couple cooperated with other households to catch, process and store the larger marine mammals (or caribou, in the case of the mountain dwelling Nunamiut) that supported the communal group through the winter. Marriage extended kinship bonds and widened the circle of people that could be depended upon for cooperative efforts and mutual aid (Spencer, 1959: 75; Van Stone, 1962: 100).

Prior to Euroamerican contact in the nineteenth century, no ceremony marked Iñupiaq weddings. A man and woman simply decided to live together, consummated the marriage, and began sharing household responsibilities. Some marriages were arranged. Dr John Simpson, at Barrow in 1852, tells of a young man's mother selecting a prospective bride. She invited the girl to work in their household during the day. If the prospective daughter-in-law proved satisfactory, she was invited to join the family (Simpson, 1988[1855]: 524). If a couple had children they usually stayed together. If they had disagreements they might divorce with no onus on either partner. Children born to an unmarried or previously married woman were not viewed as an impediment to a prospective marriage since children were welcome additions to families, providing assistance in hunting, fishing, and household work.

Euroamerican Contact

Significant contact between the North Alaskan Iñupiat and Euroamericans occurred with the advent of commercial whaling in the Arctic Ocean in 1848. The first whaling ship north of Bering Strait was a harbinger of the whalers, missionaries, and traders who followed, introducing a new way of life to northern Alaska that transformed the social and economic environment of the Iñupiat.

Whaling ships carried the material and concepts of Euroamerican culture. Technologically advanced materials and tools and a cash-based economy came hand-in-hand with intangibles: ideas, values, and religion. In addition to trade goods, the ships carried supplies, tools and equipment for whaling and ship repair. Ropes, canvas, metal knives and needles, tools, cookware, clothing, and guns all became desirable to indigenous Alaskans. Highly skilled at manufacturing from indigenous materials what they needed to survive in the Arctic, the

Iñupiat appreciated the functionality of the new materials and tools. As traders recognized the great opportunities in the north, they brought an increasing variety of goods to exchange for native furs, baleen and ivory.

Missionaries and teachers who arrived in the wake of the whaling ships introduced values rather than material goods. They came to convert the native residents, whom they viewed as underprivileged, uncivilized savages, to a Euroamerican-defined "civilized" life of cleanliness and Christian morals. Informed by the paternalistic attitudes of the times, they sought to remedy what they saw as the deplorable physical and moral state of Alaskan Eskimo people. Teachers, also trained as missionaries, imposed "civilized" food, clothing, the English language, and Christianity on the Iñupiat who were forced to abandon aboriginal customs and beliefs.[4] The United States government appropriated funds to support church organizations concerned with civilizing Native Americans. John. C. Calhoun, Secretary of War, illustrates the predominant viewpoint:

> Although partial advances may be made, under the present system, to civilize the Indians . . . until there is a radical change in the system, any efforts . . . must fall short of complete success. They must be brought gradually under our authority and laws, or they will insensibly waste away in vice and misery. It is impossible, with their customs, that they should exist as independent communities, in the midst of civilized society. They are not, in fact, an independent people . . . nor ought they to be so considered. They should be taken under our guardianship; and our opinion, and not theirs, ought to prevail, in measures intended for their civilization and happiness. A system less vigorous may protract, but cannot arrest their fate (U.S. Congress, 1820).

This attitude prevailed well into the twentieth century, affecting the treatment of all Native Americans.

Sheldon Jackson, a Presbyterian missionary who first visited Alaska in 1877, became a force for the assimilation of Alaska natives, garnering support for missions and schools by speaking to American church groups and lobbying Congress. Appointed General Agent for Education in Alaska in 1885, he used federal funds to expand evangelical activities.[5] Missionaries lived in some villages and traveled to others as circuit riders, performing religious services, baptisms, funerals and weddings. T. Brevig, a minister in Wales, performed the first Christian marriage between two Iñupiat in 1894 (*The Eskimo Bulletin*, 1895). After learning from missionaries that the church required Christian wedding ceremonies, Iñupiaq couples waited to be married until the preacher came to perform the ceremony, or they traveled to the preacher's village.

Clothing

Contact with Euroamericans dramatically affected Iñupiaq clothing. Fabric, thread, needles, sewing machines, ready-made garments and the western standards of dress offered Iñupiaq seamstresses new material, styles, and construction possibilities. Western apparel supplanted many indigenous garments but some traditional dress survived because of its supreme functionality and cultural importance. For example, unsurpassed for warmth, skin parkas and *kamiks* (skin boots) were so superior to Western dress that even Euroamericans living in the north adopted indigenous outerwear, often commissioning native seamstresses to sew special designs with elaborate trim.

Clothing was culturally important to the Iñupiat because of its role in the subsistence system. Indigenous garments and their manufacture had spiritual and social associations that were so central to the structure of Iñupiaq culture that they were never completely supplanted by Western garments. Clothing practices linked the wife/seamstress, the husband/hunter, and the prey animals in a coherent system at the core of Iñupiaq life.

Before contact, Iñupiaq parkas were made of mammal, fish, or bird skins. Caribou was most commonly used for warmth because of the outstanding insulating qualities of its hollow hairs (Driscoll, 1983: 46; Hatt, 1969: 8). In addition to the pragmatic function of protecting the wearer from inclement weather, parkas had a spiritual dimension and often incorporated animal referents such as amulets or specific construction elements. Caribou skins were cut so that the caribou head skin formed the hood of the parka; the ears were incorporated into the hood giving the hunter an animal-like appearance. Wolverine tails, ermine skins, or strips of wolverine fur similarly were attached to the backs of parkas to suggest tails. Seamstresses inserted triangular gussets (hood roots) into the fronts of the parkas, just below the hood, giving a strong impression of walrus tusks. V. Chausonnet (1988: 216) and B. Driscoll (1983: 54) have suggested that these elements symbolize the human-animal connection, a vital spiritual component of Iñupiat life. Treating animals with respect was an important aspect of the Iñupiaq belief system and included taboos against sewing land animal skins during sea mammal hunting and vice versa. To insure success, Iñupiaq hunters required new or newly refurbished garments; their clothing had to be beautiful with small, regular stitches (Chausonnet, 1988: 212; Spencer, 1959: 265). Elegant parkas from the late 1800s with precise, tight stitches and painstakingly detailed decorative trim attest to the attention seamstresses lavished on their work. Seamstresses adhered to general regional styles but individual interpretation made each parka a unique testament of their creativity.

The introduction of woven cloth had two effects on Iñupiaq clothing. It provided a means of keeping the fur garments clean and dry and it allowed the Iñupiat to conform to western standards of dress without sacrificing the warmth, practicality or cultural significance of the garments. Cotton drilling, canvas, and calico were sewn into covers for fur parkas. This extended the life of the furs by protecting them from dirt and moisture that caused the hairs to fall out (Driscoll, 1983: 46; Oakes, 1988: 274). J. Murdoch, in Point Barrow in 1881, noted, "Of late years both sexes have adopted the habit of wearing over their clothes a loose hoodless frock of cotton cloth, usually bright colored calico, especially in blustering weather, when it is useful in keeping the drifting snow out of their furs" (Murdoch, 1892: 111). In Alaska, these covers took the form of short hooded *anoraks* for the men and longer, hooded garments with ruffles at the bottom for women.

Women's ruffled parka covers had the added benefit of resembling Euroamerican dresses and of covering up the "savage"-appearing furs. Missionaries did not approve of fur clothing for indoor wear, nor did they condone the precontact Iñupiaq practice of removing all upper garments when indoors. Cloth covers, initially made to be worn over the fur parkas, solved this problem. Women wore them indoors without the fur parka underneath. The calico covers gave the appearance of dresses without making Iñupiaq women sacrifice the practicality of the loose fit and shorter length that allowed them to perform their domestic responsibilities. Euroamerican dress styles in the late nineteenth and early twentieth centuries were impractical from an Iñupiaq woman's viewpoint. Skirts fell to the floor and bodices were constricted by firmly boned corsets. Iñupiaq women could not perform the active duties required by their Arctic lifestyle if dressed in Euroamerican fashions. The *atikluks* (covers) solved the clothing dilemma from both western and Iñupiaq perspectives.

Parka covers made from cotton fabric brought by the whalers were initially sewn by hand and then, after 1856, increasingly by machine.[6] With what was little fabric variety at first, the early examples of parka covers are limited to plain white drill, coarse striped cotton, or flour sacks. The fashion column of the 1893 volume of *The Eskimo Bulletin*, an annual newspaper produced at Cape Prince of Wales, stated: "Took-twoi-na has a new pair of Safety-pin earrings. Ke-rook sports two of Dr. Drigg's glass bottle-stoppers for Labrets. Kum-nruk is out in new trowsers [sic] of the Finest Sperry's Flour cloth. A-yar-hok has a new overcloak of the fashionable 'Dried Peaches' brand. He got the bags from a ship." In early photographs all of the children in a family and even most of the children in a school are outfitted in parka covers of the same, often plaid or striped, fabric design.

As traders brought more goods north, floral calicos became popular for women's *atikluks*. Records from whaling ships document woven fabric's prevalence as a trade item. One ship's cargo included: 112 yards of calico, 161 yards of denim, 482 yards of drill, 1 sewing machine, 7 sewing machine needles, 46 thimbles, and 145 ½ yards of ticking (Bodfish, 1909). Early trim on cloth parka covers was simple bands of contrasting fabric. When commercially produced trim became available around 1900, Iñupiaq women combined bias tape, rickrack, and embroidered ribbon to create pleasing designs. Seamstresses executed the geometric patterns that decorated skin parkas in bias tape, forming intricate bands, called *qupak*, that echoed those pieced of skin.[7] The government furnished fabric for sewing and missionaries supplied other materials and donated clothing. Adept Iñupiaq seamstresses capitalized on the availability of new materials. According to Ann Bannon, a nurse working in Barrow:

> Before Christmas, when the children ought to have new dresses for the exercises, we get the cloth ready and the mothers take the cut out garments home and make them. Some mothers cut out at the club meetings and it always surprises me to watch them; they do it very well indeed. Mrs. Greist has had quantities of trimming, buttons, odds and ends of lace and insertion and remnants of cloth, and some times she lets the mothers choose from the boxes what they want and then we watch eagerly for the result and it is most pleasing.[8]

In the mid-1900s, Iñupiaq seamstresses began substituting quilted lining material purchased through mail-order catalogs or village stores for caribou skin as the inner, insulating layer of most parkas. Seamstresses also substituted mouton (commercially tanned sheepskin) for the caribou skin lining of hunting parkas; mouton was more durable and, although heavier, the increased weight of the mouton parka was not a concern since hunting became more sedentary after the mid-century adoption of snowmobiles.

Iñupiaq Weddings After 1890

Since the first actual wedding ceremonies involving Iñupiaq couples were introduced events associated with Christianity, there was no earlier indigenous practice to cite as "traditional." These missionary officiated weddings in the 1890s followed the prerequisite liturgical and cultural forms. The only models of wedding ceremonies that Alaska natives had were the occasional weddings between non-native teachers, missionaries, miners and traders.

Historical photographs illustrate the wedding clothing worn by Euroamerican couples around the turn of the twentieth century. Brides wore long white gowns and grooms donned dark suits, white shirts with stiff collars and ties, styles

Figure 2.1 Wedding in Valdez, Alaska, ca 1909. Photograph: Anchorage Museum of History and Art archives. B62.1A.484.

that, with slight variations, persist in general American culture to the present day (Figure 2.1). Most of the non-native Americans who came to Alaska at this time consciously brought their own cultural practices with them, importing as many aspects of their "civilized" life as they could. For instance, a nurse working in Gambell, on St. Lawrence Island, had a piano sent to her. It traveled by ship and dog team to her home. She describes using a white lace tablecloth and pewter candlesticks for dinner parties. A list of food brought by a teacher to the village of Wales includes tins of raspberries, white figs, minced clams, oysters, and asparagus, pints of orange juice, jars of jam and India relish, tinned lobster, bottles of maraschino cherries, and tubes of food coloring paste.[9] Newcomers continued their usual activities too, hosting dinners, card parties, and social visits, all in the manner of American society of the time. Weddings, when they occurred, followed suit as an occasion for special clothing and celebration. This microcosm of American society, transplanted from the lower forty-eight states, was the model for indigenous Alaskans who were strongly encouraged, if not forced, to conform.

Figure 2.2 Wedding in Wainwright, Alaska, 1921, ship's officer in fur clothing
officiating. Photograph: Anchorage Museum of History and Art archives.
B81.164.36.

The earliest photographs of Iñupiaq weddings show the bride, groom and
wedding party in *atikluks*. Even non-native preachers wear fancy parkas in
some of the images (Figure 2.2). As Euroamerican clothing became more
available through mail order and stores, Iñupiaq couples adopted Western
styles and purchased white dresses and suits for their weddings. By the 1950s
and 1960s Iñupiaq brides walked down the aisle wearing the short, bouffant
wedding dresses of the era.

The practice of wearing standard white gowns continued into the 1980s and,
to some extent, into the present. In the late 1980s, however, an alternative trend
appeared. Many Iñupiat began replacing the traditional American wedding
clothing with fancy *atikluks* made especially for the ceremony. Although
everyday *atikluks* had occasionally been worn for weddings when a couple
wished to avoid the time and expense of a big church wedding, the fancy
atikluks were a new fashion twist. These garments replaced the white wedding
gown but were created out of satins and laces, fabrics that were uncommon
for everyday *atikluks* but that were identical to those used for standard bridal
and attendants' gowns. The ceremonies themselves were unchanged but acquired
a new appellation; based on the clothing they were called "traditional Iñupiaq"
weddings. These ceremonies continue to grow in popularity in northern Alaska.

Traditional Iñupiaq Weddings

Just as details of Western wedding ceremonies vary, so do those of "traditional Iñupiaq." The one constant defining the ceremony is the bride's *atikluk*. Sewn by her, relatives or friends, it follows the ordinary *atikluk* form but has special details, according to the bride's desires. It may be longer, the pockets may be omitted, and the trimming is more elaborate. White satin is often used for the bride's *atikluk*, sometimes with lace overlay. Attendants' *atikluks* (including those of flower girls) are generally all the same color and are satin or, velvet for winter weddings. Groom and groomsmen either wear complementary colored *atikluks* or standard suits or tuxedos. Other than the clothing, the ceremony does not deviate from the typical Euroamerican wedding. Common practices include the procession down the aisle, the Christian liturgical religious ceremony, a reception, the throwing of the bouquet and garter, and the gifts. Only the clothing transforms it into a "traditional Iñupiaq" weddings (Figure 2.3).

Figure 2.3 Wedding in Anaktuvak Pass, Alaska, 1999, Harriet and Earl Williams. Bride's *atikluk* is white satin with lace overlay, groom's is white satin with blue and yellow *qupak* and rickrack trim. Both are wearing caribou and sealskin *kamiks*. Photograph: Privately owned, copied by Cyd Martin with permission.

Other indigenous Alaskan groups also have "traditional" weddings. One Iñupiaq bride said that she and her husband, an Athabascan Indian from Fort Yukon, had planned to have a "traditional Indian" wedding (Harriet Williams, interview by author, Anktuvuk Pass, Alaska, 31 August 1999). The groom's family would sew the necessary fringed and beaded moosehide garments for the wedding party but something came up and they were unable to provide the garments. At the last minute the bride's family stepped in and sewed Eskimo garments for all participants, making a lace *atikluk* for the bride, a white satin *atikluk* trimmed with blue and yellow *qupak* for the groom, and matching pale blue satin *atikluks* for all of the attendants and groomsmen including the flower girl and ring bearer (Figure 2.4).

Figure 2.4 Wedding in Anchorage, Alaska, 1999, Francine Hopson-Rochon and Frank Rochon. Bride's *atikluk* is white satin with *qupak* above skirt, on pockets and around hood. She wears caribou and sealskin *kamiks* with white nylon stockings with lace design. Photograph: Privately owned, copied by Cyd Martin with permission.

Authenticating Culture

The phenomena of "traditional Iñupiaq" weddings and their delineation through clothing are significant on several levels. The fact that clothing alone, and female clothing in particular, suffices to shift the status of a ceremony from contemporary to traditional demonstrates the continuing importance of clothing within Iñupiaq culture. These weddings reveal that the actions of women continue to be pivotal in defining Iñupiaq events, particularly those with spiritual implications. If the women wear *atikluks*, the wedding is "traditional", regardless of male attire. In historical times Iñupiaq clothing practices, controlled by women and associated with subsistence and spirituality, insured that women and clothing held a central role in the Iñupiaq social system. Despite changes in social, cultural and economic conditions, the relationship between clothing and Iñupiaq values has not only continued but has been augmented as clothing has acquired additional functions and meanings in contemporary contexts.

"Traditional" weddings reveal the ongoing, incremental balancing of Iñupiaq and Western values. The imposition of Euroamerican culture that began 150 years ago in northern Alaska was not at all pervasive as it may appear in the face of expanding Western globalization. Iñupiaq values survived the onslaught of introduced ideas and, in fact, the Iñupiaq tailored features of Euroamerican culture to suit Iñupiaq needs. But their wedding ceremonies, performed in churches with Christian liturgy, are more than an acquiescence to, or reflection of, colonially imposed religious mores. They are also cultural performances (Turner, 1987; Guss, 2000). Cultural performances relate to the everyday economic, domestic or political processes of a group. They not only reflect the social system but are reflexive and provide an opportunity for the group to evaluate and change its view of history. Such performances are "contested ideological terrain" that may express tradition, ethnicity, and/or resistance against the dominant culture (Guss, 2000: 8). The Iñupiaq adoption of Western weddings may be viewed as an indication of the Iñupiaq acceptance of Christian religion but, as the changing nature of these performances indicates, this acceptance is not unconditional, nor is it final. Both adherence to the doctrine and compliance with the social forms of the ceremonies remain malleable.

After the introduction of Western culture, benefits accrued to those who embraced the new social regime and complied with its educating, civilizing and proselytizing agendas. The acceptance of a Western wedding ceremony was an artifact of the imposition of Euroamerican culture on native Alaskans. The recent transformation of the ceremony into an Iñupiaq ritual reflects an increasing awareness on the part of the Iñupiat that they can renegotiate the conditions of their imposed assimilation. Recent changes in the socio-political environment of the United States, including Alaska, have empowered ethnic groups, particularly indigenous peoples, and fostered a climate favorable to claims of ethnic identity and self-determination. The adoption of Iñupiaq dress for weddings during the past decade reflects the increasingly politicized climate of Alaska, one that favors native self-determination and demonstrates indigenous groups' increasing unwillingness to conform to dictated Western policies.

A series of events, beginning with the 1967 discovery of oil at Prudhoe Bay, catapulted Iñupiaq sovereignty and self-determination issues into state and national importance. Conflicts over resources, land claims and subsistence rights drove the Iñupiat into legal battles with the State of Alaska and resulted in the Alaska Native Claims Settlement Act (ANCSA) in 1971 and the Alaska National Interest Lands Conservation Act (ANILCA) in 1980. These laws addressed land claims issues and protected native "physical, economic, traditional, and cultural existence" (U.S. Congress, 1980). A challenge to indigenous whaling by the International Whaling Commission in 1970 also mobilized the Iñupiat to defend their rights to subsistence practices. These land and subsistence issues prompted the Iñupiat to pursue native sovereignty with increasing perseverance. Through increasing economic clout and a changing social paradigm that privileges indigenous status and claims to tradition, Alaska natives are gaining power within the state and are ever more able to pursue their own political and social agendas.

This political power manifests itself in dress as well as political action. Indigenous dress is worn to conferences, legislative hearings, court proceedings and advisory committee meetings. Where the label "native" was once undesirable, it has become politically beneficial to emphasize one's native heritage. The Iñupiaq *atikluk* is a particularly expedient garment for this identification since it is distinctively ethnic, can be worn over other garments, and has a venerable origin. Because of these features, *atikluks* have been adopted by other, non-Inuit native groups. Athabascan people in Alaska and Canada also wear the *atikluk* as their "native" apparel. The garments convey an unmistakable connection with native tradition and authenticity and, in so doing, lend that authority to their wearers.

As a particularly visible type of cultural performance, Iñupiaq wedding ceremonies have been enlisted in an ongoing, society-wide negotiation of indigenous rights. The wearing of special *atikluks* in the ceremonies is one component of a trend towards self-determination in which Iñupiaq people are balancing the requirements of Euroamerican culture and the values of Iñupiaq heritage. In the realm of religion, their acceptance of an overall Christian doctrine was not total, nor did it irrevocably commit them to standard Christian practices. The recent metamorphosis of the ceremony into the "traditional Iñupiaq" wedding indicates that accommodation between the two cultures continues on many fronts. It illustrates the desire of many Iñupiat to assume ownership of aspects of culture that were imposed on them and, through a transformative process, make them their own. I asked an Iñupiaq friend why people wanted Iñupiaq weddings. She said, "People are realizing that they don't have to assimilate. They have adapted enough, they don't want to change more and they are making a statement" (Jana Harcharek, interview by author, Barrow, Alaska, 5 October 2000).

A. Boultwood and R. Jerrard (2000: 307) argue that imitation relates to behavior whereas identification relates to the adoption of values, beliefs and attitudes in addition to behavior. In the case of Iñupiaq wedding dress, an earlier period of imitation, a "trying on" of Western attitudes and beliefs as indicated through clothing, has been followed by a period of adjustment and negotiation in which a combination of non-indigenous and indigenous values are shaping contemporary Iñupiaq identity. Here, the operation of dress in reproducing the social order is seen in action. Iñupiaq-style wedding clothing is reinforcing a new social order in Alaska where Iñupiaq people are claiming autonomy and rejecting an earlier coerced acceptance of Western values and practice. Arguing for dress as an embodied practice, J. Entwhistle (2000: 328) points out that the particular context in which the dressed body operates sets constraints on what is or is not appropriate to wear. The degree to which the dressed body can express itself is symbolic of that context. Thus, in Iñupiaq weddings the bride dressed in a standard wedding dress signals the context of colonial Alaska, with its imposition of Western values, social forms and assimilative goals. The *atikluk*, however, worn in contemporary weddings, objectifies the emerging context where indigenous Alaskans are successfully asserting their rights to their bodies, lives and heritage.

Notes

1. Interviews for this project were completed in Barrow, Nome, Anaktuvuk Pass, Fairbanks and Anchorage from October 1999 to December 2000.
2. "Iñupiaq" is the singular and adjectival form of "Iñupiat." "Iñupiat" means the real people and is the accepted term in Alaska. "Inuit" is the preferred term in Canada. Iñupiat have lived along the coast and in the mountains of northern Alaska from Bering Strait east to the Mackenzie Delta, for at least 1,000 years.
3. Non-kin relationships that entail kin-like responsibilities include adoption, hunting partnership, broken marriage situations and, in the past, wife exchange. In all cases the individuals involved (and their children, in the case of marriage or wife exchange) became involved in the same cooperative relationships as blood kin (Spencer, 1959: 85).

4. The policy of contracting with church missions to provide educational services was discontinued in 1897 by Thomas J. Morgan, Federal Commissioner of Education.

5. Jackson was instrumental in the establishment of missionary-run but government-funded schools across the territory, with certain areas assigned to specific religious entities. The Presbyterian Church operated in much of northern Alaska. Although other denominations eventually moved in, the strongest religious influence within each region remained the original denomination assigned by Jackson (Stewart, 1908: 364).

6. Sewing machines did not become practical until about 1856 (Cooper, 1976: 35–7). After that time they rapidly became standard equipment on whaling ships and in traders' inventories. By the early 1900s many Iñupiaq had the portable hand crank machines (Jenness, 1991: 18, 44).

7. All geometric parka trim, skin or cloth, is called *qupak* in Iñupiaq and "delta trim" by Inuit and Athabascan seamstresses in Canada (Oakes, 1988: 202, Thompson, 1994: 103). Contemporary parkas and *atikluks* are trimmed with elaborate *qupak* made from bias tape.

8. Ann Bannon to Eva Richards, 30 October 1928, Eva L.A. Richards Papers, Special Collections, University of Washington Archives.

9. Manuscript, Richards Papers.

References

Bockstoce, J. (1986), *Whales, Ice and Men*, Seattle: University of Washington Press.

Bodfish, H., Papers, Mss 17, Library and Archives, New Bedford Whaling Museum.

Boultwood, A. and Jerrard, R. (2000), "Ambivalence, and Its Relation to Fashion and the Body," *Fashion Theory: The Journal of Dress, Body & Culture*, 4:3, 301–21.

Burch, E. (1975) *Eskimo Kinsmen: Changing Family Relationships in Northwest Alaska*, (Monograph of the American Ethnological Society 59), St. Paul: West Publishing Company.

—— (1998) *The Iñupiaq Eskimo Nations of Northwest Alaska*, Fairbanks Alaska: University of Alaska Press.

Cooper, G. (1976), *The Sewing Machine: Its Invention and Development*, Washington: Smithsonian Institution Press.

Chausonnet, V. (1988), "Needles and Animals: Women's Magic," in W. Fitzhugh and A. Crowell (eds), *Crossroads of Continents*, Washington: Smithsonian Institution.

Driscoll, B. (1983), "The Inuit Parka: A Preliminary Study," unpublished Master of Arts Thesis, Carlton University, Ottawa.

Entwistle, J. (2000), "Fashion and the Fleshy Body: Dress as Embodied Practice," *Fashion Theory: The Journal of Dress, Body & Culture*, 4:3, 323–47.

Eskimo Bulletin, 1893–1898, (Annual newspaper published by AMA Mission School), Cape Prince of Wales Alaska.

Guss, D. (2000), *The Festive State*, Berkeley: University of California Press.

Hatt, G. (1969), "Arctic Skin Clothing in Eurasia and America: An Ethnographic Study," *Arctic Anthropology* 5:2, 3–132.

Jenness, D. (1991), *Arctic Odyssey: The Diary of Diamond Jenness, Ethnologist with the Canadian Arctic Expedition in Northern Alaska and Canada, 1913–1916*, Hull, Quebec: Canadian Museum of Civilization.

Murdoch, J. (1988[1892]) *Ethnological Results of the Point Barrow Expedition*, Washington DC: Smithsonian Institution Press.

Oakes, J. (1988), "Caribou and Copper Inuit Skin Clothing Production," PhD dissertation, University of Manitoba.

Richards, E. Papers and Correspondence. Special Collections, University of Washington Archives, Seattle.

Simpson, J. (1988[1855]), "Observations on the Western Esquimaux and the Country they inhabit; from Notes taken during two years at Point Barrow, by Mr. John Simpson, Surgeon, R.N., Her Majesty's Discovery Ship 'Plover,'" in Bockstoce, J., (ed.), *The Journal of Rochfort Maguire 1852–1854*, London: Hakluyt Society.

Spencer, R. (1959), *The North Alaskan Eskimo: A Study in Ecology and Society*, (Smithsonian Institution, Bureau of Ethnology Bulletin 171), Washington, D.C.: Government Printing Office.

Stewart, R. (1908), *Sheldon Jackson: Pathfinder and Prospector of the Missionary Vanguard in the Rocky Mountains and Alaska*, New York: Fleming H. Revelle Company.

Thompson, J. (1994), *From the Land: Two Hundred Years of Dene Clothing*, Hull, Quebec: Canadian Museum of Civilization.

Turner, V. (1987), *The Anthropology of Performance*, New York: PAJ Publications.

U.S. Congress. (1820), *Annals of Congress*, 16th Congress, 1st Sess., 916.

—— P.L. 96–487, 2 Dec. 1980, 94 Stat.2371.

VanStone, J. (1962), *Point Hope: A Village in Transition*, Seattle: University of Washington Press.

3

Packaged In Japan: Elite Weddings in Osaka

Masami Suga

This essay explores how contemporary Japanese express notions of Japaneseness in a highly westernized local society. Ethnographic fieldwork in Osaka in 1995 examined elite weddings as a case study, including the role bridalwear plays in the life event. O-Young Lee's (1982) concept of compact culture provides a theoretical framework, through which I identify cultural themes critical to understanding and defining Japaneseness.

Research Setting: Osaka, a Merchant City

Osaka, the second largest Japanese city after Tokyo, is situated in the southern part of the main island, Honshu. Osaka, an urban prefecture composed of multiple cities, includes Sakai, Ibaraki, and Osaka proper. In this essay, Osaka refers to the entire prefecture. Approximately eight and a half million people live in Osaka, which covers 720 square miles (1,158 square kilometers), more than 80 per cent of which is classified as urban. Land for new housing in the city of Osaka is severely limited and the cost of living is extremely high.

Products of western origin saturate Osaka's markets and now are manufactured in, by, or for Japan; these range from household goods and food to cosmetics and clothing. Osakans pick and choose, or mix and match western material elements and incorporate them into everyday life in an ongoing open relationship with the western influence. In so doing, however, Osakans are not confined by the original purpose or context of what they select but rather remake it into something that is uniquely Japanese.

Osaka's population, most of whom have settled there for generations have developed a distinct manner of speech, a vibrant local culture, and the city is perhaps best known in Japan as the locale where many of today's business giants originated. For example, Sumitomo, Mitsui and Mitsubishi are influential players in the world's banking and investment industry, as well as in the fields of heavy machinery, life insurance, automobiles, utilities and computers.

Osakans show pride in their region's prominent business history and feel pride in the economic vitality small- and middle-scale businesses bring to the city. To this day, the spirit of a merchant town continues to dictate the way Osakans engage in the affairs of everyday life. From shopping for groceries, clothing, automobiles to wedding arrangements, many Osakans assume there is room for negotiation beyond what appears on a price tag since bargaining is a way of life and adds a flavor to the regional character.

A Shinto shrine in Osaka sponsors a large festival held annually on 10 January in honor of *Ebessan*, a well-favored merchant deity. Tens of thousands of business owners of all kinds visit the shrine and make monetary offerings, hoping for a prosperous new year. The shrine sells good-luck bamboo branches decorated with ornaments depicting elements essential to good business. Each year business people purchase these branches and bring them back to the shrine for proper disposition during the following year's *Ebessan* festival.

Osaka has long had a reputation for staging lavish weddings. Osakans continue to appreciate their old merchant spirit and demonstrate the prosperity of their region through the display of family wealth at weddings. In Tokyo and other urban centers, however, recent trends evolved into a more subdued wedding, implying that an extravagant wedding is a dated rural custom and considered less tasteful. Osaka thus enjoys an unusual city status by blending its old merchant tradition with westernized contemporary culture and continues to celebrate weddings with extravagant displays.

Data Collection

Ethnographic fieldwork focused on elite weddings, involving a highly distinctive group of ten, upper-middle- to upper-class Japanese women who lived and married in Osaka between 1989 and 1994.[1] The population represents a narrow yet powerful socioeconomic sector of Japanese society in which individuals enjoy a special degree of prestige, prominence, and privilege as a result of their financial affluence. Professionals in the wedding industry also contributed information for this study.

As urban elite, these women are likely trendsetters of fashion, compared to those from the rural or urban, working class. Because of their urban location, they are the first to encounter the newest imports from around the world. Thanks to their financial strength they are able to acquire goods even at prime price. Since they often make regular overseas trips, they bring home the latest fashions they saw firsthand while abroad. Their lead often results in local fashion trends through the popular marketing of made-in-Japan replicas of what they have purchased (e.g. Chanel tote bags, Hunting World shoulder bags and Cartier wristwatches).

Theoretical Orientations

The theoretical framework for this study comes from O-Young Lee's concept of compact culture. Lee argues in *The Compact Culture: The Japanese Tradition of "Smaller is Better"* that "it [Japan] has always borrowed well-established aspects of existing societies, things that have proven to be possible. Then it assimilates, innovates, and refashions them into something Japanese" (1982: 167). According to Lee, Japanese adopt things (often of foreign origin) by making the size smaller while retaining or improving their original quality. Through the compacting process, they "innovate" something new which they identify as peculiarly Japanese.

Lee uses the culture of reductionism as a theme to understand Japanese notions of ideal beauty at a collective level. "Given the centrality of aesthetic considerations in Japanese society" (Ben-Ari, 1990: 152), the three aspects of Lee's theme are particularly relevant to this study as an underlying aesthetic structure in Japanese life: 1) innovation by reduction, 2) inclusion by reduction, and 3) captivation by reduction (Ben-Ari, 1990: 152).

"Innovation by reduction" refers to the Japanese tradition in which Japanese create things by reducing size or simplifying function. A folding fan provides an historic example. Although invented in China as a rigid flat fan in the second millennium BC, once it arrived in Japan, it was transformed into a folding fan so that it could be stored in smaller size and be more convenient to carry (Lee, 1982: 31–2). The world's smallest electronic devices such as Sony Walkman, Sony Watchman, and wristwatch calculators offer contemporary examples of how the Japanese apply the concept of innovation by reduction for product development.

"Inclusion by reduction" embraces the Japanese love of making things smaller. A box lunch provides both a historic and a contemporary example. The principle of a Japanese box lunch differs greatly from the western sandwich. While a sandwich may be an abbreviation of a meal, a box lunch is a compact version of a formal meal in which multiple dishes are each reduced into a bite size to fit into a lunch box (Lee, 48). The Japanese box lunch originated during the Momoyama period (1568–1603) to "fulfill the need for food that could be packed in a compact, handy container and carried around"

(Lee, 48). In contemporary Osaka, children and adults regularly bring box lunches to school and work.

"Captivation by reduction" defines the way Japanese experience nature in a reduced scale. Lee argues that Japanese have traditionally brought nature closer to home rather than actually venturing into nature to appreciate its qualities. For example, *bonsai* illustrates the way Japanese capture a particular facet of nature by reducing physical dimensions to a portable size and making it readily available for personal viewing, purchase or collection. Thus, "nature is first pared down, simplified, and brought to the veranda in the form of a dry landscape" (89).

Overview of Elite Weddings in Osaka

Two common ways for a couple to meet in Osaka are arranged marriage and love marriage. Today's arranged marriages resemble a dating service in the United States, where people have a chance to study each other's résumés and portraits prior to an actual meeting. Unlike the past custom where a couple met for the first time in the full presence of their parents and a go-between, today they may talk to each other beforehand and arrange dates. They also have the right to refuse a marriage offer and to cancel further courtship at any time. Societal attitudes toward arranged marriages have relaxed, while the support and desire for, and number, of love marriages has risen in recent years.

Once a couple decides to marry, an engagement ceremony takes place to formalize the engagement publicly. During the ceremony the groom, via his go-between, gives a prescribed set of betrothal gifts and cash to the bride's family. A popular timing for the engagement ceremony is a few months prior to the wedding date. This event formerly was held at a bride's parents' home; whereas today, many families opt for hotels and restaurants. This alternative offers the convenience of catered food and accommodation of out-of-town guests. Osaka is known for the lavish contents and display of betrothal, in comparison to Tokyo and other urban centers. In Osaka, total funds invested in betrothal gifts are estimated at one-fourth of a man's annual income. If unable to come up with such funds, his parents are expected to provide the balance. The cash gift is a contemporary interpretation of a past custom in which a man gave money to his bride's family to have her wedding kimono made or bought. Today, the cash is viewed as a contribution toward rental of her bridalwear.

In Osaka, two common locations for a wedding ceremony and reception are at a hotel or in a wedding hall. Weddings in commercial venues became popular only in the mid-twentieth century, resulting in the shift in wedding locations from private homes to hotels (Edwards, 1989: 104; Katagi, 1994: 189). Smaller Japanese dwellings were not suitable for holding large weddings, especially in dense urban areas such as Osaka. The difference between the two contemporary types is the nature of their business focus. Hotels typically provide wedding services as part of their overall hotel operation; these include sleeping accommodations, restaurants and specialty boutiques. Wedding halls concentrate on the details of weddings as an event. Hotel weddings are more costly and thought to be more prestigious than wedding halls and the women I interviewed certainly preferred hotel weddings for these reasons.

Two common wedding ceremonies in Osaka are Shinto-style and Christian-style. For most people, neither Shinto nor Christian wedding ceremonies carry much religious significance. Couples select those aspects of religion in designing a wedding ceremony that they think looks and feels good in a secular and popular sense and where ambiance, aesthetics and practicality play important roles.

A wedding in Osaka usually begins with a Shinto- or Christian-style ceremony, followed by a reception, and then one or more private parties. After the marriage ceremony, the newlyweds have their portraits taken at a photography studio within the hotel. Then the bride retires into a dressing room where she has a dress change for a subsequent reception. Once she completes her change she and her husband have more portraits taken before the reception begins.

When the couple enters the reception hall, a married woman, most often their go-between or his wife holds the bride's hand and leads the couple into the event. This symbolic act of a married woman introduces the bride into the new phase of her life, from being single to being married. The couple sit in the center of an elevated main bridal table along with their go-between and his or her spouse. In Japanese weddings, the immediate families and close relatives of the couple sit at the least desirable tables to show courtesy and respect toward their guests.

A series of speeches forms part of the reception, including speeches from the go between, the couple's supervisors from work, their professors from college seminars, and other colleagues and friends. Between speeches comes a cake-cutting ceremony in which the couple inserts a knife into a sometimes six-feet (180-centimeters) tall wedding cake. Once completed, the couple withdraw from the reception hall into separate dressing rooms for another change of clothing. When they return in their new ensembles, the lights are dimmed for a candle service, a standard activity in Osakan weddings during which only a spotlight follows them as they walk. A high point of the candle service is to light a "memorial candle," composed of many small candles positioned around a large main candle forming a heart shape. The bride then may opt for yet another change of dress at the end of the reception when the couple publicly acknowledges their parents and thank the departing guests. Despite the numerous dress changes, speeches, and activities, the event takes only three hours, and Osakans call such a compacted wedding a "wedding package."

Rental Bridal Fashion

In the course of a single wedding, an upper-class bride in Osaka has three to five changes of ensemble, including Japanese and western modes of dress. For a Christian-style ceremony, she wears an *uedingu doresu* (western wedding dress) complete with a veil, followed by an *irouchikake* (colored wedding kimono) and an *irodoresu* (colored evening gown) for her reception. For a Shinto-style ceremony, she wears a *shiromuku* (white wedding kimono), followed by an *irouchikake*, *irodoresu* and *uedingu doresu* for the reception. A *furisode* (full-sleeve kimono) may also be added to the bride's choice of ensembles for both Christian-style and Shinto-style ceremonies.

The most popular way to acquire bridalwear in Osaka is to rent the clothing. A prospective bride attends a hotel-sponsored, bridal-fashion fair or visits rental bridal shops in search of her ensembles. Trained bridal consultants assist her. The two ways to rent include conventional renting and order-lease renting. All kimonos and most colored dresses belong to the first category; white wedding gowns may be rented either way.

In the procedure, the bride rents conventional existing ensembles from shops. A woman simply makes her selections among the hundreds of available items and reserves them for her wedding date. In order-lease renting, a dress is custom designed to meet the woman's taste and expectations in every way, and she is the first person to wear it. She returns both types of garments to the bridal shop when the wedding is over. It costs approximately ¥500,000 ($5,000) to rent conventionally and ¥600,000 ($6,000) to have a new dress sewn.

Rental bridalwear is sized to fit almost everyone because no single dress tightly fits the wearer's body, especially the upper bodice. The roominess allows both slender and plumper women to wear the same dress without major alterations. The dress simply hangs from the shoulders and, by tightening the ribbons in the back, the upper bodice is fitted. Bridal shops also carry an extensive collection of accessories, including veils of various length and designs, and shoes dyed to match the dress perfectly.

Renting a wedding kimono, *irouchikake* (colored wedding kimono) in particular, can be exceptionally expensive in Osaka. An *irouchikake* of the highest quality may cost approximately ¥1,000,000 ($10,000) just to have it for an event, not even for an entire day. Factors that determine a good *irouchikake* include superiority of design, intricacy of decorative work, and the region of origin. Bridal shops demand a large sum because a good *irouchikake* is one of a kind, and only a limited number of artisans today have the training and skill to create a kimono of such high artistic merit.

Because most brides wear both *shiromuku* (white wedding kimono) and *irouchikake* (colored wedding kimono), bridal shops offer a package deal. If a woman rents a *shiromuku*, she can rent an *irouchikake* at half the original price. A *shiromuku*, which usually rents from ¥100,000 to ¥200,000, is thought to be much less expensive than an *irouchikake*. In this way, the once-inaccessible, one-million-yen *irouchikake* can be worn for ¥500,000. Although the cost is still high, it may fall into a range of expected wedding expenses some families are willing to pay simply because it is a happy occasion and too auspicious to be miserly about money.

A bride almost always wears a wedding kimono with a headdress. Today's style combines a hair wig and a headdress into one. The wig replicates the earlier hairstyle created with a bride's own hair when the kimono was the everyday fashion in Japan. The wig is decorated with ornamental hairpins and a *tsunokakushi* (literally, a horn-hider, representing the hiding of a bride's horns of jealousy) or a *watabôshi* (literally, a cotton-hat, which when worn covers a bride's head except for her face). Although modern Japanese women no longer wear kimonos on a daily basis, when worn, it is important to look properly coordinated from head to toe.

The women I interviewed cited two reasons for choosing to rent and not to own their wedding outfits. A garment worn only once in a lifetime does not justify the exorbitant amount of funds to be invested into a timeless possession. A voluminous garment such as an *uedingu doresu* (white wedding gown) is too large to be stored indefinitely in a private home. When space is a scarce commodity, bridalwear without a practical afterlife deserves little consideration for permanency in Osaka.

Hotel Weddings as Packages

The women I interviewed frequently used the word "package" to describe the nature of hotel weddings. The word appeared in such phrases as "package wedding," "wedding package" and "package deal." In Osaka today, these English phrases, while pronounced in a Japanized fashion, are no longer translated into Japanese. The English words have become such an integral part of Japanese speech that Osakans, from the young to the elderly, know exactly what the words mean without explanations. In the following pages, I will illustrate: 1) how the wedding industry in Osaka, hotels in particular, packages everything customers need into a compact bundle to provide convenience and

2) how customers view, and what they expect from, such a service package for their own weddings.

Many hotels in Osaka offer wedding packages similar to the way travel agencies in the United States sell tour packages. Hotels specially set up a full-service bridal department to meet all wedding needs under one roof (e.g. Shinto shrine, chapel, rental bridal shop, betrothal gifts shop, and shop specializing in thank you gifts, florist, beauty salon and travel agency). A bridal service counter is typically found on the second or higher floors, always avoiding the busy street level and allowing the customers a more private, quieter setting. Once a couple selects a particular hotel as their wedding site, all they need to do is simply choose certain items from a list of wedding services available at or through the hotel. These services include: wedding invitations, floral arrangements, catering, rental bridalwear, entertainment, master of ceremony, ritual provider, and overseas honeymoon. Trained hotel staff coordinate and oversee the arrangements making sure that all details, before, during, and after their wedding, go flawlessly.

The women I interviewed particularly liked the fact that things were taken care of by the hotel professional staff from the beginning to the end. Hotel weddings are known for, and pride themselves in, the efficient customer service they provide. To maintain the strength of its sales, hotels go to great length to ensure that there is no service they cannot accommodate. If a hotel lacks a particular service or material requested by customers, the hotel uses its extensive business network to accommodate the request.

Hotels publish packets of written and visual materials, including an itemized list of all provided wedding services printed in a single-page in menu format along with a price sheet. By simply looking through the materials, customers gain practical knowledge of the anticipated expenses, available services, schedule for wedding preparations, details of the wedding day, ceremonial procedures, and much more. The thorough and precise information provided in the packet conveniently fits into a normal letter-sized envelope.

Let me describe the extent of the packaged wedding service hotels provide by using rental bridalwear as an example. Many hotels offer a bridal fashion fair where those who have reserved a reception hall are invited to view a runway show featuring the latest bridalwear collection. They may try on ensembles they have just seen and may reserve them at this time. The bridal fashions are brought to the customers for their shopping convenience. Hotels also house a rental bridal shop with a readily available collection of Japanese and western bridalwear, designed to help customers save time and energy.

On the wedding day, a bride is asked to do just one thing – to come in wearing no makeup. At the hotel, makeup artists, hairstylists and kimono dressers, each specially trained to handle aesthetic demands unique to weddings, await her arrival. Kimono dressing for a bride usually begins two-and-a-half hours prior to the wedding ceremony. The hotel hires the specialists and takes full responsibility for coordinating the whole affair. The bride need not bring anything; the hotel prepares all materials from cosmetics and hair extensions to undergarments, for her, including a dressing room with a full-view mirror.

The wedding ensembles the bride has reserved are delivered to her dressing room. The bridalwear package includes every item she needs for the day, including kimono slippers, shoes, jewelry, pantyhose and dressing props such as pins, strings and padding materials. Because a bride usually changes into three to five outfits during a wedding, more than one stylist attends to her dress changes. The speed and efficiency of the stylists impressed the women I interviewed who noted that the quick transformations seemed effortless. For example, as a hairstylist modifies a bride's hair from Japanese to western style, a makeup artist adds fake eyelashes, and yet another dresser helps her put on the petticoat and *irodoresu* (colored evening gown).

As illustrated in the above example, hotels provide capacious service tailored extensively to meet every need and want of each customer. In so doing, the hotel greatly increases the customer's access and convenience while significantly reducing hassles and headache.

Packaging as a Cultural Theme

As mentioned earlier, the women I interviewed used the word "package" to describe the nature of their wedding experiences. "Packaging" emerged as a cultural theme in this study, confirming the important place the notion holds in their weddings. The meaning they attach to the word "package" shows a keen similarity to Lee's three themes: 1) innovation by reduction, 2) inclusion by reduction, and 3) captivation by reduction.

Innovation by Reduction

According to Lee, the Japanese method of innovation often involves reducing the physical dimensions of objects (e.g. folding fan). In contemporary Osaka, wedding customs of Japan's non-western past mixes with influences of its westernized present and are reduced in temporal, spatial and operational dimensions to create a new ritual stage which the women identified as uniquely "Japanese."

In Osakan weddings the dress change reflects the temporal aspect of Lee's reduction process. The change, in which dress shifts from white to a color, is a contemporary interpretation of "an older Japanese practice where a bride would wear white for the first and second day of her wedding and change into a colored garment on the third" (Hendry, P: 169). The white kimono symbolized a "bride's death in her parents' home and rebirth in the groom's home. Only on the third day after her arrival did the bride formally become a member of the groom's family, and was permitted to wear colored clothing again" (Katagi, 190–1).

Previous wedding customs consisted of "a departure ceremony at the bride's home, a bridal procession, and an arrival ceremony at the groom's home. These three parts correspond to the rites of separation, transition, and union found in marriage practices of the world over" (Katagi, 189). As seen in the Osakan weddings, "a three-day wedding ritual of the past has become condensed to a day's event" (Katagi, 186) which consists of a wedding ceremony, a two- to three-hour reception, and subsequent private parties.

A case of reductionism in spatial consideration was found in the way the rites of "separation, transition, and union" are recreated during the Osakan weddings. A bride's departure (separation) from her natal home, once marked by a bridal procession from one household to the other, is symbolized now by a short walk within the same building; for example, from a Shinto shrine or a chapel to a photo studio inside a hotel.

In the past, "lanterns and torches were kept alight to prevent her (a bride) from being possessed by demons" during a bridal procession (transition) (Katagi, 190). The torch-lit bridal procession continues to exist in the form of the candle service, adopted by the wedding industry and reborn as a "western custom" to be marketed to the generation which finds things of the West appealing. As part of incorporating the western notion of romantic love, a bridal couple lights a large heart-shaped "memorial candle" during the candle service.

The cake-cutting ceremony exemplifies the final stage of the marriage rites (union). Walter Edwards (1989) draws a link between the sweet taste of cake, often broadly associated with children in Japanese culture because of their love of sweets, and fertility, a symbol of marriage as an institution where reproduction is encouraged and expected. The act of inserting a long knife, a phallic symbol, into the wedding cake is also suggestive of the sexual union in marriage (110–11).

Inclusion by Reduction

Lee uses the Japanese box lunch as an example of the Japanese love for packing things in by making things smaller. In the case of Osakan weddings, I found a similarity to his concept in the way hotels provide wedding-related businesses to customers. Like Lee's box-lunch analysis, hotels physically house everything customers will need under one roof where they can visit and purchase services and use the facilities without having to leave the building. By clustering them together, the customers minimize the time and hassle they would have experienced for coordinating their wedding affairs. For customer convenience, hotels also publish printed materials in which all information may be found at a glance. Further, Lee's notion of "packing in" was present in the psychological dimension of weddings. The women perceived hotels that sold wedding packages packed full of customer-friendly features as the seal of higher quality. Luxury hotels are especially known for their superior customer service where any peculiar demands can be readily accommodated.

Captivation by Reduction

Lee's third theme is manifested in the way Japanese experience nature. Japanese traditionally have brought nature closer to home in the form of "dry landscape" rather than by actually venturing into nature to appreciate its qualities firsthand (e.g. *bonsai*). In a similar manner, during Osakan weddings, unfamiliar things and concepts are brought closer to home in the form of wedding packages even though the weddings are no longer held at home. For those who want to wear an *uedingu doresu* (white wedding gown) and marry in a church, but who do not want to convert to Christianity, hotels offer a secular emulation of the Christian rite called Christian-style wedding. For those who think of Shinto wedding in a Shinto shrine as dated and unfashionable, but for those who wish to be a part of the ceremony, hotels similarly provide a Shinto-style wedding at the hotel.

Many Osakans think of romantic love as western. While very few Osakans display affection publicly or express love in Japanese, a diamond ring, an item of western material culture, has come to symbolize romance. The "exotic" western custom features in the Japanese ritual scene in the form of a ring exchange, both in Christian-style and Shinto-style ceremonies. Thanks to rigorous marketing by the wedding industry, diamond engagement rings also have become a standard item of betrothal gifts and cash.

For many Osakans who grow up wearing the western mode of dress, donning a wedding kimono is a more unfamiliar experience than wearing a western-style bridal gown. Hotels cater to customers' needs by supplying a team of trained wedding kimono dressers and hair and makeup artists. Not only are customers exempted from purchasing a collection of bridalwear, but they also are relieved from learning how to put on a kimono and an *obi* (sash). Hotels, not the women themselves, capture the unfamiliar and transform its complexities into a simple, convenient act through modern packaging.

Packaging as an Expression of Japaneseness

The coexistence of Japanese and the West has become an underlying structure of everyday life in Osaka. Things reminiscent of Japan's non-western past combine with western material culture and are constantly juxtaposed to create a new composition, giving Osaka the unmistakable look of a contemporary urban city. Osakan weddings are no exceptions: Japanese and western bridal fashions are worn, rings are exchanged in a Shinto-style ceremony, French dinner is served for a reception, and a wedding cake is cut by a couple wearing wedding kimonos.

Although Osakan weddings regularly incorporate customs and objects of both Japanese and western origin, the women I interviewed identified their wedding experiences as uniquely Japanese. They attributed the success of their weddings to the Japaneseness of the packaging. In Japanese culture, a stereotypically western activity, such as a chapel wedding, becomes genuinely Japanese when hotels present a professionally packaged service. On the other hand, a traditional Shinto ceremony may be viewed as less Japanese if the shrine provides only an unsophisticated wedding package or none at all.

Osakan couples certainly perceive the neatness of packaged outcome as more important than the mere bulk of things packed into it. In a highly westernized society, ". . . Western goods and practices have helped" Osakans "define Japaneseness by delineating what Japan is not" (Creighton, 55). Just as the Japanese tradition of making things smaller remains vital to concepts about Osakan weddings, so too does the Japanese urge to compact continue to play a strong role in defining the notions of Japaneseness. The act of packaging, not necessarily the country of origin of the things packaged, determines the final label of the final product.

Notes

1. The Japanese elite class has been under-represented in areas of research in general and in research on elite weddings in particular among western scholars. In current anthropological literature on Japanese weddings and other ceremonies, research has centered on the customs of rural communities or middle- or working-class persons (e.g. van Bremen & Martinez, 1995; Edwards, 1989; Jeremy & Robinson, 1989; Hendry, 1981; see also Smith, 1995 as he defends the study of urban Japanese weddings).

References

Ben-Ari, E., B. Moeran, & J. Valentine (eds) (1990), *Unwrapping Japan: Society and Culture in Anthropological Perspective*, Honolulu: University of Hawaii Press.

Creighton, M.R. (1992), "The depâto: Merchandising the West while selling Japan-eseness," in J.J. Tobin (ed.), *Re-made in Japan: Everyday Life and Consumer Taste in a Changing Society*, Binghamton, New York: Vail-Ballou Press, pp. 42–57.

Edwards, W. (1989), *Modern Japan Through its Weddings: Gender, Person, and Society in Ritual Portrayal*, Stanford University Press.

Hendry, J. (1981), *Marriage in Changing Japan: Community and Society*, New York: St. Martin's Press.

Jeremy, M. & Robinson, M.E. (1989), *Ceremony and Symbolism in the Japanese Home* (U. Hoichi, photos.), Manchester & New York: Manchester University Press.

Katagi, A. (1994), "The wedding reception: Old rituals in new disguises," in A. Ueda (ed.), *The Electric Geisha: Exploring Japan's Popular Culture* (M. Egushi, trans.), Tokyo: Kodansha International, pp. 185–94.

Lee, O-Young. (1982), *The Compact Culture: The Japanese Tradition of "Smaller is Better"* (R.N. Huey, trans.), Tokyo & New York & London: Kodansha International. [Originally *Chijimi Shikô No Nihonjin* (The Japanese who prefer reduction) by Gakuseisha, 1982].

Smith, R.J. (1995), "Wedding and Funeral Ritual: Analysing a Moving Target," in J. van Bremen & D.P. Martinez (ed.), *Ceremony and Ritual in Japan: Religious Practices in an Industrialized Society*, London & New York: Routledge, pp. 25–37.

Van Bremen, J. (1995), "Introduction: The myth of the Secularization of Industrialized Societies", in J. van Bremen & D.P. Martinez (ed.), *Ceremony and Ritual in Japan: Religious Practices in an Industrialized Society*, London & New York: Routledge, pp. 1–22.

4

Korean Wedding Dress from the Chosun Dynasty (1392–1910) to the Present

Na Young Hong

The long history of Korean dress traces its origins either from the tomb murals of the Koguryo period (37 BC–AD668) or from Chinese literature of the same period. The earliest records of the Korean wedding dress, however, date only from the Chosun dynasty (1392–1910). During this five-hundred-year period the Chosun dynasty strictly regulated the ranks of ceremonial clothes, but allowed the dynasty brides and grooms, regardless of their social status, to wear the same kind of wedding clothes as those worn by a princess and a prince. Although Korean adults usually wore white or light colored clothes for everyday, they wore a combination of bright colors, intricate embroidery, and gold-leaf imprints for their wedding dress. Furthermore, the wedding dress was decorated with various symbols and patterns which conveyed best wishes for the bride and groom. Although the materials for traditional Korean clothes, both for everyday and for ceremonial use, included cotton, silk, hemp, and ramie, silk was the usual fabric for ceremonial occasions.

Wedding rituals

During the Chosun dynasty, matchmakers arranged marriages. When both families agreed, a letter which contained the year, month, date, and hour of a prospective groom's birth was sent to the bride's family. The acceptance of the letter by the bride's family officially sealed the engagement and the groom and the bride became betrothed without knowing each other. The bride's parents used the letter to consult horoscopes in order to predict the harmony between the couple and, if auspicious, set a wedding date, usually between late autumn and early spring in order to avoid the farming season. The groom's family sent the letter wrapped in a cloth which had a red and blue color for each side, symbolizing yin and yang. In some regions, people used brilliant embroidery to decorate the cloth; today, such regional differences no longer exist. Even so, the delivery of the letter still remains an important part of the wedding in modern South Korea, although most couples who meet and marry today do so according to their own will and have a western-style engagement ceremony. Nowadays, when a bride's family receives a letter, they determine a propitious day for the wedding date.

In the past, when a wedding date was set, the groom sent a wooden box to the bride's house several days before the wedding. It contained a letter expressing gratitude for the marriage, a red and a blue cloth for the bride's skirt, and other wedding-related objects that varied by region or family.

Although the majority of modern South Koreans today prefer the western-style wedding, the traditional Korean wedding ceremony consisted of three parts: the delivery of the wild goose, the exchanges of *kowtow* (kneeling and touching foreheads to the ground) between the groom and the bride, and finally the highlight of the wedding, the couple's drinking of an alcoholic beverage. When the groom reached the bride's house, he held the first ceremony of giving a wild goose to the bride's family, drawing attention to geese who not only have many many goslings, but are faithful to their spouses (Figure 4.1).

The next wedding ritual was the mutual kowtowing of the groom and the bride for the first time. Either on a wooden floor or in the front yard, the bride's family arranged a long-legged table behind a folding screen embroidered with peony flowers, symbols of wealth and luxury. On the table, were two candlesticks, two vases containing a pine branch and a branch of bamboo, a pair of wooden mandarin ducks, a bowl of chestnuts and jujubes, and a bowl of rice. Under the table were a live hen and cock, the legs of each were bound together. Two small tables for drinks and washbasins completed the setting, one each for the bride and the groom.

When the groom and the bride entered the temporary wedding area created by the folding screen, they first washed their hands and then stood facing each other. A wedding manager lit the candles and the bride kowtowed twice to the groom while the groom kowtowed once to the bride. Then the kowtow was repeated a second time. The bride's eyes were closed by beeswax. She received help on both sides from two women, for her exchanges of kowtows because she could not see and she wore elaborate ritual clothing: several kinds of underwear, a petticoat, a red skirt decorated with elaborate gold-leaf imprints, three kinds of jacket (*jeoghori*), and a ceremonial green robe (*wonsam*) or embroidered red robe (*whalot*). She wore a head crown with ornaments (*jokduri* or *whakwan*). The groom wore an official's uniform (*samokwandae*)

Figure 4.1 The groom is going to the bride's house for the wedding ceremony during the Chosun dynasty. Painting: "Shinhan" by Kim, Hong Do. 18th century.

(Figure 4.2). There was no special dress for a bride's attendant, however, she usually wore a blue skirt and a light blue *jeoghori*. Usually in rural areas the bride's relatives assisted her in the kowtow while in the cities professional hairdressers both arranged her hair and to helped her execute her exchange of the kowtows. A ritual exchange of drinks completed the ceremonies at the bride's house. The groom and the bride then retreated to different rooms and the bride's family set a table for the groom.

The first night the groom and the bride were together was called the *sinbang*.[1] The bride's family spread a mattress and comforter in the newly-weds' room and placed pillows embroidered with mandarin ducks on the bedding. There also was a simple table for drink. In the room, the groom removed the bridal crown and untied the ribbons of her clothes. The groom and the bride saw each other's faces for the first time in this room, but many other people also peeped into the room that night through holes made in the paper door. This originated because people were both curious and worried about the newly-weds.

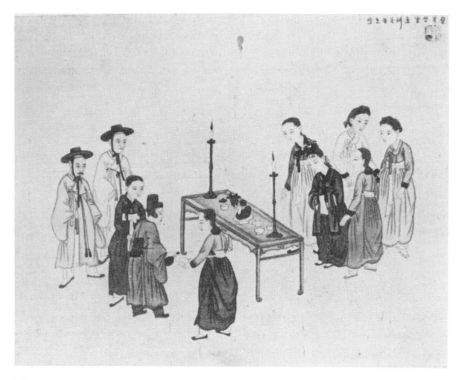

Figure 4.2 Traditional wedding ceremony during the Chosun dynasty. The groom wears *samokwandae* and the bride wears *jokduri* and *wonsam*. Painting: "Chorye" by Ki-Sen. 18th century.

The wedding feast continued for several days. In earlier times, a new couple lived in the bride's house until their first child began to walk, at about two to three years. But from the late Chosun dynasty, the newly-weds stayed at the bride's house only one or three days reflecting the Korean preference for odd numbers, and then the new couple moved to the groom's family home. On this trip, the groom rode on horseback in front of the group, while the bride followed, sitting in a palanquin. Servants followed, carrying wedding gifts, and food prepared for the first meeting of the bride with the groom's family. The wedding gifts, a kind of dowry, included objects for the bride's use, such as several rolls of fabric, clothes, a chamber pot, a washbasin, and a sewing box. Dowry items differed from region to region and their number and quality varied greatly, depending on the social status and wealth of the bride's family.[2]

Although the groom and the bride wore the same clothes for the introductory family meeting as they wore for the wedding, the wealthy provided both a green robe (*wonsam*) and an embroidered red robe (*whalot*) for the wedding and ritual family meeting so that the bride could have different clothes for the two occasions. The bride usually wore a green robe (*wonsam*) for the wedding ceremony and an embroidered red robe (*whalot*) for the ceremony of meeting the family; however, she could reverse the order of dress or wear either outfit for both occasions. The ritual meeting still forms part of the wedding tradition in South Korea, and grooms and brides continue to prepare traditional wedding dress for this occasion.

In former times, after the formal meeting, the newly-weds lived at the house of the groom's parents. The bride had to greet her parents-in-law every morning. She always dressed in a red skirt and a green jacket (*jeoghori*) or, in households that sought to maintain high standards of behaviour, in a long green jacket and a crown.

The Groom's Dress

During the Chosun dynasty, the groom wore wedding clothes similar to an official's uniform. The wedding dress of a groom was a *sangbok*, the uniform which officials wore for their everyday functions that consisted of a hat (*samo*), a loose coat (*danryung*) and black boots. The *sangbok* uniform was called *samokwandae* when the groom wore it for the wedding. After the wedding, the groom changed his wedding clothes and wore an ordinary adult robe and a wide-brimmed hat and outer coat which the bride's family prepared for him. The rich made their wedding robes at home, but the poor of a village made communal wedding robes used by all grooms and brides for every wedding.

The Groom's Hairstyle and Headdress

The Chosun dynasty groom wore a government official's stiff, black silk hat with side flaps, for the wedding ceremony. He put the hat on after wrapping a black headband made of horsetail hair around his head. The groom might place the hat over a winter cap if he married during that time of year.

Before the wedding, a young man parted his hair in the center, let the braided hair hang down his back, and put on a black hair ribbon, shaped like a swallow's beak. He affixed the ribbon to the end of his braided hair asymmetrically, like the way ribbons are fastened onto the *hanbok*, the traditional Korean dress of both men and women. An unmarried youth was not allowed to wear a hat, but rather headgear and, as an adult, he coiled his hair on top of his head. The most representative hat for the ruling class of the Chosun dynasty was one made of fine cut, black-lacquered bamboo or horse hair. This hat had a very wide brim and only a man from the upper class wore it when he went outside.

When a youth wore his wedding dress, for the first time in his life he put his hair on the top of his head. He made a knot out of his hair at the crown of his head. The man used a very small crossbar to fix the knot on his head. He also wrapped the headband around his head to prevent the hair from falling down over his forehead.

During the Chosun dynasty, if a man had not worn his hair in a knot for his wedding, he was not treated as an adult even if he grew old. If a young boy married, however, he was considered an adult if he wore his hair in this style. In principle, a young man held the ceremony for adulthood sometime between his fifteenth and twentieth birthdays, after which he made the hair knot and got married, but many young men skipped the adulthood ceremony and made the knot at the time of marriage. The ruling class regarded it as a shame if men fixed their hair in the knot without wearing hats on their heads; it was regarded as shameful as wearing only underwear.

The Groom's Ceremonial Dress

The groom's ceremonial dress was called *samokwandae* derived from two words: a *samo* which was put on his head and a *kwandae*, an official's robe and a girdle. The groom wore a blue or dark purple robe with a round neckline and wide sleeves. Tacked to the robe, both in front and in back, was a large square, embroidered with a pair of cranes. The square of civilian officials had various bird patterns on them, while those of military officials had four-legged animal patterns. Most wedding dress of the Chosun dynasty used the crane pattern, apparently reflecting the superiority of civil service to military service during that period. A groom wore trousers, a jacket, and a coat under his wedding robe.

The groom fastened his robe with a girdle. The wearer's official rank determined the ornamental material on his girdle. The leather, the base of the girdle, was wrapped in silk, and people attached various ornaments to it. Jade was the most precious material for ornaments, but only the king could use it. Government officials used a water buffalo's horn or gold or silver ornaments, according to their ranks. The girdle passed through two loops under the arms to hold it in place. Because the girdle was very large, however, it became loose behind the back when a man fixed it in the front, and vice versa. The girdle showed a man's rank and served as a decoration without any practical purpose.

The groom wore a pair of black ankle boots with red trim. He appeared in the ceremonial hall with both hands holding a square, thin, stiffened gauze fan that he raised to veil his face.

The Bride's Hairstyle and Headdress

A girl of the Chosun dynasty parted her hair in the center and braided it. She tied a red hair ribbon, shaped like a swallow's beak, asymmetrically onto the end of her braided hair in the same manner that ribbon was fastened to her jacket. Before the wedding ceremony a bride made two chignons, the symbol of an unmarried woman, on the back of her head by means of a crossbar-shaped hairpin. After the wedding, the young woman arranged her hair in a chignon on the nape of her neck and maintained that hairdo throughout the remainder of her life. The hairpin, useful in fixing a chignon, in addition served a decorative function. Hairpins came in a great variety of shapes, sizes, and materials. For her wedding a bride wore a special long and brilliant hairpin, usually of gold or silver with a dragon's or a phoenix's head.

A bride also wore two kinds of special hair ribbons at her wedding. The loose ends of a front ribbon were wound from its middle section around the crossbar hairpin and draped in front of the shoulder. The front hair ribbon had gold-leaf imprints and fringes adorned with pearls or coral beads while the back one, which was larger and longer, hung from her head, reaching below the hips. The hair ribbons were red or purple.

Today, the preparation of a bride's hair still follows ancient traditions with modest change, but brides lapse in wearing the particular regional kinds of hair ribbon decorations. For example, in the past a bride wore hair ribbons with gold-leaf imprints, adorned with small jade or amber ornaments in Seoul. The popular motif for back hair ribbon ornaments was a cicada or a butterfly. In other regions, a bride wore a back hair ribbon, decorated with small enameled, colorful silver medallions and colorful silk yarns. In Kaesung, near Seoul, a bride put on a pearl hair ribbon. In Pyongyang, a bride wound an embroidered front hair ribbon around a long hairpin and the ribbon hung over the bride's left shoulder only.

During the Chosun period, the bride put a black sateen crown on her head as the final item of the wedding headdress. In shape, it resembled a small pillbox and was decorated with jewelry. The shape and decoration of the crown differed according to family. Sometimes a bride wore a different kind of crown. Although made of thick paper and covered with black silk sateen and jewelry, it was distinctive because of its open sides. People usually adorned crowns with jade, coral, amber, or pearl beads and also placed gilt birds and butterflies which quivered on small springs on the top. In the cities of Kaesung and Pyongyang, a bride wore her crown decorated with silk flowers.

The Bride's Ceremonial Dress

During the Chosun dynasty, the bride wore a red skirt and a yellow or a green jacket (*jeoghori*) inside, and a wedding robe outside. There were two kinds of wedding robes: one was green with patterns of impressed gold leaf, the other red with embroidery. The bride could wear the same kind of ceremonial dress as a princess, such as a green robe (*wonsam*) or an embroidered red robe (*whalot*), regardless of her social status, but the dress and headdress of a bride varied according to the regions.

A common characteristic for both types of robes was that their length reached mid-calf and the backs of the robes were about four inches (twenty cm) longer than the fronts. Both had a long side slit and a front opening. A woman fastened the robe by using a pair of small silver clasps or a narrow ribbon around the bust line. The *wonsam* and *whalot* had stripes of colors around the sleeves; broad white cuffs were attached to the sleeves (Figure 4.3). The white cuffs symbolized the robe as a ceremonial dress; a poor bride used the white cloth to hide her hands during the wedding ceremony. A bride put on a

Figure 4.3 The groom wears *samokwandae* and the bride wears *whalot* in the twentieth century. Photograph: Courtesy of Choi, Suk-ro.

stiff, padded sash, 2.5 inches (seven cm) wide and 9.75 feet (three meters) long, around her chest over the wedding robe. She tied it in the middle and suspended the rest down her back.

In spite of their similarities, people could easily distinguish a *wonsam* from a *whalot* because the two robes had different shapes, colors, embroidery, and gold-leaf imprints. A *wonsam* was decorated with impressed gold leaf. During the Chosun dynasty, *wonsam* differed in their colors and impressed gold-leaf motifs according to the wearer's social status. A queen wore yellow or red, and a princess and a woman of the upper class wore green with impressed gold leaf. Commoners could wear plain green only as wedding and funeral dress. There were various patterns of embroidery for a *whalot* robe; these patterns usually symbolized the well-being of offspring and conjugal harmony. Many Chinese characters, such as those meaning wealth or longevity, were used in the patterns. People also embroidered these robes with lotus and peony flowers, children with flowers, the nine Chinese phoenixes, and pomegranates on the front, back, and sleeves. The peony flowers symbolized wealth, the phoenixes and pomegranates many children. The backside was even more brilliantly decorated because the robe's wide sleeves blocked much of the front side from view, especially when a groom and a bride held hands during the wedding. Wedding dress differed regionally. For example, a bride from Pyongyang did not wear a *wonsam* nor *whalot* robe; rather, she put on a short vest, lined and trimmed with fur, over a jacket and a skirt. One item from the traditional Chosun dynasty wedding dress, a veil of rectangular cloth of dark purple silk gauze that covered the bride's head, has not been in use since the late nineteenth century.

The Basic Bridal Clothing: Then and Now

Korean wedding dress remained conservative for nearly the whole five hundred years of the Chosun dynasty. During the first half of the twentieth century, Koreans began adopting items of wedding attire from western culture. In the past, the clothes a bride wore under her wedding dress were not very different from her everyday clothes. The basic dress for a Korean woman has been a skirt (*chima*) and jacket (*jeoghori*). Earlier, a woman's *jeoghori,* like a man's, reached the middle of her hips, like a man's, but since the eighteenth century it has been so shortened that it no longer even touches the bust line. Women tied their drawers and skirts over the bust line. A Korean woman's *chima* is a gathered skirt, wrapped around over the bust line. Women's *jeoghori* lengthened in the 1930s but since then has returned to a shorter form and remains so today.

For the wedding, a bride previously wore at least four pairs of drawers, a custom that was simplified in the twentieth century and now a bride wears only one pair. In the past, a bride also wore a petticoat-like underskirt which reached from her chest to her knees and her silhouette resembled a dome, rather than a cone. Today, a bride wears a long petticoat.

A traditional bridal skirt was red and the upper class added impressed gold leaf to the skirt's hemline. A bride wore three jackets (*jeoghoris*) for the wedding: a pink ramie *jeoghori* innermost, a small pink *jeoghori* in the middle, and an outer *jeoghori* of green or yellow. In contemporary South Korea a bride wears one or at most two *jeoghoris* instead of three. A ramie *jeoghori* had no ribbons. A bride wore a ramie *jeoghori* even if she married during the winter. This symbolized a cool married life, without distress, just like ramie clothes which were cooler for summer wear. The outer *jeoghori* had red cloths patched on the neckband, at the ends of the sleeves, at the gussets under the armholes, and on the ribbons; this type of applied decoration was called *samwhejang jeoghori*.

Koreans also wore a pair of white socks (*beosun*). In the Chosun period, a woman always wore very tight *beosuns* because, although she never bound her feet like a Chinese woman, small and narrow feet were idealized. A bride wore a pair of leather shoes which were covered with silk brocade. Shoes and socks for a woman had upturned and pointed toes.

Bridal Makeup and Accessories: Then and Now

During the Chosun dynasty, most women rejected thick makeup, although some women who entertained men applied it heavily. Those who did not use cosmetics usually took very good care of their skin. On her wedding day, however, a bride used face powder for makeup and put rouge on her lips. One week before the wedding, a bride removed all hair from her face in preparation for the makeup which was homemade and of poor quality. When a bride removed hair from her face, she tried to make her forehead rectangular; but she left long hair near her ears because people regarded it as beautiful. Once Korea began to import cosmetics from China in the nineteenth century and then began to manufacture them domestically in the late nineteenth century, the quality of makeup increased greatly.

During the ceremony, a bride put three small red circles on her face with rouge and pasted a small circle of red paper in the middle of her forehead. This tradition still remains as part of a bride's makeup. People also previously put sticky beeswax on a bride's eyelashes for a bride was not to open her eyes during the wedding ceremony, but this custom disappeared in the twentieth century.

Though Koreans wore earrings, necklaces, and bracelets before the Chosun dynasty, they never wore necklaces and bracelets during the Chosun period.[3] Rich parents-in-law gave gifts of family jewelry to a new daughter-in-law after the wedding. Many commoners could not afford wedding rings, but if a bride received rings she wore a pair of them. People engraved the bat pattern on wedding rings as a sign of good luck and the ability of the bride to bear many children, like a bat. This bat pattern became popular for brides in the late Chosun dynasty. In contemporary South Korea, a groom and a bride wear western-style wedding rings and the groom's family always gives the bride a pair of gold wedding rings.

Pendants with a silk knot and tassels hung from the sash or jacket ribbons. A bride wore bigger and more brilliant pendants for the wedding than for everyday. A woman usually wore one pendant, but put three pendants on for special occasions. In some provinces, women ostentatiously wore seven pendants.

Changes in the Twentieth Century

The western-style wedding came to Korea at the end of the nineteenth century when contact with the west began. Koreans with a western education or Korean Christians adopted this style first. In particular, the groom's wedding customs and his dress became westernized; now he wears a suit. The bride's dress became a composite of the older, Chosun customs and newer ones adopted from western culture. For example, a Korean bride began wearing a white skirt and jacket covered with a western veil and she held a bouquet. Although a woman traditionally wore white skirt (*chima*) and jacket (*jeoghori*) for mourning in Korea, they became a substitute for a bride's western wedding dress. Since the beginning of the twentieth century, the groom has worn a suit at the engagement ceremony, while the bride has worn a pink skirt and jacket. A bride still prefers to wear a traditional pink robe for the engagement.

The wedding ceremony changed again with the industrialization of South Korea after the Korean War, 1950–3, when a majority of Koreans began to hold western-style wedding ceremonies at commercial wedding halls or churches, departing from the traditional wedding ceremony held at home. The number of brides wearing western-style wedding dresses began to increase around the 1960s and a majority of brides have worn them since the 1970s.

There remain, nevertheless, many aspects of the traditional Chosun wedding procedure in contemporary South Korea. People still exchange a letter at the engagement ceremony and sending the symbolic gifts and food after the wedding is still regarded as necessary. Although a groom and a bride may wear

Figure 4.4 The bridge wears a white veil and a *hanbok* in a western-style wedding in 1930. Photograph: Private collection. Used with permission.

a western suit and a western wedding dress for their wedding ceremony, they always wear traditional *hanbok* for the ritual of feeding in-laws. If they do not prepare their own *hanboks*, a groom and a bride will borrow one from the management of a wedding hall. In this case, they only borrow an outer wedding robe because they order their basic dress or buy them from a store. A groom wears a simplified coat under the wedding robe. This kind of wedding dress, though flamboyant, is generally made of low quality fabric and with poor design because wedding-hall managers do not like to invest money in rental wedding robes.

In South Korea, major changes took place in the 1980s and 1990s. For instance, newly-weds often hold the food ritual at the wedding hall right after the wedding ceremony, at which time, some grooms put on traditional wedding dress over their western suit, mixing the two cultures. A few grooms may put on a king's robe and their brides may wear a queen's dress for this ceremony. Or, brides may wear an embroidered green robe, which deviates from the traditional wedding dress. Nonetheless, with the recent renewed awareness of traditional Korean culture, upper-class grooms and brides are increasingly returning to more traditional Chosun dynasty wedding dress.

Notes

1. Before the *sinbang*, the groom must undergo harsh treatment because youths from the bride's village hit the soles of the groom's feet with sticks, after hanging him upside down. This was a kind of mischievous retaliation by the village youths, thinking the groom was stealing a girl from their village. This activity seldom occurs these days.

2. Nowadays the word *pyebaek*, however, has changed to mean the formal process of introducing the bride to the groom's family and close relatives after the wedding.

3. When they put on earrings, they put earrings on both earlobes without piercing them, because Confucianism, the state ideology, prohibited people from impairing any part of their body, a gift from their parents. People usually wore rings without gemstone settings. Enameled silver rings were worn more often than gold rings. Amber and jade were also used widely for rings, but people usually wore these in the summer.

References

Hong, N. Y. (2000), "A Study of Changes in Wedding Dress for Paebaek during 20th Century," *Journal of the Korean Society of Clothing and Textiles* 24:4, 594–604.

—— (2000), "A Study of *Whakwan*," *Journal of the Korean Society of Dress* 50:3, 31–42.

Hong, N. Y., Lee, E. J., and Lim, J. Y. (1995), "A Study of Folk Dress Culture-Field Research Around the Mt. Kumo Area," *Journal of the Korean Society of Clothing and Textiles* 19:1, 71–9.

Kim, J. Y. and Hong, N. Y. (1999), "A Study of *Jokduri*," *Journal of the Korean Society of Dress* 43:1, 243–58.

Suk, J. S. (1971), *Hankook Bokshiksa* [History of Korean Dress], Seoul: Bo Jin Jae.

Yang, S. (1997), *Hanbok – The Art of Korean Clothing*, Seoul: Hollym International Corp.

You, H. K. (1972), *Hankook Bokshiksa Yonkoo* [A Study of Korean Dress History], Seoul: Ewha Womans University Press.

5

Marriage and Dowry Customs of the Rabari of Kutch: Evolving Traditions

Eiluned Edwards

Introduction

The Rabari are Hindu pastoralists who inhabit the desert region of Kutch district in the extreme west of Gujarat, where India borders Pakistan. There are three main subgroups of Rabari in the district: Kachhis in the central and western area, Dhebarias in the east and south-east, and Vagadias in the east and north-east. Their dress is distinguished by the signature use of black wool by the women and white cotton by the men. Much of it is decorated with elaborate hand embroidery (Figure 5.1). Rabari women are renowned through-out north-west India for their artistry and dense bas-reliefs of mirrorwork and embroidery that embellish not only items of dress, but also the domestic textiles and animal trappings used by the caste.

For the Rabari, the impetus behind the production of these embroideries is marriage. Apart from their livestock, textiles and dress are their chief material resources, and they are distributed by means of the dowry system. The occasion of a wedding provides a showcase for the women's artistic prowess and vividly illustrates the community's coherent sense of aesthetics (Figure 5.2). But these textiles constitute far more than the simple material assets of the Rabari, they also embody the "spirit and substance" of the community (Bayly, 1986: 286). Amendments to the textiles' composition are indicative of fundamental changes within the caste.

Since Independence in 1947, there has been widespread social change in India resulting in dramatic alterations to the rural way of life, and among the nomadic Rabari, to an emerging pattern of sedentarization. These changes have generated ongoing discourse in the Rabari community about the nature

Figure 5.1 Vagadia Rabari (migratory group). The Rabaran are wearing black wool skirts and veilcloths. Their blouses are synthetic. Their male relative wears a white cotton turban, smock and loin cloth. Photograph: the author.

of individual and group identity; the continuing negotiations in this respect have been expressed most notably through the medium of textiles and dress.

Embroidery ban

In April 1995, the council of the Dhebaria community issued an edict that banned the making and use of embroidery within that subgroup (Sri Rabari

Figure 5.2 Dhebaria Rabari wedding, 1997. The bride and groom are linked by a skein of white cotton that symbolizes their union. The wedding took place after the embroidery ban of 1995, and the dress of both bride and groom is decorated with brocade and lace. Custom dictates that the bride is shrouded in deep veiling for the entire wedding ceremony. Photograph: the author.

Samaj, 1995: 1–4). In addition, jewelry was to be restricted to a bare minimum and all the property transfers of marriage were to be completed within three years of the wedding ceremony. The Vagadia council followed suit in August of the same year. Any contravention of the new rules would be met with the imposition of a substantial fine. The ban was intended, in effect, to end the transmission of an embroidered dowry for Dhebarias and Vagadias.

Among Dhebarias, application of the ruling has been stringent and any early dissent was publicly quashed:

> This is an illiterate community. What is the tool to scare them? If we tried to catch everyone, it would not work. So we caught one, a Rabari from Haboi. We had a procession and brought him into the main square. We began to beat him and took him to the community headquarters. He is a good man, you can sit and talk to him. But if we don't do something like this, it won't work. That day we spent fifty rupees on tea to make him see that if someone like him who can really bring change in the community, does something like this, how will it work? He said that it was his own wish, his wife did the embroidery for him and he wanted to wear it. We made him sit in the community headquarters with half his clothes on. We tore his smock and tied it to the headquarters gate and told him to go home. (Personal communication, Arjanbhai Hirabhai, Dhebaria council member, 21 June1997).

The comparative wealth of Dhebarias, especially that of key members of the council, meant that they were able to take time away from their businesses to monitor and to enforce the ban. Among Vagadias, there has been no such coercion and the prevailing attitude is less compliant, with the women insisting on their right to make embroidery and to wear their full compliment of jewelry.

> Of course we need to wear it. Why do we have jewelry if we are not allowed to wear it? We definitely need embroidery. When we send a girl to her in-laws, we send her wearing all her embroidery and jewelry. Dhebars – they are plain like us old women. They aren't allowed to wear anything and there is no difference between a married woman and a widow. Widow and married, both are equal. What is the point? (Personal communication, Maliben Rajabhai, Vagadia Rabaran, 28 August 1997).

The ban was the result of a long campaign on the part of a number of Dhebaria council members. Their primary aim was to reduce the costs of dowry and bridewealth, which had become punitive by the early 1990s. Many council members perceived the burden of these costs and the lengthy transfer procedure of a woman and her dowry to her husband's home as social evils.[1] They were damaging to individual Rabaris and held back the community as a whole.

> Five or six of us decided that like Gandhi, who was starved and beaten and went to jail for the independence of the country, we were prepared to go through the same process to abolish this sin from our society. We were prepared for that. We were prepared to beat and to be beaten. For three months we moved through the villages like an election campaign and campaigned for this thing (Personal communication, Arjanbhai Hirabhai, Dhebaria council member, 21 June 1997).

In the Dhebaria and Vagadia subgroups the process of marriage, the key social institution of the community, was fraught with difficulties. Completing a dowry had become increasingly protracted because of the cost of its making, especially if there were several daughters in the family, and the amount of time needed for the women to complete the rising number of goods required. There was a corresponding increase in the cost of a bride and the installments of bridewealth were taking years to complete: "Rangka would not be migrating this year because he was on honeymoon. He had waited for his wife for over twenty years, travelling back and forth to his in-laws' house, begging them to send her to him" (Davidson, 1996: 84). Pride, too, was at the root of the problems with marriage. The "conspicuous consumption" of an ostentatious dowry could enhance a father's social standing. "Among Dhebarias there is one particular problem: they are economically better off. Not in the world but at the level of Kutch, so they have that ego. One thing is ego and the second is economic power, so they think they are better than anyone else" (Personal communication, Arjanbhai Hirabhai, Dhebaria council member, 21 June 1997).

It seemed that the established system of marriage brought little but grief to all concerned: women were not transferring to their in-laws until their late thirties and early forties, at an age when fertility starts to decline. "On the one hand, a father's economic situation weakens. On the other hand, a daughter's life is spoiled. He has to feed his daughter and spoil her life at the same time" (Personal communication, Arjanbhai Hirabhai, Dhebaria council member, 21 June 97). Driven by a sense of crisis within the subgroup, it appeared to Dhebaria council members that action was required urgently to alleviate the financial burden placed upon families. The capital released by the embroidery ban could then be redirected into community development. This could only be achieved, however, by a radical revision of the existing process of marriage.

The Traditions of Marriage

The importance of marriage in Indian society is paramount. For a man, it is a transformative ritual that marks his passage into the third stage of life recognized in Hindu scriptures, that of householder.[2] The life stages of a woman are defined in relation to men, thus marriage transforms her from being her father's daughter to being her husband's wife (cf. Wadley et al., 1991; Nabar, 1995).

A woman is perceived as requiring marriage to make her worthy of respect. With the onset of menarche, her fertility and female energy associated with the great goddess are seen as capricious and only to be effectively controlled within the institution of marriage. Marriage channels her sexuality into bearing children, it also makes her "auspicious" and, as such, she is accorded a measure of status, albeit refracted from her husband. That status, however, relies upon his being alive and is withdrawn in the event of his death. A widow is inauspiciousness personified and, as such, may not attend important rituals such as weddings (Fuller, 1991: 22–3).

In India, marriage, although transformative at a personal level, more generally maintains social continuity. It is the institution that consolidates the bonds of kinship and secures posterity. Caste endogamy is the norm that preserves the ritual purity of caste and clan, and sustains the continuity of social custom. When these patterns are disturbed, the very fabric of a community is threatened.

Marriage Customs of the Rabari

Among the Rabari of all three subgroups, negotiations to secure a good match for a son or daughter begin early and an engagement is often formalized by the time a child is two years old. Betrothal is signified by a small gift of jewelry, usually an amulet worn about the neck, made to the girl by her prospective in-laws. There may be a hiatus of several years before the ceremony at the heart of the wedding. For this, the bride and groom, linked by a skein of cotton that symbolizes their union, make four circulations around the sacred flame. It is their first meeting. Dhebaria and Vagadia marriages all take place at the festival that marks Lord Krishna's birthday; Kachhis may marry on any auspicious day in the year.

The central wedding ceremony takes place in the bride's village at an hour declared auspicious by the officiating *Brahmin* priest. After traveling with his wedding party, the groom sits in state attended by two assistants, waiting to be summoned by the *Brahmin*. His assistants must anticipate his every want as he may not speak for the duration of the wedding and his movements are impeded by his elaborate regalia.

The groom's dress is influenced by warrior caste court dress and traditionally consists of *mashru* (a satin with a silk warp and a cotton weft), trousers heavily gathered at the waist and tight at the ankle, a long *mashru* smock, and a generous red turban, to which is affixed an embroidered or beadwork triangle now often decorated with a set of flashing lights. He also wears an embroidered scarf that goes under his chin and wraps around his turban and a small shield on his back. In the warrior tradition he carries a sword sheathed in an elaborately decorated textile. The celebratory nature of the event is captured in the flamboyance of his dress.

In contrast, his bride observes deep veiling. The honor code dictates that she must manifest the utmost modesty. She is swathed in two layers of veilcloth, the uppermost formerly of red tie-dyed *mashru*, now often of synthetic fabric or silk, with a tie-dyed woollen one underneath. These conceal her blouse and skirt, both of which are heavy with decoration. On her wedding day she eschews the flat-paneled blouse of an unmarried girl and wears the blouse of a married woman for the first time. This is customarily a fully embroidered blouse, although it may now include bands of purchased metallic braid as well. The style of the blouse is distinguished by heavy ruching across the breasts, which connotes the fuller proportions of a lactating mother. A preoccupation with fertility is also evident in the embroidered devices that cover the blouse. Scorpions, phallic symbols associated with the god Shiva, the tree of life, and an abundance of floral forms fill the garment, blessing and encouraging a woman's latent fecundity. Implicit in the styling and decoration of her blouse is a woman's future role as a mother. She will wear this style of garment thereafter.

Once the ceremony is over and all the guests have been fed, the bride accompanies the groom to his village where she will stay, perhaps only for a single day. This is the first stay in her husband's home. She spends most of the visit veiled and secluded in the back room of her in-laws' house, with a guard of female relations outside the door, before returning to her natal village where she will stay until the next visit.

The lengthy process of marriage is punctuated by such visits that are, in fact, transfers of property negotiated by the families involved. The resources transmitted consist of different types of material goods and the primary instance of transmission is the dowry, a gift from father to daughter that is intended to meet her needs for starting out on married life. In addition to this, Rabaris also give bridewealth.[3]

Bridewealth

Bridewealth, also known as brideprice, is a gift usually of cash and jewelry, made to a bride's family, not the bride herself, by her husband-to-be's family. Always regarded as a degraded form of marriage, akin to selling a daughter, the instances of bridewealth in India are few and the practice is now declining. It is for the most part restricted to low-caste and tribal groups. Although Rabari fall into neither of these categories, two of the three subgroups in Kutch, the Dhebarias and the Vagadias, give both bridewealth and dowry.

Prior to the ruling of April 1995, Dhebaria women commanded a substantial brideprice, reputedly between eighty and a hundred thousand rupees ($2,580–3,225), much of it as jewelry (Personal communication, Pababhai Rajabhai, Vagadia Rabari, 26 January 1997). This cost could be circumvented to a certain extent by a custom which exchanges pairs of brothers and sisters in marriage. Both Dhebarias and Vagadias still arrange this type of symmetrical exchange marriage which keeps cash transfers to a minimum (Personal communication, Pababhai Rajabhai, Vagadia Rabari, 30 November 1994).

Dowry

Dowry remains the favoured type of marriage in India as it most closely resembles the Hindu ideal of "the gift of a virgin." The practice is thriving across all sectors of society, despite legislation to outlaw it, particularly the Dowry Prohibition Act 1961.

A Rabari dowry continues to consist primarily of a trousseau of heavily embellished blouses, skirts and veilcloths, and similar ornately decorated household textiles and animal trappings (Figure 5.3). In terms of cash, relatively little is given. The number and nature of items included in the gift is dictated by the rules of each subgroup. As previously discussed, a new austerity has ruled dowry in the Dhebaria community since 1995. Prior to that, a Dhebaria dowry was comparable with that of Vagadias in terms of the range of goods produced, although the quantity of each item was far greater.

Current practice in the Vagadia community specifies that a girl should complete two blouses entirely covered with embroidery, three blouses made from tie-dyed silk or satin fabric with embroidery covering the stomach panel and cuffs, a minimum of five blouses made from synthetic fabric and decorated with purchased braids, three plain black woollen skirts, three tie-dyed woollen veilcloths decorated with embroidery along the centre seams and end borders. She must also have a selection of dowry bags decorated with appliqué and embroidery, embroidered envelope bags for holding items of special value, shopping bags embellished with embroidery and purchased braids, quilts, and decorations for the house.[4] (Personal communication, Renuben and Deviben Arjanbhai, Vagadia Rabaran, 22 June 1997). Formerly, a woman also would have made animal trappings, chiefly camel decorations, for her dowry; however, the need for these items has all but gone due to Rabaris' increasing sedentarization and the loss of their vocation as camel-breeders in the years since Independence.

The Making of Dowry

The production of dowry embroidery begins in earnest in a woman's teens and accelerates once an approximate date has been fixed for her marriage. This is

Figure 5.3 A dowry installment of a Vagadian Rabaran, ca 1955. Photograph: the
author.

very often prompted by the onset of menarche. Her trousseau may not be
completed until several years after the wedding ceremony and, indeed, many
women use the excuse of an unfinished dowry to avoid leaving home.

Making her dowry prepares a woman, in part, not only for the relocation
she must make but also for the social and psychological adjustments incumbent
upon her as she leaves the familiarity of her natal village. Often the experiential
boundaries of her world do not extend much beyond that. She must cope with
being joined in marriage to someone she does not know and then living in a
household of strangers.

Dowry embroideries are made in the nurturing environment of a woman's
home. She embroiders among other young women who have the prospect of

a similar transition ahead of them, and with older women who have weathered the experience of becoming wives in sometimes hostile surroundings (Elson, 1979; Sharma, 1980). Embroidery is produced in a space that is physically and temporally almost exclusively female. After the first round of water collection of the day and the completion of other domestic duties, the women gather on the platform of one of the houses in an area of a village usually belonging to a single caste and settle to their embroidery. Security is centred in the secluded area and home (Niranjana, 1997), and the structured decorum of the code of modesty, required when the men are about, vanishes. Veiling is relaxed or abandoned altogether as the women gossip and apply themselves to their embroidery surrounded by small children. It is in this environment that girls start to learn the repertoire of stitches, design devices and the color palette of Rabari embroidery. There is no systematic formal instruction as such, they learn by observation and by simply being around senior females at work.

Style of Embroidery and Types of Stitches

A number of stylistic influences are evident in Rabari embroidery. The extensive use of chain stitch (now a solid open chain stitch but previously simple chain stitch) reveals the influence of *Mochi* embroidery. Men of the *Mochi* or cobblers caste flourished as professional embroiderers in the nineteenth and early twentieth centuries. Under the patronage of the royal courts of Kutch and neighbouring Saurashtra, they produced exquisitely embroidered items of dress such as skirts and bodices. These were worked with a refined version of the cobblers awl. The style of hook embroidery was adopted by local women for their domestic embroidery, although they reproduced the effects with a needle. They also absorbed the palette of the *Mochi* which favoured "auspicious" colors such as yellow, green, red and pink, with white or yellow outlines used to define forms. Recurrent borders of flowers and parrots, the use of elephant and peacock motifs, all link the embroidery of the Rabari women with the professional embroidery of the *Mochi*.

Another notable influence is that of the local Muslim clans. The Rabari have had close contact with their fellow Muslim herders in the Banni area in north Kutch. The Muslim embroidery reflects the Quranic proscription against the use of figurative imagery. It consists of geometric designs worked in complex interlacing stitches, bands of satin stitch and borders of couched thread bracketed between outlines of open chain stitch. The surface of the cloth glitters as the light catches small mirrors secured in complex webs of herringbone stitch. According to Indo-Persian philosophy, the divine quality of light is a visible manifestation of God's reason working in the world. The Muslim women of

Banni literally fill up their textiles with light to make them auspicious (Pandya, 1998: 54–5). Rabaris' tendency to abstraction in their embroidery, the use of interlacing stitches and the extensive use of mirrors, all suggest that they have absorbed the aesthetics of the Banni Muslims.

The Property of Dowry

Although ostensibly a "gift," dowry is a thoroughly negotiated transaction between two families. Congruent with general patterns of property ownership in India, Rabari women do not own "immovable property" such as land and buildings; this is vested in males and is inherited patrilineally. As "movable property," dowry offers fewer opportunities for producing wealth (Goody and Tambiah, 1973; Sharma, 1980 and 1984; Nabar, 1995). It is true that a woman may sell her dowry jewelry but this merely realises its cash value and does not generate further income. It has also been categorized as "invisible" or "intangible property," which includes special skills, knowledge of rituals, and, significantly, honor and reputation (Sharma, 1980; Hirschon, 1984). A woman's honor and reputation come under particular scrutiny throughout the procedures of marriage and these concepts are embodied in the substance of her dowry.

In India the belief prevails that different types of cloth are imbued with particular qualities that they impart when used (Bayly, 1986). Unlike most Hindus for whom silk is the purest of fibres, Rabaris accord that status to wool, which they believe to be the gift of Lord Krishna (Frater, 1995). As the gift of a god, its ritual purity surpasses that of all other fibres. This is said to be the reason why Rabaris have traditionally favored wool as the chief fabric for caste dress. Pragmatists maintain that their choice of wool has been governed by its ready availability to them. As herders of sheep, amongst other animals, they have a plentiful supply of the raw material. In addition, many villages throughout Kutch are jointly inhabited by Rabaris and a caste of untouchable weavers who have traditionally woven items of Rabari caste dress.

Wool is used for the women's veilcloths and the men's shawls. Men's turbans also were formerly made of wool, although these have been made of cotton for the last three decades. The ritual purity of wool offers protection from pollution and, embodied in the veilcloths of the women, it is particularly instrumental in maintaining the honor code of the Rabari community. Veilcloths are understandably key components of a Rabari dowry (Figure 5.4). The bride uses a different veilcloth for each visit to her in-laws, culminating in the use of a distinctive veilcloth to mark her final visit. This is still the custom among Vagadias, although it has been modified among Dhebarias since

Figure 5.4 Vagadia Rabaran wearing one of her dowry veilcloths. It is made of local wool and has a tie-dyed design. The centre seam and end borders are heavily embellished with embroidery and mirrorwork. She also wears ivory bangles, a symbol of her married status. Only Vagadias persist in the use of this ornament which is considered somewhat old-fashioned by the other subgroups. Photograph: the author.

1995. In effect, veilcloths mark the progress of the property transfers of marriage.

Inasmuch as a veilcloth carries the "intangible property" of purity with which it protects a woman from pollution and safeguards her honor, by extension, the dowry in its entirety protects the reputation of her family and clan. Choices of fabric and dress are governed by the desire to secure maximum auspiciousness for the proceedings of marriage. To this end, skirts and veilcloths should be made of wool, and dowry blouses should be made of silk or *mashru* which are categorized by Rabaris as "true" or "authentic cloth". *Mashru* literally means "permitted" as it was devised for Muslims for whom the use of pure silk is proscribed (Bayly, 1986: 290).

Cheaper printed synthetic copies are being used, however, with growing frequency in place of both the original wool and *mashru*. Embroidery is being replaced in a similar manner by purchased metallic braids known as *jari* and lace. Although Rabaris use these terms interchangeably, originally *jari* applied only to thread made from gold or silver wire wound around a silk or cotton core. Cheaper versions are now produced from plastic foils and lace is the braid made from these (Personal communication, Pareshbhai Jariwala, *jari* manufacturer, 29 April 1997). These have been fashionable for the last ten to fifteen years, although the longest standing use of braid is white rickrack braid which has been used for twenty-five years as a substitute for the embroidered border design (Personal communication, Matuben Rajabhai, Vagadia Rabaran, 7 September 1997).

The use of the cheaper synthetic fabrics and *jari* reflects both the industrialization of India and the inflation of the Rabari dowry over the last quarter of the twentieth century. The substitution of *jari* for embroidery has allowed women to economize in terms of the labor of embroidery as the quantitative demands of a dowry have risen. Nonetheless, a young Kachhi woman preparing her dowry expects to make no less than twenty-five or thirty embroidered blouses and possibly up to fifty. Two generations ago, before Independence, her forebear would have made only five (Personal communication, Paliben Megabhai and Nathiben Kanabhai, Kachhi Rabaran, 27 June 1997).

At a practical level, a dowry is intended to set up a woman up for life. Its particular value, however, has traditionally resided in its "bio-moral substance" (Bayly, 1986), that is the ritual purity and talismanic qualities Rabaris believe to be embodied in the wool, silk, and *mashru* of which it is composed. In the eyes of some Rabaris, the substitution of synthetics for "true" or "authentic cloth" and *jari* for embroidery, has compromised the ritual purity of a dowry and reduced its protective properties. "It was pure in the past but now all these impure things have come" (Personal communication, Nathiben Kanabhai, Kachhi Rabaran, 27 June 1997). According to another school of thought, chiefly that embraced by young, educated men from all subgroups, this is modernization: embroidery connotes nothing but backwardness, a lack of education and resistance to change.

Outcomes of the New Rules: Evolving Traditions

As yet it is only Dhebarias who have abandoned entirely the tradition of an embroidered dowry. Since the introduction of the new rules, they have started to feel the benefits of the acceleration of the visitation system, as far more women have transferred to their in-laws within three years of the wedding ceremony. "So for girls, there is at least fifty per cent gain: the thirty-five year old girls have started going. It will happen slowly, but it is better than before" (Personal communication, Arjanbhai Hirabhai, Dhebaria council member, 21 June 1997). In terms of community development, education is being targeted, including that of girls, which was not previously deemed to be important: "Education for girls was nil, but now, this year, fifteen have come for admission to the [Rabari residential schools]. That is the first step" (Personal communication, Arjanbhai Hirabhai, Dhebaria council member, 21 June 1997). Thus, one of the main arguments in favour of the embroidery ban – that Rabaris released from the burden of dowry could invest money in community development, especially education – is being acted upon.

The sacrifice has been the loss of a distinctive aspect of Rabari culture, "Now we have the question of embroidery. Here we have lost as well as gained because our culture is going" (Personal communication, Arjanbhai Hirabhai, Dhebaria council member, 21 June 1997). The brunt of this has been borne by women. Although their style of dress remains in terms of garments, Dhebaria women have been stripped of their distinctive, visually coded embellishments, and the stored wealth of thousands of dowry chests initially was consigned to redundancy and later to embroidery dealers.

For a Dhebaria woman, denied the distinction of married woman's dress which marked her as "auspicious," and with the property of dowry reduced to mere utility, the ban has signalled a loss of status: "The married woman's symbol, that is gone" (Personal communication, Lasuben Devsibhai, Dhebaria Rabaran, 21 June 1997). Thus the positive benefits of differentiation identified by a number of authors (Dunlay, 1928; Flügel, 1930; Bush and London 1965; Polhemus 1978; Tarlo 1996) as a primary function of dress, now appear lost to these women. Lacking voices on the council, and denied entry to the open meetings held periodically at the community headquarters because of the restrictions of caste codes, they have no say in the decisions that have radically affected their lives.

Despite this, since 1998, there has been something of a resurgence in the use of decorated dress among the younger Dhebaria women. They are shrewdly doing nothing to contravene the letter of the law but they are manipulating it. Their dress now bears extensive borders of purchased braid, beads and sequins that are machine-stitched into place. Unsurprisingly, the braids they choose have a number of the symbols embedded in the older embroidery. These tend to be pan-Hindu symbols such as the tree of life and florals. It remains to be seen if the manufacturers will respond to this growing market and develop braids with specific Rabari designs.

The Dhebaria council tolerates this "renaissance" because the time spent applying commercial braiding to a dress is far less than that spent on hand embroidery. In many respects, the council members see it as the future style of dress for all three Rabari subgroups in Kutch. They are aware that as women start to enter the wage labor market, the time available to them for traditional pursuits, such as embroidery, is much reduced, although the compulsion to decorate, evidently is not. Thus, the use of braids for dress has been absorbed into the overall strategy for community uplift (Personal communication, Arjanbhai Hirabhai, Dhebaria council member, 21 January 2001).

Rabari women are seen as the guardians of tradition. This is due, in part, to their steadfast use of embroidered dress, although this has been imposed upon them by the Rabari sartorial code and the rules of honor. Honor also dictates that they integrate little with other communities and are unfamiliar with the urban environment, adhering to the ways of the village and, indeed, the migratory group. On the one hand, this is seen as laudable behaviour: V. K. Srivastava refers to "the pristine lustre of their caste, rooted in the virtue of simplicity" (1997: 188). On the other hand, their adherence to embroidered caste dress, emblematic of the negative aspects of tradition, has resulted in their becoming scapegoats.[5] "Our women are holding us back. If they improve, our community will improve" (Personal communication, Hirabhai, Kachhi Rabari, 25.6.1997).

For others, embroidery is perceived conversely as an important component in the overall strategy for the upliftment of the Rabari of Kutch. The women's embroidery skills, honed by years of fashioning their dowries, may provide a steady source of future income and a means of retaining a vestige of their artistic heritage: "We are thinking of doing something to preserve our culture and give women work" (Personal communication, Arjanbhai Hirabhai, Dhebaria council member, 21 June 1997).

The decision to develop commercial embroidery in the Dhebaria community has been influenced by the experience of Kachhi women over the last two decades. They work at home stitching small, decorative mirror pieces to shawls for entrepreneurial weavers for which they are paid an agreed amount for a fixed number of mirrors. The arrangement accommodates their domestic responsibilities and does not bring them into conflict with codes of honor, which work outside the village might do. The young unmarried women balance their time between making their dowries and doing other labor, either "shawl business" for the weavers, or seasonal agricultural laboring on nearby farms.

Two villages from the Dhebaria community and a few from the Kachhi community are now also doing labor-work embroidery for two NGOs (non-governmental organizations) working in Kutch. The aim of these projects is broadly income-generation.

The gradual involvement of Rabaran from all subgroups with commercial embroidery remains a core element in the strategy for community development: "If they do embroidery, they will get both work and money" (Personal communication, Arjanbhai Hirabhai, Dhebaria council member, 21 June 1997). The realization of these plans may well be accelerated as Rabaris devise ways to cope with the impact of the January, 2001, earthquake in Gujarat which laid waste to their villages and devastated their lives (Personal communication, Kantibhai Ros, Patanwadi Rabari, Principal, Rabari Ashramshala Anjar, 15 February 2001). It would seem that the women's embroidery skills – an aspect of the "intangible property" of dowry – will be restored to their previous high status.

Notes

1. According to the Rabari rules of marriage, husband and wife do not live together immediately after the wedding ceremony. Over a number of years, a woman will make a series of short visits to her husband's home. Each visit usually lasts between one and three days and marks the transfer of an installment of dowry property. Three to five such visits traditionally take place before all property transfers are completed and a woman co-habits permanently with her husband.

2. The four stages of a man's life referred to in the Hindu texts are: birth; a boy's investiture with the sacred thread; marriage, when a man becomes a householder; death and the release of the soul. These define the roles that he is expected to fulfil (Kramrisch, 1968).

3. To contextualize this amount, the average daily wage for an agricultural laborer at that time (1997) was fifty rupees ($1.30).

4. A *toran* is a home decoration hung over the door facing the main entrance to a house. It has triangular flaps hanging from it, the form being derived from the practice of hanging clusters of asopalav or mango leaves above the door to ward off malign spirits. *Toran* is very often accompanied by two L-shaped textiles known as *barsankhiya* which hang down the sides of the door, thus the door is framed by protective textiles. *Chakla* refers to two square votive textiles, usually hung on the wall, one on each side of the door facing the entrance of a house.

5. While Rabari men do not entirely escape the negative associations of caste dress, they are permitted greater flexibility within the dress code. Many change their apparel to suit the situation, donning *shirt-pants* (western style trousers and shirt) for activities in urban areas, and caste dress of *dhoti*, *kediyun* (smock) and *pagadi* (turban) for community occasions. These garments are supposed to be worn for weddings; as well, they are worn for formal council meetings known as *nat*, or admission is denied.

References

Appadurai, A. (ed.) (1986), *The Social Life of Things: Commodities in Cultural Perspective*, Cambridge: Cambridge University Press.

Bayly, C. A. (1986), "The Origins of Swadeshi (home industry): Cloth and Indian Society, 1700–1930," in Arjun Appadurai (ed.), *The Social Life of Things: Commodities in Cultural Perspective*, Cambridge: Cambridge University Press, 285–381.

Bush, G. and London, Perry (1965), "Age and Sex Roles," in Mary Ellen Roach and Joanne Bubolz Eicher (eds), *Dress, Adornment and the Social Order*, London: John Wiley and Sons, Inc., 64–72.

Davidson, R. (1996), *Desert Places*, London: Viking.

Dunlay, K. (1928), "The Development and Function of Clothing," *Journal of General Psychology* 1: 64–78.

Elson, V. (1979), *Dowries from Kutch: A Women's Folk Art Tradition*, Los Angeles: University of California.

Flügel, J. C. (1930), *The Psychology of Clothes*, London: Hogarth Press.

Frater, J. (1995), *Threads of Identity: Embroidery and Adornment of the Nomadic Rabaris*, Ahmedabad: Mapin Publishing Pvt Ltd.

Fuller, C. J. (1991), *The Camphor Flame: Popular Hinduism and Society in India*, Oxford: Princeton University Press.

Goody, J. and Tambiah, S. J. (1973), *Bridewealth and Dowry*, Cambridge: Cambridge University Press.

Hirschon, R. (ed.) (1984), *Women and Property: Women as Property*, London and Canberra: Croom Helm.

Jacobson, D. and Wadley, Susan S. (1977), *Women in India: Two Perspectives*, New Delhi: Manohar.

Kane, P. V. (1941), *History of Dharmasastra*, Poona: Bhandarkar Oriental Research Institute.

Kramrisch, S. (1968), *Unknown India: Ritual Art in Tribe and Village*, Philadelphia: The Philadelphia Museum of Art.

Nabar, V. (1995), *Caste as Woman*, New Delhi: Penguin Books India Ltd.

Niranjana, S. (1997), "Femininity, Space and the Female Body: An Anthropological Perspective," in Meenakshi Thapan (ed.), *Embodiment: Essays on Gender and Identity*, Delhi: Oxford University Press, 107–24.

Pandya, V. (1998), "Hot scorpions, sweet peacocks: Kachchhe art, architecture and action," *Journal of Material Culture* 3: 1, 51–75.

Parry, J. (1986), "*The Gift*, the Indian Gift and the 'Indian Gift,'" *Man* 21: 3, 453–73.

Polhemus, T. (1978), *Social Aspects of the Human Body*, Harmondsworth: Penguin Books.

Reynolds, H. B. (1991), "The Auspicious Married Woman," in Susan S. Wadley (ed.), *The Powers of Tamil Women*, New Delhi: Manohar, 35–60.

Sharma, U. (1980), *Women, Work and Property in North-West India*, London and New York: Tavistock Publications.

—— (1984), "Dowry in North India: Its Consequences for Women," in Renée Hirschon (ed.), *Women and Property: Women as Property*, London and Canberra: Croom Helm, 62–74.

Sri Rabari Samaj (1995), *Bandharano ni Thadi*, Anjar: Sri Rabari Samaj.

Srivastava, V. K. (1997), *Religious Renunciation of a Pastoral People*, New Delhi: Oxford University Press.

Tarlo, E. (1996), *Clothing Matters: Dress and Identity in India*, Chicago: University of Chicago Press.

Thapan, M. (ed.) (1997), *Embodiment: Essays on Gender and Identity*, Delhi: Oxford University Press.

Wadley, S. S. (ed.) (1991), *The Powers of Tamil Women*, New Delhi: Manohar Publications.

Pragmatism and Enigmas: The "Panetar" and "Gharcholu" Saris in Gujarati Weddings

Donald Clay Johnson

The state of Gujarat on the western coast of India has long been one of the prominent Indian centers of worldwide mercantile activity. Its merchant communities, found throughout the world, retain remarkably strong ties to their homeland, Gujarat. Starting in 1991, in response to the opening of the Indian economy and the resulting greater participation of India in world trade, the number of Gujaratis leaving India for careers in other parts of the world noticeably increased. Wedding ceremonies and traditions within the merchant communities in Gujarat itself thus provide an opportunity to observe change in a culture in which a noticeable percentage of its population lives abroad. This essay focuses upon members of the Gujarati Hindu and Jain merchant communities who primarily live in Ahmedabad, the most populous and dominant economic city of the state. Research for it derives from attending more than twenty Gujarati weddings between 1990 and 2001, viewing picture albums and videos that documented weddings over a fifty year period, interviewing women about what they wore at their wedding, and accompanying families when they went shopping for wedding attire. For a variety of reasons, the last decade of the twentieth century saw significant changes in weddings, in their length of ceremonial time, declining from three to four days to one or at most two days, as well as changes in the component wedding activities. The core wedding ritual and especially what the bride wears, however, faithfully continues earlier traditions.

As in most cultures, Gujarati marriages are family events and each member of the large, extended families who possibly can do so returns to India for the wedding ceremonies. These abbreviated visits by family members, usually for a week or two, result in the concentration of as many weddings as possible during these trips back to Ahmedabad. The need to hold several weddings during such a short time thus has contributed to the shortening of some ceremonial events and to the elimination of others. Although abridged, the rich sense of tradition remains nonetheless and the spirit of earlier times duly receives attention. For instance, family members who return from abroad for weddings overwhelmingly dress in traditional, rather than non-Indian or western, clothing for most, if not all, of the wedding events. These family members similarly wear heirloom jewelry, often many generations old.

Within the wedding ceremony itself two saris mark the transition of the bride from her natal to her husband's family. The Indian sari, the garment tradition- ally worn by urban Hindu and Jain Gujarati women, is an unstitched textile between forty and forty-eight inches (102 and 130 centimeters) wide and either six or nine yards (5.5 or 8.3 meters) long, depending upon the style of draping. The sari completely covers a floor- length petticoat, has pleats in the front to facilitate walking, and the final segment goes over either the right or left shoulder partially covering the *choli*, an abridged blouse that covers the shoulders and breasts. The typical fabrics for saris are cotton or silk and, more recently, synthetics. Numerous techniques, done either in weaving or sub- sequent surface application, have resulted in innumerable, visually distinctive saris. This discussion deals with two such techniques, the *panetar*, a sari which features a white central area and these days a red border that may be a brocade, embroidered, or tie-dye, and, the *gharcholu*, a tie-dye sari.

At the marriage rite the bride wears the *panetar* sari, considered the last garment she receives from her parents although she receives saris from her family as part of the wedding events. Then, during the ceremony, her mother- in law gives her a *gharcholu* sari which serves as a visible symbol that her new family will always take care of her, feed her, and clothe her. The *gharcholu* is so important, in fact, that among some Gujarati groups the bride is required to change into it immediately after she receives it and to wear it for the rest of the wedding ceremony (Personal communication, Mrs. Viraj D. Patel, 4 December 1994). In other communities, the *gharcholu* simply is placed shawl-like on the head or shoulders of the bride as a public statement that demonstrates the groom's family's ability to clothe and to take care of the bride (Personal communication, Mrs. Sanjana N. Parekh, 14 December 1996). After a period of time during the ceremony, the *gharcholu* sari is removed from her shoulders and taken to her new home. The two saris thus symbolically portray the transition of the bride's life from her parents' home to the home of her husband.

The use of textiles from two different families marks a major life event that contains insights into the roles and attitudes of the two families. Gujarati weddings demonstrate a definition of roles and responsibilities between the families of the bride and groom regarding attire. Since the bride is going to her husband's home, the groom's family must naturally be perceived as the dominant family in the wedding and the wedding saris play a role in demonstrating this. Hence, the *panetar* sari of her natal family should not be more elaborate or expensive than the *gharcholu* from the groom's family. The bride's choice of a specific style or design in a *panetar* sari thus presents a challenge as the *gharcholu* sari is made from cotton while the *panetar* is a silk sari, reflecting the Hindu and Jain tradition of wearing silk at auspicious events. Silk is considerably more expensive than cotton; thus, among other characteristics, the relative cost of the two saris plays a role in defining the new relationship between the two families. In most instances this conflict is resolved by the gold brocade work (*jari* or *zari*) in the *gharcholu*. Although the two wedding saris reflect relations between the two families, the ever-practical Gujarati merchants recognize there are times when the family of the bride is more prominent than the groom's. Such families wishing to demonstrate their economic situation are easily able to do so in the jewelry worn by the bride in or on her forehead, ears, nose, neck, arms, wrists, hands, fingers, and toes, as it all comes from her family. Hence the ritual relationships between the families of the bride and groom find ways of stating true reality.

In a time of great change in the content of weddings, the *gharcholu* has remained remarkably consistent in its designs and its motifs. The *gharcholu* has even been introduced into the wedding ceremonies of other communities outside Gujarat. In strong contrast, the *panetar* survives more as a name than as a specific sari. The differences between these two saris and their functions in Gujarati society reflect changing societal attitudes.

Panetar

In its evolution over the last century the *panetar* demonstrates the practicality of a merchant community well used to evaluating costs and uses of merchandise. Although now always white with a red border, this is only the latest manifestation of the *panetar* as a sari type that carries great ritual significance. Reflecting Gujarati culture and taste, the panetar sari traditionally has had a plain white body and a tie-dye border as well as one or three tie-dye medallions portraying dancing women in its central area. Gujarat has long been famous for its tie-dye textiles and these motifs in the *panetar* sari reflect this. Sixty years ago, green was commonly used as the border color since it blends two colors, blue and yellow (Personal communication, Mrs Lilavanti Harjivandas Kotecha [Bardanwala], 27 December 2000). To Hindus, blue is associated with the God Krishna while Radha, his consort, has yellow as her color. The divine union of Radha and Krishna finds expression in the color green, a blend of blue and yellow, and serves as a visual statement that a marriage unites two people.

Around the time of India's independence in 1947, Gujarati wedding fashion introduced the colors orange and saffron, and subsequently red, the symbol of joy, for the *panetar,* and red quickly became the preferred color (Personal communication, Mrs Vrajbalaben C. Shodhan, 20 January 2001). Once established, red has remained the preferred color for the *panetar*. However, even though the color has remained constant, the definition of what, precisely, is a *panetar* sari has changed greatly.

During the post-independence period in India, questions began to be asked about the practicality of a sari which would only be worn once. While rigidly continuing the use of red for its border, brides began to wear saris which incorporated decorative elements other than tie-dye, usually either embroidery or brocade. When questioned about this departure from tradition, women consistently say that if they did not wear a tie-dye *panetar* in their wedding they could wear the sari at subsequent events and functions and it would not be as noticeable that it was the same sari they had been married in. Some women have even had portions of their panetar saris dyed other colors after the wedding to further reduce their identification as the saris they wore at their weddings. Thus the situation has evolved in Gujarati merchant communities that the bride wears a white sari with a red border at the wedding ceremony and that this sari is called a *panetar*. However, the decorative elements of this sari are not consistent and the newer *panetar* saris may include brocade work, embroidery, or tie-dye.

Gharcholu

In contrast to the *panetar*, the *gharcholu* is a tie-dye fabric of great complexity. The tying of the cloth traditionally is done in Kutch, a remote area in western Gujarat that borders Pakistan. The cloth then is shipped south across the waters of the Rann of Kutch to Jamnagar in the Saurashtra region of Gujarat, where it is dyed and sold. The dots on the sari are finely tied designs within square blocks between four and six inches (ten and fifteen cm) per side. The borders of the blocks are defined by undecorated *jari* brocade work, woven from strands of extremely fine gold wire or silk thread wrapped with gold or silver. The number of blocks in a vertical row on the *gharcholu* is either ten, twelve, or, fourteen. Since the overall dimensions of the sari are fixed, a *gharcholu* with ten blocks has larger surface squares for portraying its motif than one with fourteen blocks. The smaller the square, the more elaborate and finely tied the tie-dye work within it. Whereas the *gharcholu* traditionally had twelve or fourteen blocks in a vertical row, these days it is far more common to have ten or twelve blocks per row because of rising labor costs and the need to produce *gharcholu* saris in a timely manner. The result has been a decline in the quality of craftsmanship. Although old *gharcholu* saris are highly prized by connoisseurs and actively collected, the groom's family has to secure a new one as there are other life cycle events which require women to wear their *gharcholus* and wearing a used one is unacceptable.

The cloth is either mill- or hand-woven cotton with the gold *zari* bands already woven into the borders and body of the fabric. The production of the *gharcholu* design takes three stages. First, the designs are stenciled on the cloth which then is given to a craftsman who may take several months to tie the cloth and, finally, it is sent to Jamnagar to be dyed.

The designs or motifs used in a *gharcholu* vary among the different Gujarati communities. For instance, the Jains, a religious group which practices strict nonviolence, will not use a *gharcholu* with designs portraying animals or people (Personal communication, Mrs Nita N. Parekh, 6 December 2000). Hindus, on the other hand, freely incorporate elephants, dancing women, and birds into their *gharcholu* saris. The design repertoire for Hindus contains arabesques, flowers, animals, birds, and people (Personal communication, Mrs Anjoo M. Sheth, 10 December 2000). Since the initial use of a *gharcholu* is for a wedding, its predominant color is red. Red and white thus are the dominant colors but in the reverse of these colors' proportionate use on the *panetar*. Whereas white with a red border forms the color scheme of the *panetar*, the *gharcholu* reverses this with red as the color of the fabric body and with all other colors modified as tie-dye accents to produce the designs and motifs. Yellow or white, the original color of the cloth, are the areas of the fabric protected from the dye in the resist dyeing process and thus form the accent and design colors. In addition, some green tie-dye work is found in the *gharcholu* reflecting, as with the *panetar*, the symbolism of Krishna, Radha, and marriage.

The *gharcholu*, however, remains an enigma and numerous questions arise about it. Whereas Hindus always wear silk at auspicious rites and events, the *gharcholu*, as indicated earlier, is made from cotton. Although the gold content in it means it is an expensive sari, the less-expensive base fabric, cotton, presents a riddle if one wishes to explain its role in such an auspicious event as a wedding.

The word "*gharcholu*" means "house dress," which indicates the perception of it as an item of clothing worn at home rather than at propitious events where silk is traditionally worn. Indeed, Indian women usually wear cotton fabrics at home both because silk requires far more care and maintenance and because cotton is far more comfortable in the hot climate. However the *gharcholu* is far too elaborate a sari for daily attire at home. Rather, the *gharcholu* has ritual functions for the entire duration of the marriage of the man and woman. Cotton, far more durable than silk, of necessity, became the fabric for this important sari since it is ritually required for decades after the wedding. As a woman ages, the palette of colors for her clothing changes from bright, vibrant hues to more sombre tones, and cotton, rather than silk, often becomes the fabric usually worn. Since the *gharcholu* will be worn throughout a woman's life, the preference for cotton when she is elderly plays a role in a sari given to her at her wedding. Although red is the dominant color of the *gharcholu*, it is of a hue which can be worn by any age group.

Within a wedding ceremony, the mother-in-law gives the *gharcholu* to the bride, thus ritually signifying the bride's acceptance into her new household. As well, this gift serves as the public expression that her new family will always provide her with clothing. The gift of a *gharcholu* also demonstrates the role or importance of the bride within a traditional family structure. Demanding that the bride change into the clothing given to her by the groom's family demonstrates the departure of the bride from her own family and her entrance into her husband's family. Changing from her wedding sari into the *gharcholu* shows the dominance that her husband's family can now exert over her. One thus sees the role of the *gharcholu* in the wedding ceremony as the visible statement of the position that the bride will have within her new family and the expectations held of her in this social structure. Thus, although the *gharcholu* is an elaborate textile, its role within the wedding ceremony actually places the bride into a new role in society.

Research has not yet determined the origin of the *gharcholu*. An initial possibility I pursued was that it derived from the Jains since they practice nonviolence not only to people but also to animals. Jains traditionally did not wear silk since extraction of the silk thread from the cocoon requires killing the moth. But Kutch, the area which is generally accepted as the origin of the *gharcholu*, is not an area with many Jains. It thus appears to be a Hindu contribution to the wedding ceremony.

The enigma regarding the *gharcholu*, however, does not end with the wedding ceremony. Since the *gharcholu* represents the acceptance of the bride into her new family, she and her sisters-in-law must wear the *gharcholu* saris they received at their weddings at one related ceremony or event at every subsequent family wedding (Personal communication, Mrs Vandana S. Parekh, 10 December 2000). Since families wish to impress guests at the wedding ceremony proper, they seldom wear the *gharcholu* then, although in some families they do. There are many traditional activities and events connected with weddings and the women usually wear their own *gharcholus* at one of these other ceremonies. A common, but by no means the only, time when this is done is at the ceremony when gifts from maternal uncles of either the bride or the groom are received (Personal communication, Mrs Vandana S. Parekh, 10 December 2000). Others, however, prefer to wear it at the ceremonial blessing of the house and wedding area. Whenever worn, the wearing of the *gharcholu* is a collective activity during which all the married women of the household take part; this consequently demonstrates the unity of a family, and is a most important public statement of a joint family. The *gharcholu* thus remains a part of the bride's life for as long as her husband lives and serves as a visible reminder of her status and position within her husband's family whenever worn as part of ceremonies after her wedding.

Tradition varies regarding other ritual events when women wear their *gharcholu*. It often, for instance, is worn when a son has his first haircut. The elaborate ceremony, performed in the first, third, or fifth year of the boy, signifies formal admittance into his Hindu tradition. His mother, who sits beside him during the ceremony, by publicly wearing her *gharcholu* tells the assembled guests of her role and status within the family as well as marks an important event in the continuation of family traditions.

When her husband dies, however, the wife's role within the family changes to that of widow and she loses the privilege of wearing her *gharcholu*. This loss of privilege is marked by the widow giving her *gharcholu* to one of her daughters-in-law and demonstrates her changed status in life. The presentation of her *gharcholu* to younger, married women of her family formally states the end of her marriage. If the wife, however, precedes her husband in death, her *gharcholu* plays one final role for her – serves as her shroud as her corpse is taken to the cremation area (Personal communication, Mrs Harsha A. Doshi, 30 January 2001). The *gharcholu*, given to the bride by her in-laws as part of the wedding ceremony, defines her role and status within her new family for the rest of her life.

Conclusion

A Gujarati bride wears two different saris during the marriage ceremony. The contrast between the *panetar* and *gharcholu* saris reflects values and attitudes of Gujarati society. The *panetar*, a traditional tie-dye garment worn by the bride only once for a specific event – her marriage – has been transformed into a generic textile incorporating a variety of design motifs that can be used for other purposes. The traditional decorative motifs no longer are confined to tie-dye but often now are of embroidery or brocade. After the wedding, the *panetar* sari becomes an elegant garment worn at other social events and may even be dyed a different color to further remove its identification as a wedding sari.

The *gharcholu* is a garment worn many times specifically to serve as the symbol of marriage itself. The bride wears it at subsequent wedding events and it becomes her funeral shroud if she precedes her husband in death. The *gharcholu* sari thus plays an integral part during her married life and visibly demonstrates her roles and responsibilities within her husband's family. Given these functions in Gujarati society, and unlike the changes in the *panetar* sari's motifs and colors over the last half of the twentieth century, the *gharcholu* design motifs and colors have remained constant over time.

References

Census of India, 1961. Gujarat. Vol. 5. Pt. 7A. no. 13, *Jari Industry of Surat,* Ahmedabad: Government Printing Office.

Census of India, 1961. Gujarat. Vol. 5. Pt. 7A, no. 21, *Bandhani or Tie and Dye Sari of Jamnagar,* Ahmedabad: Government Printing Office.

Dhamija, Jasleen (1985), "Textiles," in *Crafts of Gujarat,* Ahmedabad: Mapin, pp. 65–98.

—— (1987), "Embroidery of Gujarat: Living Traditions," in Nizam, M. L. (ed.), *Decorative Arts of India*, Hyderabad: Salar Jung Museum, pp. 151–61.

Haynes, Douglas (1986), "The Dynamics of Continuity in Indian Domestic Industry: Jari Manufacture in Surat, 1900–1947," *Indian Economic and Social History Review*23: 127–49.

Jaitly, Jaya (1985), "Embroidery," in Dhamija, Jasleen (ed.), *Crafts of Gujarat*, Ahmedabad: Mapin, pp. 1–40.

Jhala, Umade and Bhowmik, M. P. (1992), *Brocades of Ahmedabad*, Ahmedabad: National Institute of Design.

Mukhopadhyay, Santipriya (1983), *Catalogue of Embroidered Textiles from Cutch & Kathiawar in the Indian Museum,* Calcutta: Indian Museum.

Murphy, Veronica and Crill, Rosemary (1991), *Tie-dyed Textiles of India, Tradition and Trade*, New York: Rizzoli.

Tarlo, Emma (1996), *Clothing Matters: Dress and Its Symbolism in Modern India,* Chicago: University of Chicago Press.

Westfall, C. D. and Desai, D. (December 1987), "Gujarati embroidery," *Ars textrina* 8: 29–41.

7

Swazi Bridal Attire: Culture, Traditions and Customs

Lombuso S. Khoza and Laura K. Kidd

The Kingdom of Swaziland: Cultural Background

The Kingdom of Swaziland, a small, landlocked, mountainous country in southeastern Africa, 6,704 square miles (17,364 square kilometers) in area, is surrounded by South Africa in the north, west and south, and bordered by Mozambique to the east. The country's current estimated population is 1,083,289. The Swazi people, descendant from the Nguni, historically have been able to maintain homogeneity and may be considered a "tribal-less" nation, sharing a common language and common cultural traditions.

Drawn into the Boer War, Swaziland became a protectorate of Great Britain until independence in September 1968. Swaziland has a king who continues to help Swazis maintain their traditional culture and values.[1] Swaziland has two official languages, *Siswati* and English. Christianity coexists with indigenous beliefs. Traditional rites, rituals and customs prescribe codes of social behavior through every stage of a Swazi's life and remain an integral part of it despite increasing modernization. Swazis preserve and practice traditional customs as a reflection of their great pride in their history and culture and they continue to balance living in a modern society while maintaining strong ties to the past.

Dress continues as one way Swazis maintain their traditional cultural heritage. People wear it everyday in rural areas and to a lesser degree in urban areas. Traditional dress is worn for national celebrations and other annual festivals.[2] Traditional attire also plays an important role in maintaining cultural ties during the Swazi wedding ceremony.

Swazi Courtship and Marriage Rituals

According to oral tradition, a young man courts a young woman by the river before he proposes marriage.[3] The river, a public gathering place, serves as a convenient place to meet since the young woman would collect water with her sisters and friends. Once the man proposes, the groom's delegation of elders, selected by the groom's father, goes to the future bride's home to ask for her hand in marriage and to negotiate the dowry bargaining. Upon arrival at the future bride's home it is customary for the groom's elders to provide a gift "to open the mouth," in the form of a goat or a cow to the bride's family, indicating their desire to open marriage negotiations.

After accepting the gift, negotiations begin. In traditional courtship practice, the bride's father plays no role in the bargaining process but he chooses male elders to negotiate the dowry. These negotiations center on determining the number of cattle the groom's family sends to the father of the bride. Cattle in Swaziland, as in many agricultural societies, indicate the family's affluence and prosperity. Once the number of cattle is agreed upon and the wedding date set, preparations begin for the main event of the wedding, the formal delivery of the bride.

Before the wedding ceremony begins, the bride's party comprising her family, relatives, friends and other members of her community prepares beer from the *marula* tree after which the bride's party sets off to the groom's homestead, timing their arrival to occur at dusk. Upon arrival, the bride's party enters the home of the groom's parents after a goat is slaughtered and skinned. They all share a meal made from the goat. After the meal, the bride's party then retires to their sleeping quarters. The dried and tanned skin of the goat becomes the material for two of the bride's garments: an apron-like diagonally draped upper body cover (*sidziya*) and a goat-hair bracelet (*siphandla*).

The following morning, the groom's father slaughters an ox that was part of the dowry and the young people of both families go to the river to bathe and don their attire for the wedding celebrations. After feasting on roast ox meat and drinking the beer made by the bride's party, wedding dances begin. Both wedding parties perform dances. During these, the female members of the bride's party perform for the assembled audience but the bride dances only for her husband-to-be. The high point of the marriage celebrations occurs in the afternoon and consists of a number of speeches made by men from the groom's and the bride's families. Of particular importance is the speech by the groom's father, welcoming the bride into his family. The bride's father usually responds to this speech by praising his daughter and handing her over to the care of her new family.

The official marriage ceremony (*kuteka*) occurs in a cattle byre. Within the byre the bride holds spears; the number of which symbolize the number of cattle given as her dowry. With those spears in hand, the bride cries and laments the end of her unmarried life in a part of the ceremony called *kumekeza*. A proper demonstration of crying by the bride indicates her willingness to adapt to her new life and duties within her husband's family. If she refuses to lament, her future in-laws torment her until she cries.

A mixture of clay, fat and red ochre smeared on the bride's forehead and body as a symbol of her new status as a wife makes the marital union official. The groom's family then presents a young girl to the bride. Known as the "bride's own," the girl is nurtured by the bride, a process that helps prepare the bride for her eventual role as a mother. The bride does not adopt the girl and the real parents retain their parental rights.

After the marriage ceremony, the celebrations continue with the presentation of gifts from the bride to her new in-laws. Important gifts have symbolic cultural meanings. These gifts traditionally consist of everyday home and bath items, such as grass mats and brooms, washbasins, washcloths, and bath soaps by which the in-laws remember the new bride.

Swazi Traditional Bridal Attire

The core garments worn as Swazi bridal attire are virtually indistinguishable from everyday traditional dress. Swazis previously fashioned their dress of cow, ox, or goatskins and added ornamentation from natural materials such as grass and seeds. In the 1840s, European settlers arrived in Swaziland bringing trade goods such as cloth and beads, which soon appeared in Swazi traditional dress. Changes in traditional Swazi bridal dress became part of this acculturation process, just as new materials continue to be added to the available materials used for clothing. Acculturation of Western dress elements into traditional Swazi dress mirrors other changes Swaziland experienced upon contact with the West and supports H. Applebaum's observation that a culture "adopts, rejects and molds its life and in so doing selects what is consistent and fits within its culture" (1987: 67).

Social classes exist in Swaziland but the divisions between them are not rigid. Acknowledged distinctions between royalty and non-royalty, nevertheless, do exist. The quality of the garments and lavishness of the accessories convey social class distinctions. The basic elements of traditional bridal attire, however, remain consistent across classes: the bridal hairstyle (*sicholo*), two lower body covers (*sidvwaba* and *sidvwashi*), two upper body covers (*sidziya* and *lihiya*), and accessories (Figure 7.1).

An important part of traditional Swazi bridal fashion is the beehive-shaped hairstyle (*sicholo*).[4] On the wedding day, women help the bride prepare for

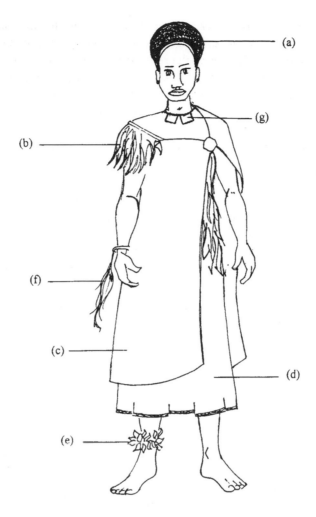

Figure 7.1 A Swazi woman in traditional bridal attire. (a) *Sicholo* with *intsambo*. (b) Goatskin *sidziya*. (c) *Lihiya*. (d) *Sidvwaba* (the *sidvwashi* is under the *sidvwaba*). (e) *Lifahlawane*. (f) *Siphandla* (g) *Ligcebesha*. Illustration: Laura Kidd.

her day and mold the bride's hair into this beehive arrangement using a mixture of animal fat and clay to hold the hair in shape. The natural color of the bride's hair is changed from black to shades of brown or red when it is dusted with colored soil. The bride wears a thin headband woven from tree bark around the base of the hairline. Women may add long pins, similar to hat pins, and barrettes to decorate the beehive hairstyle.[5] This hairstyle traditionally is only worn by married women as an important indicator of their marital status.

The bride wears a skirt-like garment wrapped around the hips (*sidvwaba*) and tied to the left, made of tanned oxhide or cowhide. Because of the rough nature of the hide, the bride wears an underskirt made of a rectangular woven cloth (*sidvwashi*) underneath the outer skirt (*sidvwaba*) to protect the lower body against chafing. On her upper body the bride drapes a flat goatskin apron (*sidziya*) diagonally across her chest and over her right shoulder. Over this the bride wears a flat rectangular woven print-cloth (*lihiya*) twice as wide and long as the underskirt. The print-cloth (*lihiya*) falls below the knee and covers much of the skirt and underskirt. It drapes diagonally over the left shoulder, around her body under the right arm and ties just above the left breast in an intricate knot. The knot is known by several different names, among them "monkey knot" and "dog knot." The method of tying this knot is complicated because all ends of the knot must be hidden.

Accessories are also important components of Swazi bridal attire. Traditional accessories include wooden earplugs worn in the bride's earlobes. A special necklace with two square pendants in a woven beaded "love letter" pattern adorns the bride's neck (Figure 7.2). Bead or seed bracelets are also worn. Brides also wear a goatskin bracelet around the right wrist.

Figure 7.2 The outline of the *ligcebesha* necklace with one style of "love letter" pendant. The "love letter" symbols are woven into a background of beads. Illustration: Lombuso Khoza.

Around one ankle, the bride wears an anklet formed of natural seed pods strung together. This makes a crackling sound when the bride walks and dances. Other females in the bridal party wear two anklets. Shoes and sandals are not part of bridal attire because foot coverings are not part of traditional everyday Swazi dress.

In Swazi culture, the bridal clothes of a woman are the finest garments in her wardrobe. She wears them not only for her wedding ceremony but also for other important cultural occasions. A married Swazi woman typically wears her bridal attire whenever she visits her in-laws, a sign of respect for them and the community at large.

Differences in Traditional Attire Across Social Classes

Although basic bridal garments remain consistent between Swazi social classes, the quality of the garments reflects the bride's family's social and economic status. If the bride marries a chief, a prince, or the King, she wears additions to her attire. If the bride is of royal descent, she adds additional pieces to her basic attire, no matter into what social class she marries.

The most important additions to the traditional bridal outfit occur in the attire worn by women who become one of the King's brides or are part of the royal family. In addition to the basic garments, the King's bride or a princess wears long black feathers in her hair that radiate around her beehive hairstyle. These brides also wear an additional upper garment (*sigeja*), a cape-like garment made from shredded cow tails. During one stage of a dance performed during the wedding ceremony, female in-laws remove the cape and the royal bride appears bare-breasted.

Changes in Swazi Marriage Customs

Although many Western influences came to Swaziland with British colonization, perhaps the most rapid and perceptible changes occurred after Swaziland's independence in 1968. Because of an emphasis on education, many young people seek higher education in Swaziland, Great Britain or the United States. Travel, education, and a more global perspective challenge Swazis to maintain their traditions during a time of increasing influence from the West.

Swazis retain many courtship and marriage rituals, yet they often modify these traditions and rituals in response to a changing society. Career-oriented young adults now rarely meet their future spouses at the river; instead they meet at university, at work, or at social functions, a change most parents accept. Nonetheless, nearly all Swazi families continue to participate in dowry and marriage negotiations. Cattle, as a cultural "symbol of wealth, status, and sentiment" remain the preferred method of dowry payment, although the cash value of the cattle is sometimes an acceptable substitute (Godeffroy, 1999: 62).

The majority of Swazis practice Christianity but certain traditional Swazi wedding rituals appear to be in conflict with Christian tenets. For example, Christianity prohibits the Swazi custom of polygamy. When a couple has a Christian church wedding, it is assumed the husband will not enter into polygamous relationships; however, if a couple marries in the full traditional ceremony, the assumption is that all cultural traditions, including polygamy, may be practiced. As a compromise to these conflicting belief systems, a Christian Swazi couple may have a church wedding on Saturday and then perform some of the traditional rituals the next day. Many Swazis who marry outside of the country may also carry out parts of the traditional wedding ceremony on their first visit home after their wedding. The parts of the traditional marriage ceremony still most commonly performed include the bridal negotiations and the presentation of gifts from the bride to her new in-laws.

Today, the type and value of the gifts from the bride to her new in-laws have changed radically from the household and bath items traditionally given. The value of the gifts has escalated and the gifts may be valued more for their monetary than their symbolic value as home and personal items. In some instances, the gifts include expensive blankets, bedroom and lounge suites, all indicative of conspicuous consumption.

Changes in Traditional Swazi Bridal Attire

The changes in Swazi traditional bridal attire reflect the influence of Western fashions, technology and popular culture. Her dress indicates the economic and social status of the bride and her family. The modern Swazi bride, however, uses the type and quality of her attire and accessories to reflect her groom's social status particularly if she marries into a higher social class.

Changes in the beehive hairstyle reflect changing lifestyles with the incorporation of synthetic fiber technology in wedding attire. Today, modern brides who typically wear their hair in Western styles prefer prestyled beehive-shaped wigs of human or artificial hair which are easier to style and maintain than the traditional molded beehive style. The white headband continues to be worn in the hair, but is now braided out of white acrylic yarns instead of tree bark. Some married women do not wear the beehive hairstyle every day after their marriage, especially if the women do not typically wear traditional Swazi dress. Still, when married women wear traditional dress, they customarily wear the beehive-shaped hairstyle with the white yarn headband.

The skirt (*sidvwaba*) and the underskirt (*sidvwashi*) also have changed. Traditionally made from ox or cow leather, the modern bride's skirt is now constructed from black terrycloth (towelling) fabric. Because terrycloth does not chafe the skin of the wearer, she no longer wears the traditional underskirt for comfort. Instead, many modern Swazi women wear Western-style petticoats or lingerie half-slips under the terrycloth skirt.

The diagonally draped upper body garment of goatskin (*sidziya*) is worn under the rectangular print-cloth upper body drape (*lihiya*) as part of the traditional attire; however, the word *sidziya* is also used for another garment worn by Swazi married women. At some point in the late twentieth century, the word *sidziya* began to be used to describe a cut-and-sewn garment made from print-cloth that resembles Western-style jumpers or wrap-around dresses (Figure 7.3). Now, many married women wear these types of *sidziya* during

Figure 7.3 One modern style variation of *sidziya*. This is a pink gingham wrap-around dress, with appliquéd shoulder embellishments and flat trim in darker pink. Illustration: Laura Kidd from a photograph in the personal collection of Lombuso Khoza.

visits to in-laws as a sign of respect. As with Western-style jumpers and dresses, the fashionable *sidziya* garment has style characteristics such as pockets, decorative piping, appliqué, embroidery and other creative sewing applications.[6]

The rectangular upper body drape (*lihiya*) remains the most fashionable part of the bridal dress (Figure 7.4). The modern *lihiya* is made of polyester fabric woven in floral or geometric designs, or among elite groups, of silk fabrics with gold yarns, a fashion attributed to one of the present King's wives.[7] Today, the bride often replaces the traditional knot with decorative pins or brooches.

Figure 7.4 A typical print-cloth *lihiya*. Illustration: Lombuso Khoza and Laura Kidd.

Accessories worn with bridal attire have undergone changes that also may be attributed to the impact of Western culture. Designer fashion accessories in Swaziland, as in the West, indicate wealth and social status. Modern brides wear Western fashion accessories such as earrings, necklaces, wristwatches, rings, and designer sunglasses with traditional bridal attire. In addition, they wear Western shoes or sandals.

Accessories also maintain and identify social class distinctions. Brides who marry into the royal family wear accessories indicative of their family's high social and/or economic status. Brides from wealthy families also wear accessories to designate their social position. As in the West, they use accessories as a sign of conspicuous consumption and to reveal the wealth of their families.

The changes occurring in traditional bridal dress create dilemmas for many Swazis. The use of brooches or pins instead of the knot used to tie the out print cloth (*lihiya*) is one such example. Many elders fear the absence of the traditional knot indicates the bride had never been taught or could not master the method of tying it (Personal interview, Fakudze, 2001). The position where the knot is tied also concerns many elders. The knot traditionally resided on the right side above the breast for males and on the left side for females so they could be free to dance. Today, however, the appropriate side for either sex has become blurred; for example, males might tie a knot on the customary female side (Personal interview, Fakudze, 2001).

One recent trend in modern Swaziland has been the adoption of the married woman's beehive hairstyle by unmarried women. Some unmarried women with children wear the beehive-shaped hairstyle with no white yarn headband. The presence or absence of the narrow headband in the traditional hairstyle is now an important visual cue in determining a woman's marital status.

Cross-Cultural Perspectives

Similarities exist between Western and Swazi bridal attire. In both cultures, the quality of the bride's attire varies depending upon her family's social and economic status. A consistency exists between the two cultures in selecting or designating a dress culturally recognized as bridal attire. In both cultures, the introduction of synthetic fibers eases fabric maintenance and changes aesthetics. A notable difference is the Swazi use of bridal attire after the wedding ceremony. A Western bride packs her bridal gown away with great care, and usually does not wear it again; a Swazi bride, in contrast, continues to wear her bridal attire for visits to in-laws or for special national festivals and ceremonies.

In both Western and Swazi cultures, the wedding ceremony and festivities symbolize social and economic status. In Western wedding ceremonies more opportunities arise to create activities that involve great expenditures. Many Swazis, however, incorporate creative ways of working within older customs and rituals to display their economic status. For example, the gifts given by the bride to her new in-laws continue to be domestic household goods but now may include expensive items such as furniture or household appliances.

The Maintenance of Symbolism Through Continuity and Change

Documenting the changes in traditional Swazi bridal attire is not a straight-forward process. As H. Kuper writes, "[T]he historical method is particularly difficult because of the approach of the Swazi to time, and the absence of written records" (1986: 8). Traditionally, each generation orally passed down customs of the culture, such as dress. Oral transmission of cultural history and traditions has, along the way, been tweaked and customized to accommodate social changes. Accordingly, "the absence of written records" of correct attire results in modifications by each generation that are incorporated into traditional ways of dressing.

The basic bridal garments and accessories remain symbols with a shared meaning for the people of Swaziland that bridges the past and present. When a Swazi bride elects to wear traditional bridal attire, she provides "some degree of continuity and structure from one context to another, as well as providing some variety and change" (Franks and Seebruger, 1980 article, cited in Kaiser 1997: 42). In adapting outside customs and molding them into the traditions within her culture, the Swazi bride faces choices that must balance the maintenance of cultural traditions with the Western influences that now are a part of Swazi life. In making these choices, the community expects the bride to consider her socio-cultural environment.

While the Western bride freely does what she wishes when it comes to her choice of gown and accessories, the Swazi bride, if she decides to marry with considerations of her cultural traditions, faces a limited choice in the attire she may wear. Nevertheless, the Swazi bride may creatively introduce changes to traditional attire by integrating selected Western fashion accessories acceptable within cultural bounds. There are no specific boundaries as to how far the changes will occur. Although Swazi elders may be disappointed in some of the changes that have occurred, the continued use of the basic traditional bridal attire demonstrates the integration of cultural change and continuity in the context of everyday social life. Change, then, becomes intimately connected to the past and to the future (Khoza, 1992).

Traditions within a culture are never static because circumstances or events cause them to change. Swazi pride in their culture and their determination to maintain their traditions, however, assure that the changes they introduce will not dilute the shared cultural meanings inherent in traditional rituals and dress. In the case of the Swazi bride, she melds her bridal attire by retaining certain cultural traditions with her adoption of Western influences.

Notes

1. The present monarch of Swaziland is King Mwsati III, who ascended to the throne in 1986.

2. National celebrations include the King's birthday and Independence Day. National festivals include the sacred *Incwala*, performed by young males, that celebrates the strengthening of the kingship as well as the harvesting of new fruits. Another national festival is the popular Reed Dance (*Umhlanga*), performed by young females, which affords the King the opportunity to select a new bride. In Swaziland, polygamy is a traditional practice.

3. The account of the courtship and wedding rituals has been derived from M. Kohler's account, found in A. Kuper (1982: 128–31). Further information was received from L. Fakudze during a personal interview on 7 January 2001 in Swaziland.

4. Interestingly, the beehive shape is also the shape of the traditional Swazi house.

5. The addition of these hair accessories is documented in pictures of women from the early twentieth century. In twenty-first century Swaziland, wearing these types of hair accessories is considered an "older" person's style. Modern Swazi brides rarely wear these types of hair accessories in their hairdos.

6. Why one word is used to describe two dissimilar garments is unknown and there is no pronunciation difference that distinguishes between these garments. A direct English translation of *sidziya* is "apron."

7. Most silk fabrics are imported from Thailand and sold in local fabric shops.

References

Applebaum, H. (1987), *Perspectives in Anthropology*, Albany: State University New York Press.

Godeffroy, D. (1999), *Edladleni*, Swaziland: Jubilee Printing and Publishing.

Kaiser, S. B. (1997), *The Social Psychology of Clothing*, New York: Fairchild.

Khoza, L.S, (1992), "Gender Symbolism of Swazi Infant Dress," Master's Thesis, University of California at Davis.

Kuper, A. (1982), *Wives for Cattle: Bridalwealth and Marriage in Southern Africa*, London UK: Routledge and Kegan Paul Ltd.

Kuper, H. (1986), *The Swazi: A South African Kingdom*, New York: Holt, Rhinehart and Winston, Inc.

8

Gender, Identity and Moroccan Weddings: The Adornment of the Ait Khabbash Berber Bride and Groom

Cynthia Becker

Ait Khabbash Berber women typically live quiet lives at the edge of the desert in southeastern Morocco, yet celebrate weddings with a fervor that matches the scorching August heat of the Sahara. They will spend hours sitting with the bride in a tent constructed specifically for the occasion, singing songs, beating drums and dancing for three days, carrying out the marriage rituals of their Berber ancestors. Ait Khabbash Berber women dominate weddings, thereby preserving the cultural distinctiveness of their group despite other societal influences that have changed the nature of daily life. French colonial occupation of the area in the 1930s drastically changed life for the Ait Khabbash, who gradually began to sell their livestock, fold up their tents, and leave their desert existence. By the 1960s, most had moved into houses in the nearby oasis of the Tafilalet. This transformation from a nomadic to a sedentary lifestyle led to changes in economic activity, patterns of labor, ideology and daily forms of artistic and cultural expression, such as dress.

Although fashions and styles of everyday clothing and jewelery changed and continue to evolve for Ait Khabbash women and men, the adornment of the bride and the groom has barely changed over time. During weddings, women unfold a dusty and infrequently used nomadic tent and construct it as a temporary home for the bride. Women carefully dress the bride in a red scarf, white clothing, wool belt and the silver jewelry their ancestors wore on a daily basis. They sing the songs of their mothers and grandmothers while applying henna to the bride's hands and feet. They also sing for the groom as he is being dressed in a similar red scarf and white clothing. While life continues to evolve for the Ait Khabbash, they maintain their identity as a discrete ethnic group and weddings are important events that allow them to express their distinctiveness.

This essay focuses on the process of dressing the bride and groom in order to address why women, rather than men, are responsible for maintaining the artistic symbols of Ait Khabbash Berber identity. Not only do women manage weddings, but the bride's decorated body is a symbol of what it means to be Ait Khabbash. Although the adornment of the groom also forms a central focus of weddings, his dress reflects cloth normally associated with Ait Khabbash women, demonstrating that men rely on women to provide the group with symbols of their identity.

Issues of identity are crucial to Berbers or Imazighen, who consider themselves to be the indigenous inhabitants of North Africa.[1] Berbers lived in the region before the Punic and Roman occupations, and the arrival of Arabs to Morocco in the seventh century deeply influenced them religiously, culturally and linguistically (Sadiqi, 1997: 9).[2] Although Berbers gradually adopted Islam and most learned to speak Arabic, a language vastly different from their indigenous language, the existence of a distinct Berber culture continues to be important.[3] This feature distinguishes Morocco from other North African and Middle Eastern countries and most Berbers are proud of their distinct heritage (Sadiqi, 1997: 18).[4]

Ait Khabbash Berbers live in the multi-ethnic region of southeastern Morocco in and around the Tafilalet oasis, Morocco's largest oasis. Although the everyday dress of the various groups in the Tafilalet is becoming more and more similar, weddings serve as occasions when the Ait Khabbash Berbers publicly express their ethnic identity through dress. Weddings which draw attention to fertility and the propagation of the group are crucial to Ait Khabbash identity. Nickie Charles and Helen M. Hintjens argue that when identity is ethnically based, tight control over a woman's sexuality is necessary in order to define and maintain the boundaries of the community because the biological capabilities of women associate them with the continuation of the society (1998: 2). Uncontrolled female sexuality threatens the integrity of the group; therefore, the adornment of the bride is crucial to Ait Khabbash identity because it represents the control of female sexuality, fertility and ensures the preservation and maintenance of the group's identity.

Teaching Gender Identity: Dressing the Bride

The dress associated with weddings teaches gender roles, instructing the bride what is expected of her in society. Although gender roles and opportunities continue to change for young Ait Khabbash women, the process of dressing the bride teaches her the ancestral values and behaviors expected of a married woman. The bride's dressing ceremony refers to the night before the actual wedding and specifically designates the occasion when the bride is dressed in her wedding clothes. The act of dressing the bride is so crucial to the wedding ceremony that one woman specifically carries out this ritualized duty. The woman called *tamaccat*, that literally translated means "the woman who brushes" states one of her primary responsibilities is to brush and to style the typically long hair of the bride. Women consider it an honor and a privilege to perform the services of *tamaccat* because it suggests that they have extensive cultural knowledge.

A group of women assist the artistic endeavors of the *tamaccat* by accompanying her actions with ritualized songs called *izlan*. These women sit in a circle surrounding the bride, perform *izlan*, and carefully watch the *tamaccat* (Figure 1.1). Only married women circle the bride, because these women have the cultural knowledge and life experience to teach her. The circle of women around the bride serves as a ritual of protection and provides the bride with emotional support. Like most brides, she becomes very nervous at the prospect of her first sexual encounter with her husband.

One of the songs begins by praising God and comparing the bride to the Prophet's daughter:

My daughter, God be with you.
Yelli zzureg zar-m rebbi.[5]

Daughter of the Prophet, hey my daughter.
Yellis n nnabi a yelli.

While the song is sung, the *tamaccat* begins to style the bride's hair and to apply perfumed herbs. Ait Khabbash believe the thickness and the length of a woman's hair directly reflects her fertility and the brush used on the bride's hair absorbs the essence of her reproductive power. A bride who does not want to get pregnant immediately after her marriage asks her mother to hide the brush used during her wedding. Tradition suggests if a bride does not see the brush, she can avoid an unwanted pregnancy.

After the application of the perfumed herbs, the *tamaccat* braids the bride's hair. Her bound hair exemplifies the control of female fertility within the institution of marriage. The song continues:

Wear white clothes.
Les-imt ikebran mellulnin.

Throw old clothes away and use silk.
Ger s-uderbal ag leḫrir.

These *izlan* use the metaphor of the bride throwing away her old clothes and using silk to refer to the bride's change in status from unmarried virgin to married woman. The words suggest a symbolic transformation but, in fact, the bride does throw away her old clothing. Indeed, prior to her wedding, a young girl may not be very concerned with her appearance. Young girls often wear old skirts and faded t-shirts because they do most of the housework for which it is not practical for them to wear nice, new clothes. Girls who are concerned with clothing prior to their marriages are considered frivolous and possibly promiscuous.

After the bride is dressed in her white clothing, she sits down so the *tamaccaṯ* can apply her headdress and jewelry while women sing:

Aâbroq tops the head and looks nice.
Yuley ukenbuc igef izil.

Aâbroq refers to the headdress placed over the bride's head that she wears during the entire wedding ceremony (Figure 8.1). The bride only removes the

Figure 8.1 A group of women surround the bride while she is dressed and henna applied to her hands. Photograph: the author.

aâbroq when she and her husband are alone for sexual relations. In the morning after their sexual encounter, she places any type of covering over her head and returns to her family, who redresses her in the *aâbroq*.

The *aâbroq* has several components. Its square shape is made when a red, striped silk cloth is placed over a long, thin cushion tied on top of the bride's head and layered with jewellery and sashes. The red cloth covers the entire head and neck of the bride down to her chest (Figures 8.1 and 8.2). In order to secure and insure it properly covers the bride's face and neck, the sides of

Figure 8.2 A fully dressed Ait Khabbash bride. Photograph: the author.

the cloth are sewn shut after the bride is dressed. As her head is completely encased in the cloth, it forms a type of mask. The fabric near the eyes of the bride is moistened with water and rubbed in order to make it thin enough for the bride to see through. A small band of multicolored embroidered fabric binds the cloth to the head more securely to insure it holds its position. This band has sequins that trim its bottom edge and simulate bangs, the preferred hairstyle of Ait Khabbash women prior to the 1970s. A green cord with a thick tassel on the end is also wrapped around the bride's head and the headdress is then topped with a silver chain and pendant (Figures 8.1 and 8.2).

The several layers of ties, sashes and silver jewelry that create the bride's headdress symbolize the containment of her fertility within marriage and protect her during this liminal, in-between stage. The bride keeps her face covered during the entire wedding and only her husband and one or two very close female relatives are allowed to see it during this period. The act of covering the bride's face places a barrier between the bride and the outside world.

Covering the bride's face also protects her from the evil eye and conceals the bride's facial orifices, openings that are vulnerable to invasion by the *jnoun*. The *jnoun*, ambiguous beings not quite human, are mentioned in the Qur'an. They eat, drink, sleep and have children, yet are quick-tempered beings who can guide and serve humans one moment or cause illness or even death the next. Strokes, paralysis, mental illness, epilepsy, and other forms of illnesses are believed to be signs that people have angered the *jnoun*. *Jnoun* inhabit physical passageways, such as wells, drains and doorways and are particularly active during rites of passage. People passing through life's social changes, such as childbirth, circumcision, and weddings are particularly vulnerable to their attacks. Covering the bride's facial orifices, tying small bags of incense and herbs to her dress, and putting sweet-smelling herbs in her hair are all done to please the *jnoun* and avoid a harmful incident.

The *aâbroq* is also believed to protect the wedding guests from the power of the bride and her ability to steal the "beauty" or outer physical essence of other women. As noted earlier, binding the bride's head additionally represents the symbolic control of female sexuality. Before the bride and groom have sexual intercourse, the groom must untie the bride's body from the sashes, jewelry and cloth that bind her. The act of untying and unbinding the bride represents the act of sexual intercourse.[6]

The *aâbroq* also has a practical function. Weddings are intense experiences for a young bride who is the center of all attention during the wedding ceremony. People discuss how the clothes drape around her body, the length and thickness of her braids, and even the shape and texture of her hands. The *aâbroq* protects the bride from publicly demonstrating emotion while being evaluated by women in the community. The Ait Khabbash believe that a person's outer body should not reveal too much about a person's thoughts or beliefs. The *aâbroq* protects the bride from revealing too much about her inner joy or sadness concerning her marriage.

Since the sexual encounter between the bride and the groom is the culminating event of a wedding, the bride also covers her face out of modesty. While I attended a wedding, one Ait Khabbash woman explained the significance of the *aâbroq*: "The bride wears the *aâbroq* because she is shy. She is from far away and maybe never saw her husband and he never saw her. She pokes small holes in her *aâbroq* so she can see her surroundings but no one can see her. The *aâbroq* makes her more comfortable."[7] The bride is central to the wedding ceremony, but at the same time the silk cloth and silver jewelry that mask her face serve to distance her from the event socially.

The use of a red cloth to adorn the bride calls to mind the multifaceted position of women in Ait Khabbash society. Although the fertility and sexuality of women are crucial to Ait Khabbash society because they ensure the continuation of the group, nevertheless, female fertility and sexuality also have the power to disrupt the society. Red indicates both the polluting effects of blood and a positive fertility symbol. The red color of the *aâbroq* symbolizes virginal blood, menstrual blood, and the blood of childbirth, all associated with female reproduction.

The *aâbroq* contains other colors the Ait Khabbash associate with female fertility. For example, green tassels are wrapped around the top of the *aâbroq* and the cloth itself has yellow and black horizontal stripes near the bottom. Red, green, yellow and black are colors associated with female fertility, and three of these four colors appear in the *aâbroq*. The Ait Khabbash link the colors red, green, yellow and black to objects found in the natural environment. Several women linked them to ripening dates. Unripe dates are green, and eventually turn yellow, red and then a dark brown, almost black color. An analogy may be made between the ripening of dates and the development and blossoming of a girl's body into womanhood. Others felt these four colors used in the bride's dress symbolize the rainbow. The rainbow symbolizes fertility to the Ait Khabbash, and the name of the rainbow in Tamazight is *tislit n unzar*, which literally means "bride of the rain." Rainbows are highly valued in southeastern Morocco because they are a rare occurrence in an area with less than ten centimeters of rainfall each year.[8]

As demonstrated above, while bridal adornment celebrates female sexuality, it also represents its control, and songs performed by women reinforce this idea of containment and control:

Hey my dear, get the leash.
Qen-d a âezza taguni.

Hey my dear, get the fibulae.
Qqen-d a âezza tisegnas.

The idea of binding and containing the bride's body is evident in the verse: "Hey my dear, get the leash". The word "leash" refers to the amber choker necklace the bride wears around her neck (Figure 8.2). This very large piece of jewelry may contain over thirty amber beads and surrounds the neck of the bride like a collar or "leash." Many believe amber to have protective and healing qualities and it is frequently ground up to make medicine.

The song also calls for the bride to wear *tisegnas*, or "fibulae," a type of jewelry worn by Berbers throughout Morocco. Fibulae may be described as large silver pins with a thick silver chain that drapes down between them and are used to hold the front and back of the bride's garments together at her shoulders (Figure 8.2). Two small round boxes with bulging carved lids that conspicuously resemble breasts are filled with perfumed herbs and attached to the chain. Two pairs of cast silver bracelets adorn both her wrists. One pair, called *izbian n iqerroin*, or "bracelets of animal horns," are very heavy, solidly cast bracelets with twelve triangular-shaped points radiating from their central band (Figure 8.3). The large size of these bracelets visually emulates the ideal

Figure 8.3 The groom's family fills a tray with silver bracelets, an amber necklace, a red silk cloth and green and red tassels and presents this to the bride. Photograph: the author.

of the physically strong woman. Prior to the 1970s, brides continued to wear these bracelets on a daily basis to mark their marital status.[9]

The sharp pins of the fibulae and the radiating points of the bracelet of animal horns symbolically protect the bride. James Bynon writes that pointed motifs are common to Berber art and are stylized representations of dangerous and repulsive objects, animals and insects, such as serpents, scorpions, knives, or swords (1984: 145). These motifs protect also against the evil eye by having the ability to symbolically burst or pop the eye (Bynon, 1984: 147).

As the bride continues to be dressed, the clothing used to adorn her body physically and metaphorically binds and further protects her. For example, the bride stands up and a wool belt is wound around her waist several times. Since the Ait Khabbash herded sheep, goats, and camels, the wool used to make the belt symbolizes both the fertility of women and their association with the continuation of the Ait Khabbash community. On the one hand, the act of tying and binding the waist, the area where female reproductive organs are located, draws attention to female sexuality. On the other hand, the belt wrapped around the bride's waist relates to fertility and its control within the boundaries of marriage. In the past, after marriage a woman continued to wear this belt around her waist, but this is rarely done today by newly married women.[10]

The bride's mother and not her future husband gives her the wool belt. Women braid these red, green, yellow and black wool belts for their daughters, usually when the girl is still very young, and save them for their weddings. Since the bride is not yet a part of her husband's family, the control of female sexuality is the responsibility of her own family. The belt is bound and tied around her waist for the first time on the eve of her wedding night, a time when her virginity will be tested and her family's reputation and honor will be upheld or destroyed.

The final stage in the wedding preparation is the application of henna (Figure 8.1). When the bride's hands and feet are decorated with henna, women sing:

Give your right hand, give your hand to be decorated.
Ara-d afus n iffus, ara-d afus s-igman.

Applying henna, an elaborate form of body adornment, has become one of the central features of almost all wedding ceremonies in Morocco. In many areas, a professional *neggafa* spends as many as eight hours elaborately decorating the bride's hands and feet, requiring the bride to sit silently and to be completely still for hours at a time (Combs-Schilling, 1989: 212). The Ait Khabbash do not practice the elaborate henna ceremony typical of most areas of Morocco, the henna process for them takes only fifteen minutes. The woman dressing the bride uses her index finger to smear henna on the palms and tops of the bride's extended hands up to her wrist (Figure 8.1). The tops and bottoms of the bride's feet are decorated up to the ankles. The hands and feet are then covered with a cloth and left to dry for several hours to insure that the skin is stained a deep red color.

During the henna ritual, the physical and the social body "cooperate" and henna protects both the spiritual and the physical body (Kapchan, 1993: 7). Henna designs are not important to the Ait Khabbash; rather, the auspicious nature of the henna itself is crucial to its application. Henna designs accompany transitory events where blood is shed and status changes. Henna is believed to have "divine blessing," and protects the bride against danger from the evil eye and the *jnoun* that accompanies the change from one status to the next.

The action of binding and containing the bride's body with cloth and jewelry represents the control of female sexuality and fertility and ensures the continuation of the group into the future. Several scholars argue that the control of women in various ceremonies in many Muslim countries represents attitudes that Muslim women are weak, morally inferior beings who are devoted to sexual pleasure and flesh-centered desires. For example, Fatima Mernissi, a Moroccan sociologist, argues that Islamic doctrine and belief associate women with chaos and men are instructed to avoid women and direct their attentions to God rather than female seduction (1987: 41–2). Daisy Dwyer, in her book *Images and Self-Images: Male and Female in Morocco*, however, argues that Muslim women do not see themselves this way. "Men, in women's eyes," she writes, "can be consumed with desire of a sexual sort, and can be shamefully profligate, quite like the female sex according to the male view" (1978: 153).

The cloth and jewelry binding the bride's body are not worn to control the bride's sex drive but to complete the association of women with the essential qualities of Ait Khabbash identity – fertility and containment – and to empower the Ait Khabbash community against the outside world. Ait Khabbash weddings and their associated art forms express a gendered ideology on which to base identity constructions. Women give life to Ait Khabbash identity and ensure the continuation of the group into the future. Women are agents of boundary making and bearers of the values associated with Berber identity.

Dressing the Groom

In order to appreciate the power of women in Ait Khabbash society fully one must also consider the adornment of the groom. The role of women is so crucial in the preservation of Ait Khabbash identity that the groom wears garments similar to the bride in order to harness some of her power.

The aesthetics of the forms and motifs used by the Ait Khabbash typically are symmetrical, balanced, and reflect the complementary and opposing relationships that exist between men and women. Although men and women appear to occupy separate and opposing worlds, they influence each other. The mutually dependent relationship between men and women may be seen on the body of the groom. The artistic expressions at weddings can be understood as a codified ideology that expresses gender order. Because women, who do all of the weaving, are closely connected to arts, men rely on women for the creation of artistic symbols of identity.

While a small group of men from his family dress the groom in appropriate wedding attire, women accompany this action with song. Other women present at the event are not allowed to see the groom and a white cloth is hung before him to block their view of the proceedings. This is done less for modesty and more to protect the groom from both the positive and the negative powers of women (Figure 8.4). Women, who may secretly be jealous or resentful of the groom's marriage, have the ability to affect the groom with the evil eye that will cause his impotence. Anger that her daughter was not chosen to marry the groom may cause a woman to seek revenge against him. The white cloth stops the potentially harmful power of women by setting up a physical barrier of protection. White protects because it is a color associated with the innocence, purity and the prestige of Islam. Pilgrims to Mecca wear white clothing and men who pray in a mosque frequently dress in white. When the white cloth shields the groom, women begin to sing:

In the name of God, the compassionate and the merciful.
Bismi Llah Rrahman rrahim.

Allah guides you my son.
Izwar-ak Rebbi a memmi.

He guides you, and he follows you.
Izwar-ak i gger-ak.

The pigeon enters his clothes.
Ikjem dig utbir timelsa.

As these *izlan* are sung, a groom is dressed in a white "hooded gown", and a white "hooded cape" (Figure 8.4). While he is dressing, a verse compares him to a pigeon. The metaphor of the pigeon also refers to the bride at different times during the wedding. The use of similar metaphors to describe both the bride and the groom is unusual in Morocco. Scholars, such as Edward Wester-marck, write that during most Moroccan weddings the groom is typically

Figure 8.4 A groom covers his face with a women's red silk belt and white turban. The same type of red silk belt is also draped across his chest. Photograph: the author.

transformed into a sultan or king[11] (1972: 97). Unlike in other areas of Morocco, the Ait Khabbash groom is instead compared to a pigeon, a symbol with feminine connotations typically used to refer to women. The lack of cooperation that historically existed between the Ait Khabbash and Morocco's central government may explain why the metaphor of the sultan or king is not important to Ait Khabbash identity.

The pigeon, a metaphor for women, is a symbol of purity and denotes the sacredness of the occasion. Both the bride and the groom wear white clothing, a color associated with cleanliness and purity. Purity is physical and both the bride and the groom ritually wash their bodies with water in order to cleanse themselves before the wedding ceremony. Purity is also metaphoric; the Ait Khabbash construction of identity involves attitudes concerning the purity of group identity. Group purity is something the Ait Khabbash desire to control during weddings, since they believe group purity can only be maintained when Ait Khabbash men marry Ait Khabbash women.

After the groom is dressed in his white clothing, a long, red silk cloth with multicolored stripes is wrapped around his face so that his entire face is covered except his eyes (Figure 8.4). The silk cloth is actually a woman's silk belt, thus another symbol clearly associated with women. A similar belt is then draped over the groom's right shoulder, brought across his chest and tied at his left hip (Figure 8.4).

The use of the silk belt to dress the groom demonstrates that the feminine construct is a powerful means through which group identity is created and maintained. The Ait Khabbash groom wears clothing associated with women because women are models for group unity. The silk belt, a metaphor for the controlled sexuality and fertility of women, is a potent symbol for the male reliance on women's fertility to ensure the continuation of Ait Khabbash identity into the future.

The red silk belt is then covered with a powerful symbol of masculine identity, the turban, when the following song is sung:

Oh groom with the turbans.
A yisli a bu leâmamat.

The turban is a symbol of masculinity and honor, and a white turban is wrapped around the groom's head until it almost completely covers the silk belt (Figure 8.4). Both the red silk belt and the white turban create a boundary between the facial orifices and the outside elements. The act of covering the mouth and nostrils during ritual occasions prevents the *jnoun* from entering the body. Furthermore, the male turban, by covering the female belt, seems to act as another metaphor. The turban also embraces imagery that associates men with Islam and the qualities of modesty, honor and dignity.

While women continue to sing, the groom's hands and feet are adorned with henna in a fashion similar to the bride. Henna completely covers the palms of his hands and the soles of his feet, which are then wrapped in pieces of white cloth. Afterwards, women sing the following lyrics:

Hey owner of yellow shoes.
A bu tkurbyin tiwragin.

Stand up, the days stand for you.
Tubedda bedant-ak liam.

These phrases refer to the purified state of the groom. After henna dries on his feet, he slips into yellow, leather shoes without backs. The shoes, imported from the city of Fes, are only worn on ritual occasions. A needle is placed in the right shoe of the groom; its pointed shape protects the groom from harmful forces, such as the evil eye and the *jnoun*.

After the groom is dressed he must be removed from public and shielded from the evil eye and *shur*. *Shur* is an Arabic word used by the Ait Khabbash that can be translated to mean "sorcery or conjury" (Kapchan, 1996: 239). There are many types and forms of *shur* practiced in Morocco. Some types are socially acceptable, such as the act of visiting a *fqih*, a religious scholar, in order to obtain a written charm or the purchase of herbs and spices to create a remedy for an illness. Other forms of *shur* are very secretive, typically have evil intent and are forbidden by Islam (Kapchan, 1996: 241).

The most dangerous type of *shur* is *thiqaf*, an Arabic term that refers to a type of *shur* that can stop someone from achieving something. In this situation, *thiqaf* can be used to cause the groom's impotency. In order to decrease his vulnerability to *thiqaf*, the groom is not allowed to walk to the nuptial tent. Instead, the groom is carried on the back of one his close male friends who will remain isolated with him for the next twenty-four hours. This is the only person, male or female, to remain with the groom until the bride is brought in to spend the night with her husband.

Conclusion

Both visual and verbal arts reveal gender attitudes that unite members of the Ait Khabbash community. Bodily adornment of both the bride and the groom contains powerful metaphors that express the importance of female fertility to the continuation of Ait Khabbash identity. The dress of the bride binds and ties her body. This action reinforces a model of inner unity that determines the aesthetic system of the Ait Khabbash and protects it from the outside world. The groom wears clothing associated with women, but one of the most striking differences between the bride and the groom is the public role the bride plays in the wedding ceremony, which contrasts so markedly with the groom's concealment from the public eye. The groom is taken away from the public event and confined to the nuptial tent, and only one man is allowed to make contact with him. The groom does not become a public part of the wedding ceremony until he successfully pierces the hymen of the bride. Thus a woman is transformed into a public symbol of Ait Khabbash identity, while the groom is hidden away from sight in order to protect his reproductive abilities from outside manipulation.

Although everyday dress has changed and continues to change for the Ait Khabbash, weddings continue to promote the central role of women in the creation and maintenance of Ait Khabbash identity. The dressing of the bride expresses the crucial role women play in Ait Khabbash society by publicly reinforcing the connection between social identity and women. The colors, forms and motifs of the arts used to adorn the bride's body express the importance that the Ait Khabbash community places on values of fertility, cooperation and group preservation.

Notes

1. This study uses the word "Berber" to refer to the indigenous inhabitants of North Africa because it is a term familiar to most readers; however, the term "Imazighen" is preferable because of the negative connotations associated with the word "Berber." The term 'Berber' is problematic because it is derived from the word *barbaros*, a term used by the Greeks to describe anyone who was not Greek, therefore, "barbarian," "primitive" and "alien" (Sadiqi, 1997: 12). *Amazigh* is the masculine, singular form of the plural word *Imazighen*, which means "free men."

2. It is probable that the whole of North Africa, from Egypt to Morocco, was occupied by Imazighen at one time, although the numbers of Imazighen that occupy North Africa today are relatively small. Approximately 140,000 Berbers live in small isolated pockets in Egypt, Tunisia and Mauritania. One million are scattered through Niger, Mali, Burkina Faso and Libya; another 5.5 million live in Algeria. The Berber population is the largest in Morocco and is estimated to be approximately 9.5 million (Ennaji, 1997: 24).

3. The diverse Amazigh groups throughout northern and western Africa speak various Amazigh languages. In Morocco alone, three different Amazigh languages are spoken: Tarifit in the Rif mountains, Tashelhit in the Sus Valley, High Atlas and Anti-Atlas Mountains and Tamazight in the Middle Atlas and southeastern desert oases (Ennaji, 1997: 12–13).

4. The existence of a large Amazigh population (between 40 and 50 per cent of the total population) is believed to be one of the major ingredients that makes Morocco different from other North African and Middle Eastern countries (Sadiqi, 1997: 18).

5. Transcriptions conform to the standard system followed by Salem Chaker (1984: 113–14). Addi Ouadderrou transcribed the songs in Tamazight. The songs presented in this essay are not complete; rather I have included only verses that explicitly refer to wedding dress.

6. Edward Westermarck also notes the connection between untying the bride's body and intercourse:

> This "tying up" of the bride may be, or may have been, a sham attempt to protect the bride by laying obstacles in the bridegroom's way, or a means of protecting the bride from being by magic deprived of her virginity before the conjugal intercourse, or a means of ensuring the consummation of the marriage by compelling the bridegroom to untie the knots; but in any case the untying of them is regarded as a necessary preliminary to coition (1968: 583).

7. I quote from an informal interview at a wedding in October 1996.

8. The actual spectrum of colors associated with the rainbow is red, orange, yellow, green, blue and purple. The Ait Khabbash often use the colors black and purple interchangeably. While red, green, yellow and purple are indeed found in the rainbow, they are only a sample of the entire color spectrum.

9. Jacques Rabaté and Marie-Rose Rabaté (1996: 159) estimate that the weight of these two bracelets on one arm is between 600 to 900 grams. Women commented that prior to French colonization, the Ait Khabbash were involved in various battles with other groups in the region. Bracelets served as protective weapons.

10. In many other areas of Africa, belts are metaphors for the control of female reproduction. For example, Kalabari women in Nigeria also tie a cloth around the waist of a girl who has begun to menstruate in order to demonstrate that she has reached sexual maturity (Michelman and Erekosima, 1992: 175). Lila Abu-Lughod writes that married Bedouin woman in Egypt also wear belts around their waists. If a married woman does not wear a belt, this means she is promiscuous and is "ready for anything" (Abu-Lughod, 1988: 136).

11. M. Elaine Combs-Schilling also states that the groom is compared to a king:

> To become an adult male, the body first becomes the quintessential male, the Moroccan king, the blood descendent of Muhammed who reigns from Morocco's throne. The transformation is dramatic. The young man takes on the ruler's persona, embodies his postures, affects his attitudes, adopts his authority, and becomes central and pivotal to all that transpires (1989: 190).

According to Combs-Schilling, the groom symbolically becomes the Moroccan monarch. This idea is debatable, and Henry Munson, for example, disagrees that the groom represents the actual Moroccan monarch. He writes that the transformation of the groom into a sultan "is certainly a significant metaphor, reflecting among other things a homology between the authority of husbands and that of kings' and reinforces Moroccan concepts of manhood" (1993: 122).

References

Abu-Lughod, Lila (1988), *Veiled Sentiments*, Berkeley: University of California Press.
Bynon, James (1984), "Berber Women's Pottery: Is the Decoration Motivated?," in John Picton (ed.), *Colloquies on Art & Archaeology in Asia No. 12*, London: University of London, 136–61.

Chaker, Salem (1984), *Textes en Liguistique Berbère: Introduction au Domain Berbère*, Paris: Centre national de la recherche scientifique.

Charles, Nickie and Helen M. Hintjens (eds) (1998), *Gender, Ethnicity and Political Ideologies*, London: Routledge.

Combs-Schilling, M. Elaine (1989), *Sacred Performances: Islam, Sexuality and Sacrifice*, Columbia University Press: New York.

Dwyer, Daisy (1978), *Images and Self-Images: Male and Female in Morocco*, New York: Columbia University Press.

Ennaji, Moha (1997), "The Sociology of Berber: Change and Continuity," *International Journal of the Sociology of Language* 123, 23–40.

Kapchan, Deborah (1993), "Moroccan Women's Body Signs," in Katharine Young (ed.), *Bodylore,* Knoxville: University of Tennessee, 3–34.

—— (1996), *Gender on the Market: Moroccan Women and the Revoicing of Tradition*, Philadelphia: University of Pennsylvania Press.

Herbert, Eugenia W. (1993), *Iron, Gender, and Power: Rituals of Transformation in African Societies*, Bloomington: Indiana University Press.

Mernissi, Fatima (1987), *Beyond the Veil: Male-Female Dynamics in a Modern Muslim Society,* rev. ed. Bloomington: Indiana University Press.

Michelman, Susan O., and Erekosima, Tonye V. (1992), "Kalabari Dress in Nigeria: Visual Analysis and Gender Implications," in Barnes, Ruth and Eicher, Joanne B. (eds), *Dress and Gender: Making and Meaning in Cultural Contexts*, New York: Berg, 164–82.

Munson, Henry, Jr. (1993), *Religion and Power in Morocco*, New Haven: Yale University Press.

Rabaté, Jacques, and Rabaté, Marie-Rose (1996), *Bijoux du Maroc: Du Haut Atlas à la Valée du Draa*, Aix-en-Provence: Édisud.

Sadiqi, Fatima (1997), "The Place of Berber in Morocco," *International Journal of the Sociology of Language* 123: 7–21.

Westermarck, Edward (1968), *Ritual and Belief in Morocco*, 2d. ed., Vol 1, New York: University Books.

—— (1972), *Marriage Ceremonies in Morocco*, 2d. ed., London: MacMillan and Co., Ltd.

9

An Athenian Wedding, Year 2000

Helen Bradley Foster

On 11 June 2000, Katerina Kontogianni and Miltiadis (Miltos) Katsaros married in Athens, Greece.[1] They, like ninety-seven per cent of the Greek population, are members of the Orthodox Church and wed under its auspices.

Until the 1960s, Greek couples courted only with the approval and under the scrutiny of the woman's parents. Today, young people choose their own partners and date without chaperones. With the loosening of certain mores, civil weddings became popular in the larger cities for about two decades. Now, there is a noticeable return to formal church weddings. Despite the changing expectations of greater freedom for women in the secular realm, the Orthodox Church remains patriarchal; no women hold any positions of power within its hierarchy.

The Orthodox Church conducts its rites in a conservative manner using a liturgy that dates to the first and second centuries AD. In contrast to Roman Catholic and Protestant wedding ceremonies in which the bride and groom respond to a series of questions posed by the priest or minister, during the Orthodox church wedding service, the bride and groom remain silent while the priest informs them of their duties and responsibilities as wife and husband.[2] Within these seemingly static rituals, however, individuals may insert their own personalities. Dress in particular often serves as the means by which this is achieved.

The Orthodox Wedding Ceremony

A couple may not marry during Lent. With this exception, a wedding may take place in any month, with May, June and September being the popular choices primarily because of the fine weather. A wedding may be held on any day, but most occur on weekends, especially on Sundays, the day preferred by priests. Because of the limited number of Sundays, three or four marriages commonly take place on the same day in a religious ceremony that lasts about thirty minutes.

A newly developing pre-marital custom, perceived as emanating from the United States, is for the woman to receive a diamond engagement ring; but, for now, this remains an uncommon practice, found only in cities. Usually, the future bride receives no engagement ring as a material declaration of the couple's intention to marry. Some women and men, however, wear the wedding band on their left hand before marriage as a symbol of their intentions, switching it to the right hand after marriage.

The wedding begins at the church door as the bride's father gives her to the groom, whereupon the groom presents the bride with flowers. Preceding the guests into the church, the couple moves to a marriage table set up in front of the sanctuary. A white cloth covers the table upon which lie the large, gold-encrusted book containing the New Testament liturgy, the wedding rings and the wedding crowns (*stephana*).[3]

The wedding party stands at the table; the bride to the right with her parents and family members, the groom and his family to the left. Two sponsors, usually a male and a female, attend the couple during the service. The sponsors may be godparents, family members, or close friends. Orthodox churches in Greece contain no pews or chairs; therefore, the wedding guests stand and face the sanctuary, forming a semi-circle around the couple.

Even if the bride and groom have already been given a secular engagement party and she an engagement ring, a priest performs the betrothal as the first part of the church ceremony with an exchange of rings. After a prayer offering, the officiating priest takes the bride's ring, makes the sign of the cross with it three times, and places it on her left ring finger, repeating these formalities with the groom's ring. The priest then removes the bands, makes the sign of the cross with them three times, and places them on the bride's and groom's right ring fingers. The couple then drinks three sips of wine, as do the sponsors, and kisses the Bible.

The second half of the ceremony entails the dramatic crowning of the bride and groom when each of them receives a headdress: a thin circle fabricated of metal, covered with satin or silk cloth, and embellished with real or artificial flowers and beads.[4] A ribbon, about one meter long, ties the two crowns together as a symbolic uniting of the couple.

In this part of the ceremony, the priest joins the couple's hands. He then lifts both crowns from the wedding table and, holding them in a crossed position, he crosses the crowns three times over the bride's head and repeats the same motions over the groom's head. The couple's sponsor, standing behind them, then crosses the crowns over each of their heads three times.[5] Next, the priest places the crowns on the bride's and groom's heads. If the bride wears a veil, her crown is placed on it. With the crowns still tied together, the priest holds the Bible before him, joins hands with the couple, and leads them in the joyous and exuberant "Dance of Isaiah," circling the table three times while the sponsor holds the joining ribbon aloft (Figure 9.1).[6] At this point, the ceremony becomes noisy and raucous as the guests interact in the rites by throwing rice and rose petals at the newlyweds during each of their three passes around the table. The priest uses the Bible to shield his face from the hail of rice and flowers, while the couple's sponsor struggles to keep the crowns on the bride and groom's heads.[7]

With the dance concluded, the service continues with the priest offering more prayers, after which the bride and groom kiss.[8] This ends the wedding ceremony. The priest removes the crowns, binds them together with the ribbon and gives them to the couple along with a copy of the New Testament. Accompanied by their families, the bride and groom move between the wedding guests and form a receiving line at the church entrance. After greeting the couple and their families, the guests are presented with bundles of white, sugared almonds. A reception with food and dancing follows at another venue.

Figure 9.1 The priest leads the couple in the "Dance of Isaiah". Photograph courtesy Katerina Kontogianni and Miltos Katsoros.

Country Wedding – City Wedding

Approximately two-thirds of the Greek population live in urban areas. Athens, with its population of five million, is home to about one-half the total population. This phenomenon is recent, however, and most Athenians can count back no more than two or three generations, if that, to ancestors who migrated from villages throughout greater Greece into the capital. For instance, Katerina and Miltos both were born and raised in Athens, but all four of their parents were born and grew up elsewhere. The pull to the former villages occurs when great hoards of people leave Athens, returning to their ancestral homes for festivals, particularly Easter, the Assumption of the Virgin, the village saint's name day, and for baptisms, weddings and funerals. On a more subtle level, reinforcing such ties to the past continues even in the urbane, cosmopolitan city when the traditions and beliefs learned in the home village are practiced on a day-to-day level and most especially are acted upon during major family events.

Place certainly plays a role in whether the wedding remains conservative or stretches the boundaries of adherence to custom. In villages, for example, the entire population usually attends both the church ceremony and the festivities afterwards. In cities, the guests are limited to those invited by the couple and their families.

Commercial bridal shops in cities and towns offer every item of dress the bride may want, as well as decorations for the church such as candles and floral arrangements (Figure 9.2).[9] Like her urban counterparts, many a rural bride now takes advantage of the services and goods of these shops located in nearby towns. Nevertheless, in villages, the fashion statement of the wedding party, particularly the bride's dress, tends not to be on the cutting edge. In fact, all material aspects of a village wedding are circumscribed by just how much is known and adapted of newer, urban trends—trends that lag before penetrating into the countryside.

The ages of the bride and groom also influence the style of a wedding. The younger the couple, the more likely the parents will orchestrate the wedding in a manner known to their own generation. Education presents another factor. Attendance at a university exposes the couple to modern ideas not available to a man or woman whose formal education ended at the village high school. Finally, social status plays a part in the accoutrements of a wedding. Quite simply, in any social group, the upper classes expose their position and wealth in a display of the best, newest, and costliest material goods.

Katerina, born in 1968, was thirty-two at the time of her marriage and is a medical doctor as well as a PhD. Miltos, born in 1965, was thirty-five, received a master's degree in the United States, has his own architectural firm and is a

Figure 9.2 Commercial bridal shop, Pyrgos (Eleia), 2001. Photograph: the author.

professor of architecture. Rather than the longer, formal, chaperoned, and often arranged betrothal period of former decades, Katerina and Miltos became acquainted when a mutual friend introduced them. They began dating and then lived together before their wedding. Athens, as the place of their marriage, contributed to the particular style of their wedding. But their ages, educations and social positions further determined how Katerina and Miltos's wedding reflected creativity within the framework of the proscribed church ceremony. As Miltos comments, "We selected our wedding activities; but in Athens, weddings have become 'industrialized,' planned by professionals. We wanted our marriage to be with our friends and beloved family, not to be a social event to show off."

Although purposely disregarding the professionally organized marriage, intertwined with the modern ideas with which this couple planned their marriage are the older, village customs advocated by their parents. Katerina's parents came from the Epiros region, Miltos's mother near Delphi, and his father from Corfu. Throughout this description of Katerina and Miltos's wedding, I will note the particular customs each mentioned as having been advanced by one or the other of their parents. While many of these customs appear to be widespread or are variations on a similar custom, some are unknown to the people whom I interviewed from other areas of Greece. Greeks retain a number of marriage customs which remain particular to specific regions of the country.

Katerina's and Miltos's remarks about their own wedding demonstrate a high degree of sophistication. This is most obvious in the desire to mark their own wedding as individualistic, not pretentious, while still conforming to the structure set by the church ritual. Miltos neatly summed up the contrast between country and city weddings: "In villages, marriage is the whole community's affair; they are more conservative with traditions. In Athens, the couple is more able to individualise their marriage."[10]

Dressing the Bridal Bed

Several events lead up to the actual wedding ceremony. Among the gifts received, the bride's family gives a substantial dowry as its contribution towards the couple's future life together. Until recently, a Greek bridal dowry consisted of household linens, furnishings and animals. Brides from wealthier families also usually came to the marriage with a dowry that included gold jewelry and real estate. Since 1983, bridal dowries are illegal in Greece, yet they remain a part of the unwritten marriage contract. Today, real estate, particularly in the form of a city apartment, is the most common large item given by the bride's parents.

In the past, as part of her dowry, a young woman prepared the linens for her future home. Of these, the most important were heavily embroidered and crocheted bed linens, the most elaborate being those used to cover her marriage bed.[11] Today, because of the availability of both Greek and imported machine-manufactured household linens, rarely do young women labor over these items.[12] Even in remote villages, status now is attached to factory-made textiles, although rural mothers and grandmothers still may spend much time and effort making these decorative linens in anticipation of the eventual marriages of their female descendants. In more urban areas, instead of hand-decorating household linens, women merely buy them as dowry items. Nevertheless, even in the cities, earlier customs prevail in a rudimentary form – particularly in the custom of "dressing the bridal bed." Three days before the wedding, female relatives of the bride made up the marital bed with the linens hand-embroidered especially for this purpose. In the past, the other dowry items and gifts were also brought out at this time and the women sang a special song for the bride.

In Athens, Katerina's mother arranged this event prior to her daughter's wedding. Unlike the solemnity of the occasion in former times, however,

Katerina describes it as a pre-marital event organized "just to have fun with friends." In the past, only women participated. On the evening Katerina's bed was dressed, along with older female relatives, Katerina and Miltos's fathers, their sponsers, female cousins, girlfriends, and even Miltos and his brother attended. These guests brought sweets to eat and they drank together during the time the women spent dressing the bed.

Katerina's mother purchased the bed linens which Katerina describes as "the best you can afford – silk sheets." The bed was further dressed with a blanket hand-woven by Miltos's grandmother and given by his mother. The women make up the bed the same as for everyday use with sheets, a blanket and large pillows; the difference being that the linens for the marriage bed are finer. According to custom, the bed is not slept in until the wedding night, after which the linens are not used again except for special occasions, such as a wedding anniversary.

As part of the custom, the women always make the bed three times. The first two times, Katerina's mother instructed her daughter to pull off all the linens and say that it was not made well enough. When the bed was finally ready, the guests threw rose petals and rice on it.

If a small baby (preferably a boy) is present, it is put on the bed to ensure a future child for the couple. For Katerina, an eight-year-old child was placed on the bed. Carolyn Mordecai mentions a variation on this custom, but does not note where in Greece it took place: "After the wedding, young children were briefly placed on the marital bed so that the bride and groom would be fruitful and give birth to many children" (1999: 184). This folk custom again signals the link between the bride and future motherhood.

At the completion of dressing the bed, Katerina went out drinking with her girlfriends. Perhaps as a complimentary celebration for the future groom, friends gave Miltos a bachelor party, but this is a new concept for Greeks and not widely done as yet. A more widespread custom pertaining to the groom is having his relatives or the male attendant dress and shave him, to the accompaniment of music, just prior to the marriage ceremony. Miltos reports his uncles tried to shave him, but he refused and shaved himself.

Wedding Participants' Attire

For the marriage ceremony, the groom and male sponsors wear a good, but not formal, dark suit, often without a tie. For his wedding, Miltos purchased a new suit, and he and his father and brother wore ties (Figure 9.3). The female family members wear good dresses and, at this wedding, each wore long ones.

Figure 9.3 Wedding dress of Katerina and Miltos. Photograph courtesy Katerina Kontogianni and Miltos Katsoros.

Although the couple usually has a male and female sponsor, Katerina and Miltos chose two women friends as their attendants: one of the sponsors, Katerina's best friend, introduced them; the other was a younger woman whom they met after they began dating who told them they were "a match" and whom they consider "lucky" for them. Female attendants do not wear matching outfits. At this wedding, however, their dresses matched in color because mauve was currently popular in Athens and they both happened to choose it.

More Greek brides now wear long white gowns, but earlier in the twentieth century, the bride had three options. A short dress or suit of any material and color could be worn, particularly by those women who could not afford a dress that would be worn only once. At least by 1930, however, some village brides had adopted white. A photograph of the 1930 wedding party of Miltos's maternal grandparents in the village of Lidoriki shows his grandmother in a white, mid-calf-length dress and wearing a simple, white veil that does not cover her face (Figure 9.4). Finally, during the same period, in some regions, women continued to wear very colorful, localized, regional bridal attire that included embroidered chemises, bridal aprons and ornate headgear.[13] And, in what may portend an emerging style for the most sophisticated, Miltos describes what he saw at a wedding he recently attended in Metsovo (Epiros) where the wealthy bride and groom wore the older, traditional, regional wedding costumes in retroactive acknowledgement of their local heritage.

Seamstresses regularly make the modern, white gowns, but specialty wedding shops, found in all but the smallest villages, now serve many brides-to-be. Katerina says that because she had little time to have a dress made or to shop for one, she went to only one bridal store. Her mother found the shop and

Figure 9.4 Wedding dress of Miltos's maternal grandparents, Panayotis and Ephrosyni Apostolopoulos, Lidoriki, 1930. The groom wears a fedora, dark suit and vest. The bride wears white. Their sponsor wears a boutonnière. The entire village and local musicians escort the couple from the church. The boy in the foreground carries the wedding crowns. Photograph courtesy Miltos Katsoros.

recommended it as "one of the best" in Athens. Katerina's choice of bridal gown demonstrates the cross-cultural fertilization of wedding fashion currently available because of the expanding global economy. The shop her mother advised her on specializes in gowns from the United States. Katerina says her American-made gown is designer created, but the designer, Dimetrios, a Greek-American, is not well known.

Having chosen the style from among the various models, the US manufacturer then made the dress to fit Katerina's figure. She requested only one modification, that the fabric shoulder straps be replaced by thin straps of rhinestones "to feel better, more formal." Many brides change out of their bridal gowns into other fancy, but less restrictive, outfits for the wedding reception and the extensive dancing they will do. Patricia Storace reports that at Athenian weddings, "time is made between ceremony and reception for the wedding party and guests to change from their grand church clothes to grand evening clothes" (1997: 212). Because Katerina was so pleased with her own bridal gown, she continued wearing it for the entire night. She was well aware of the impression she made in her dress. To emphasize this, Katerina describes what she looked like when Miltos's uncle pulled a table to the middle of the dance floor and lifted her up on it to dance.

Katerina remarks that she was satisfied with the dress except for problems she had with the train after the wedding ceremony. She says the hooks meant to hold the train off the floor did not work and the train kept falling down. She found it difficult to walk and the falling train proved to be especially troublesome when she danced.

Katerina's gown is of white taffeta overlaid with fine white silk (Figure 9.3). The full-length gown with a train is constructed with very simple, elegant lines: a smooth bodice and a gradually flaring skirt from the waist. No flounces, no lace; a band of applied embroidery around the top of the bodice being the only trim. Although Katerina describes the gown as "strapless," it does have very thin straps of small rhinestones. Katerina may have been just ahead of recent American bridal fashion because a year after her own wedding, *The New York Times* reported on the current trend in "sexy" bridal wear wherein strapless gowns have replaced the high-neck, sleeved ones popular during the preceding five years (Bellafante, 15 May 2001:A22).

Echoing the sparkle of the gown's straps, Katerina wore a necklace of same-sized rhinestones, given to her previously by her father. She wore single-stud diamond earrings, a gift from Miltos at the time they made a "secret commitment" to each other. With this token, Miltos eschewed the American-style engagement ring, while at the same time giving Katerina diamonds.

Katerina wore sheer, silk white gloves as do many Greek brides. Greek-made bridal dresses come with matching gloves as part of the ensemble. The bride wears the gloves throughout the wedding ceremony and during the period immediately following as she shakes hands with, and embraces, the wedding guests in the receiving line. The American-made gown Katerina chose did not come with matching gloves, so, at the suggestion of the saleswoman in the bridal shop, Katerina purchased them from her.

More unusual than the gloves were her wedding shoes, hand-made by the only cobbler in Athens who specializes in this item of attire. He covered her shoes with the same white silk fabric as her gown. The ankle-strap shoes are closed only over the toes. At a height of 5 feet 3 inches (1 m 60 cm), Katerina is petite in comparison to Miltos's height of 6 feet 3 inches (1 m 90 cm). To offset the 12 inch (30 cm) difference, Katerina wanted to wear very high heels for her wedding. The shoemaker, however, limited her heels to 3.5 inches (9 cm), saying she could not walk properly in anything higher. Because she danced the entire evening, Katerina says that her bridal shoes were destroyed. The original white silk slippers, now black, cannot be worn again, but she has saved them nonetheless.

Kostis Kourelis relates a contemporary custom involving the bride's shoes that seems to have begun in the 1960s with the women's rights movement as a way for modern women to negate St Paul's well-known strictures on the wifely role. At the point in the liturgy when St Paul's *Epistle to the Ephesians* is read, the bride covertly stamps her heel as hard as possible on the groom's foot as the priest intones the lines: "Wives, submit yourselves unto your own husbands . . . For the husband is the head of the wife . . . Therefore as the church is subject unto Christ, so let the wives be to their own husbands in everything" (*Eph.* 5: 22–4). Younger wedding guests wait expectantly for this to happen to see if the groom can control grimacing from pain. According to Kourelis, the priests are unaware of this subversion of the prescribed rites. Eleni Konstantinidi says the priests must know what is going on because once the bride stomps on the groom's foot, the guests all respond by laughing out loud. Katerina did not stomp on Miltos's foot.[14]

Folk custom around the world often dictates certain other additions to the bridal outfit. Mordecai notes a Greek-related one, but again does not indicate where this is done and it was unknown to any of my informants: "Single women would also sign their names under the hem of the bride's wedding dress to receive good luck in finding their own husbands" (Mordecai, 1999: 184). In Katerina's case, her mother told her to wear borrowed jewelry. Katerina wore a ring belonging to her cousin. Her mother also told her to place a small blue bead on her wedding gown. Katerina attached the bead to the inside of her bodice.

The Greek bridal, blue-bead custom relates to the widespread fear of the evil eye. It is known "throughout the Middle East – there are charms against the evil eye in Arabic, Hebrew, Turkish, Persian" (Storace, 1997: 30). This custom stems from the belief that some people possess the evil eye, usually interpreted as envy, with the power to harm those whom are envied. Wearing a blue, eye-shaped bead acts as an apotropaic device.[15] Mary Coulton says the Orthodox church offers a special prayer service for those who have been afflicted by the evil eye (Personal communication, Mary Coulton, August 2002). Just when and where the belief began may never be ascertained, but the fear that envy is harmful goes back to at least the Apostle Paul, who warns of it in his *Epistle to the Galatians*.

Flowers adorn the bride in Greek weddings. Five bunches of small white flowers were woven into Katerina's hair across the crown of her head. She also carried a bouquet of white roses and green ivy given her by Miltos which, at the reception, she threw backwards to be caught by an unmarried woman. Mordecai reports on another Greek custom related to the bridal bouquet: "[A] pair of scissors was (and still is) often inserted in a bridal floral bouquet to cut the evil eye" (184); she does not cite where this is performed. Towards a different purpose, in the Peloponnesos, scissors are placed under the pillow of a woman during childbirth "to cut the pain." In addition to the floral bouquet that Miltos presented to Katerina, he gave wrist corsages to the two attendants. These were Katerina's idea. She had seen wrist corsages in the United States and requested them for her own sponsors because she was aware of the visual effect they would have: "They looked very pretty on their wrists when they helped switch the crowns".

The couple's attendants provided the customary decorations for dressing the church: the flowers that adorned the wedding table and two, very tall, white candles wrapped with artificial flowers that stood nearby. These candles are expensive, costing between $300 and $1,000. At the conclusion of the ceremony, the candles are extinguished and are often taken to decorate the reception and then given to the church. Katerina's and Miltos's mothers each expressed concern that the tips of the burnt candlewicks must be cut. Katerina's mother actually brought a pair of scissors to the church to do this "so that no one else gets the wicks," an apotropaic gesture meant, like the blue bead, to ward off the evil eye. The custom also relates to the recurring charms which entail cutting, such as placing scissors in the bridal bouquet and placing scissors under the bed of a woman in labor. In these instances, each custom is associated with women, either as brides or as mothers.

The Wedding Crowns

The groom purchases the wedding rings. Katerina and Miltos conformed to tradition by exchanging the customary simple, gold bands, each engraved inside with the first name of the other and the marriage date or some other special date (for example, when the couple met). Katerina and Miltos deviated from custom, however, with their choice of wedding crowns.

1. Origins of the Wedding Crowns

The wedding ceremony divides into two parts, each with a symbolic object of bodily adornment: the exchange of finger rings and the crowning of the bride's and groom's heads. Scholars diverge, however, on the overall importance of one or the other of these material symbols of an Orthodox marriage. On the one hand, Gary Vikan says, "During the early Byzantine period, as today, the single object most intimately associated with marriage was the ring" (1990: 146).[16] Eurydice Antzoulatou-Retsila, on the other hand, writes: "In the eyes of the church and the law, the crowning ceremony is the only valid and binding confirmation of the marriage" (1999: 185). The rings, of course, will be worn forever, while the crowns, though carefully preserved, are donned only once. Nevertheless, the crowning ceremony is the highlight and final rite signifying the couple's union by the church.

Headdresses incorporating real or symbolic plant material predate Christianity in Greece. Eleni Konstantinidi reports on head wreaths as part of Greek dress as early as the Bronze Age. She writes that about 3000 BC, diadems appear and were used by men and women. "It seems diadems form a special class of jewelry destined to denote the social or religious character of the owner." Konstantinidi describes two such headpieces that resemble the modern wedding crown in appearance: an "elaborate gold diadem with attached gold leaves from Lebena, dated to the Early Palatial Period [2000 BC]; it bears similarities to a gold band from Mycenae . . . which was found around a woman's skull and on it were strengthened gold leaves in the form of a cross" (2001: 24). Also resembling the modern wedding crowns were the ephemeral head wreaths of real plants awarded to winning athletes at the four major ancient Greek games (776 BC to the fifth century AD): the Olympic wreath of olive branches, the Pythian (Delphi) wreath of laurel, the wreath awarded at Isthmia of bay leaves, and the Nemean wreath of celery (Raschke, 1988: 4).

Debate and discussion circulate about the relative importance of the rings and crowns, yet even more confounding has been the scholarly speculation about the origins of the crowns in the Orthodox wedding ritual. In a recent essay, Vikan offers strong iconographic evidence to argue convincingly that crowning the wedding couple began as a pre-Christian Roman custom, popularized later among the Greeks, which only gradually gained acceptance by the Orthodox Church during the Byzantine period (1990: 152).[17] Vikan also discusses the symbolism that the Romans gave to marriage customs, some of which continue to this day: "[For] the Roman wedding . . . the ring finger was chosen for its supposed connection with the heart . . . crowns were worn to ward off dangers . . ." (1990: 155).

2. Contemporary Wedding Crowns

Antzoulatou-Retsila, specifically writing on Greek Orthodox crowns (which she terms "modern wedding wreaths"), examines their religious and family ritualistic functions from the early nineteenth through mid-twentieth centuries (1999: 185–6). She also describes the materials used to make wedding crowns for the same period. These, she says, were fabricated from either local plants, metal, cloth or wax (183). Hand-gathered olive leaves and branches or, more usually, grape vine, were the materials most commonly used as the base material. She dates the beginning of the use of metal – silver, gold, and tin – to the Byzantine era. The betrothed couple usually rented metal crowns from the church, except for wealthy families who had the crowns hand-wrought by a craftsman and then passed them down through generations (184). According to Antzoulatou-Retsila, the materials used to decorate modern crowns included woven gilt cloth, silver braid, and wax. "The latter material – from which store-bought wedding wreaths are made – achieved popularity in Greece only within the course of the last few decades, coming in time to replace other traditional material" (185).

Today, as part of his or her wedding duties, the sponsor purchases the couple's ready-made crowns from shops specializing in wedding attire. The basic model consists of a thin metal ring covered in white fabric with attached cloth or wax flowers and leaves. Avoiding the more generic styles and conventional materials, Katerina and Miltos instead chose to individualize their matching crowns. Miltos commissioned a sculptor friend to design and make them. The artist crafted these uncommon crowns from a thin base of flattened, brushed silver. He encircled the silver base with an asymmetrical, raised ring of flattened aluminum that, in a highly abstract manner, only hints at the traditional floral motif. In fact, upon seeing their crowns on the wedding table, the priest remarked to the couple on their uniqueness, saying he had never seen anything like them. To continue the thematic element of these crowns, the sculptor also designed the abstract, spherical aluminum rings that encircled each of the white cloth bundles of sugared almonds given to each guest. In this sense, each guest carried away a tangible memory of the couple's individualized crowns.

The husband and wife, meanwhile, retain the actual crowns. A religious couple customarily places their wedding crowns, along with other items, in a small, family altar that hangs in a corner of their home. Katerina and Miltos, who consider their crowns to be works of art, plan, instead, to frame and hang them for display in their home.

Conclusion

A Greek wedding is both a sacred and a social contract: an official church sanction and a secular compact, each ensuring communal cohesiveness. Greek wedding celebrations extend into the secular realm both before and after the actual half-hour church ceremony. In addition to the church rituals, Katerina and Miltos had to make room for the customs traditional to the regions of their parents' upbringing, which they indulged in with good humour. Yet for all the secular events, both before, during and after the religious ceremony, the Orthodox service remains the focal point around which these other events revolve. Of all the events, the church ritual remains the one part of the festivities that can not be changed and is the most difficult to personalize. The prescribed rites of the Orthodox marriage ceremony, therefore, narrowly circumscribed Katerina's and Miltos's ability to individualize their own wedding.

Much of the dress this couple chose for their wedding conform to contemporary Greek practice. The most important symbolic deviation they made from the norm was the choice of an uncommon pair of crowns, whose crafting they so carefully planned. The church has long blessed wedding crowns as icons of marriage, a tradition that finds its beginnings nearly two millennia ago when Greeks adopted it from an even more distant Roman religious custom. Thus, the wedding of Katerina Kontogianne and Miltiades Katsaros on 11 June 2000, in the city of Athens, while thoroughly modern, nevertheless preserves the couple's connection to a heritage, both sacred and secular, both urban and rural. Their crowns, those items of dress most closely identified with an Orthodox wedding, highlight the individual style that Katerina and Miltos brought to their own wedding. Yet, on a deeper level, their crowns are the items of wedding dress which symbolically link them to all Greek couples over time and over place.

Notes

1. Interviews with the couple took place during July and August 2000 and August and September 2001. I wish to thank Katerina and Miltos for the time, patience and thought they gave to answering my queries. My thanks also to Kostis Kourelis and Mary Coulton who, during the same periods, provided insights into regional and historical Greek wedding customs. I am also grateful to Eleni Konstantinidi who added final, helpful insights a month before her own Athenian wedding in October 2001.

2. Athenian-born Mary Coulton married an Englishmen, Jim Coulton, in 1969, in Athens, in an Orthodox ceremony. Mary remembers that before the wedding, Jim, who speaks and reads Greek, remarked that he wanted to read over the marriage liturgy to know to what he would be responding. Mary says that Jim, raised in the Anglican

faith, was surprised when she told him, "you just keep quiet, the priests do all the talking, the rest of us don't say anything."

3. I transliterate all Greek words in this essay into phonetic English spelling.

4. The Greek word, *stephanos* (pl. *stephana*), the name of the headdress, means "floral wreath;" the word *stemma* means "crown." In English, however, *stephanos* is always translated as "crown," so I retain that term here even though this headdress is more accurately a "wreath."

5. If there is one sponsor, he or she crosses the crown; if there are two, then the couple decides who will perform this rite.

6. In several verses of the Old Testament book of *Isaiah* (King James Version), crowns and newlyweds each serve as metaphors for the acceptance of God as the one savior: 28.5, 62.3, 61.10 and 62.5.

7. Mary Coulton's parents married in an Orthodox ceremony in 1933. Mary says that in those days, sugared almonds also were thrown at the bride and groom and that her father told of receiving a nasty bump on his ear from the almonds thrown at him.

8. While a bride may wear a veil, it is uncommon for a modern, Greek woman to wear one that covers her face. If she does, it is lifted for the kiss.

9. These shops also sell baptism outfits for children who go through this Orthodox rite at age one. I first thought of the displays of bridal gowns being sold alongside infant clothes as incongruous. Upon remarking to Greek women about this, they found it odd that American specialty dress stores did not offer the same array. In their opinion, shops sell both types of fancy dress because each will be worn for important church rituals. As an outsider, I see the close proximity of bridal gowns and baptism outfits as a link between the bride and the community's expectation of her future role as a mother.

10. Mary Coulton's Greek mother immigrated with her family to Athens in 1922 from Smyrna, an urban centre in Turkey. During the celebrations for Mary's Athenian wedding in 1969, her mother offered not a single folk custom because, Mary reasons, her family had been city dwellers for many generations and folk customs are retained longer by villagers.

11. The Benaki Museum in Athens houses one of the foremost collections of eighteenth- and nineteenth-century examples of hand-decorated, Greek wedding bed linens. Noteworthy pieces come from the Aegean Islands and Epiros. Among these is a glorious and very rare seventeenth- or eighteenth-century embroidered tent from Rhodes that served to isolate the sleeping platform from the lower sitting area and hid the bridal bed "from prying eyes."

12. For an interesting comparison of the assembling of modern dowries by three women from the Argolid, each with a combination of hand-made and purchased textiles, see Koster (307–13).

13. The Benaki Museum collection includes illustrations of Greek brides; of note here is a watercolour by N. Sperling (dated *ca.* 1930) of a woman from Salamis in "bridal peasant costume." She wears a grey-blue, ankle-length, finely pleated skirt overlaying a white, laced-bordered petticoat. A short, gilt-embroidered, blue vest covers the sides and back of her white bodice with attached deep-red, gold-embroidered

sleeves. Chains of gold coins hang over her chest and over the front of her long, gold-embroidered, lace-bordered, deep-red apron. A single string of gold coins loops around her forehead. Over her head, she wears a long, white, gilt-embroidered veil, fringed in gilt at the ends. The veil drapes loosely under her neck and hangs down her back below knee level.

14. Both Kourelis and Konstantinidi witnessed this during urban weddings. I do not know if village brides also do it.

15. It is not uncommon in Greek villages today, for example, to see a tiny blue bead pinned to the back of a baby's shirt in the belief that the bead will ward off the conscious or unconscious envy of others which might prove harmful to the infant.

16. For some, the ring may be regarded as more than a symbol of marriage. In the early 1990s, I stopped to admire an enormous potted basil plant sitting by the house entrance of an older woman in Achaia (northwestern Peloponnesos). I brushed the plant with my fingers and was stung by a wasp. Observing my pain, the woman immediately removed her gold wedding band and, holding my hand, crossed the ring three times over the wasp sting while saying, "Christos, Christos, Christos". In this instance, the wedding ring acted as a healing device; indeed, for me, the pain instantly vanished.

17. Vikan illustrates his essay with a Middle-Byzantine marriage miniature from the Biblioteca Nacional, Madrid, that shows a priest crowning a bride and groom (Fig. 1: 161).

References

Antzoulatou-Retsila, E. (1999), "Summary" [in English], in *Wedding Crowns in Modern Greece* [in Greek], Athens: Alexandros Publishers, 183–6.

Bellafante, G. 15 May (2001), "In Rush Hour of the Brides, The Word is Sexy," *The New York Times*, A22.

Konstantinidi, E. M. (2001), *Jewellry Revealed in the Burial Contexts of the Greek Bronze Age*, London: Bar International Series 912.

Koster, J. B. (2001), "'Nobody Weaves Here Anymore': Hand Textile Production in the Southern Argolid," in Susan Buck Sutton (ed.), *Contigent Countryside. Settlement, Economy and Land Use in the Southern Argolid Since 1700*, Stanford: Stanford University Press, 290–318.

Mordecai, C. (1999), "Greece," in *Weddings: Dating and Love Customs of Cultures Worldwide Including Royalty*, Phoenix, Arizona: Nittany, 184–5.

Raschke, W. J. (ed.) (1988), "Introduction," in *The Archaeology of the Olympics: The Olympics and Other Festivals in Antiquity*, Madison: University of Wisconsin Press.

Storace, P. (1997), *Dinner With Persephone: Travels in Greece*, New York: Random House.

Vikan, G. (1990), "Art and Marriage in Early Byzantium," *Dumbarton Oaks Papers* 44: 145–63.

10

An Historic Perspective of English and Soviet Bridalwear Between 1917 and 1960

Janice Mee and Irina Safronova

The reality of greatly expanded interactions of peoples and cultures in the twenty-first century mandates understanding of the historic and aesthetic perspectives which determine cultural values. Each society perceives its own unique cultural development, yet seemingly disparate societies often exhibit amazingly similar qualities. Comparing bridalwear of England and the Soviet Union during the first half of the twentieth century reveals that European society on either side of what became the Iron Curtain for half this time shared many common values and aesthetics. Research for this essay was undertaken for the Museum of Ethnography, St Petersburg, exhibition "Princess for a Day" which compared British and Soviet wedding attire 1917–90.

Russian Traditions

Weddings in the Soviet Union overwhelmingly derived from Russian traditions of the earlier Czarist period. Russian folk dress changed from national costume to the attire of only the lower classes during the reign of Peter the Great (1673–1725) who ordered the nobility to wear European dress. Not until the twentieth century approached did Russian and English wedding dress begin to have commonalties largely attributable to the dominant role Paris played in European fashion. By the end of the nineteenth century, a Russian wedding consisted of two parts, one sad and one cheerful. The bride's attire reflected these emotions in the various rites and rituals which comprised her wedding. The sad portion of the wedding reflected leaving her life of freedom and her fears of an uncertain future in the unfamiliar house of her husband. Weeping and

singing songs that portray the potential gloomy life in a strange family dominated this segment of a wedding. Reflecting such a pensive and sombre mood,
the sleeves of the bridal dress reached the hemline and were called weeping
sleeves since the bride moaned, wept, and waved them as she left her natal
home. Blue or black were the predominant and sombre colors of the *sarafan*
(traditional women's dress), worn over a shirt at these sombre events.

Wearing a white veil marked the transition from sadness to joy in the sequence
of wedding events. The veil, an essential component of Russian bridal costume,
covered not only the bride's face but often extended to the floor. This enveloping cover protected her from both evil spirits and people who harboured
evil intentions. Traditional colors for this bridal veil were white and black with
red trim. White, as in most European societies, signified not only purity and
innocence but also sorrow and death. The proverb "to a wedding as to a
funeral" stresses the seriousness and responsibilities inherent in a wedding. The
anxiety and sadness of the bride disappeared with the conclusion of the wedding
ceremony as the joy and celebration of married life quickly overtook her. The
newlywed wore her best clothing and headdress on the first day of her married
life. The dominant color of this apparel was red, a color of joy.

Twentieth-century wedding dress combines aspects of earlier ones. White
dominates as the color for the modern dress, a carefully selected garment which
identifies the bride as the centre of the event both by use of the color of purity
as well as by its length. The decline in belief in such things as the "evil eye" found
expression in a modified veil whose purpose changed from being a talisman
against evil to a decorative element that projects image, nobility of character,
mystery, and even enigma. Gloves, a notable part of the earlier traditional
wedding dress, remain a part of the bride's dress since the tradition of her not
touching the groom with her bare hands has continued as a societal attitude.

England: Before 1917

The origins of many customs connected with English weddings derive from
early pre-Christian pagan festivals, particularly those celebrating the coming
of spring. The Victorians readily adopted these earlier traditions and infused
symbolism into their colors and flowers. The color white thus not only was
the symbol of purity but was further enchanced in meaning to be a force which
deterred evil spirits intent upon seducing virgins. The popular flowers in a
Victorian bride's bouquet included orange blossom for fertility, myrtle for
romance and happiness, and red roses for passionate love.

A horseshoe, an emblem of fertility, was thrown by the bride into a crowd
of guests. Tradition held that the lucky person who caught it would be the next

to marry. The horseshoe now is relegated to being tied to the "going away" car and the bride now throws her bouquet. The British rich storehouse of superstitions ranges from good luck in the belief that having a chimney sweep at a wedding is fortuitous, to bad luck when the bride and groom see each other on the day before the ceremony. The strongest and most respected wedding proverb remains "something old, something new, something borrowed, and something blue". The traditions related to this proverb are that old and new signify the transition from single to married life, something borrowed signifies happiness and security, while the color blue represents constancy.

Russia: 1900–1915

After the death of Peter the Great in 1725, the elite classes continued his decrees concerning dress; but in villages, Russian folk costumes could be seen in weddings into the twentieth century. As the twentieth century began, elite Russian women abandoned the stiff corset which resulted in smooth lines in the dress form. Critics observed that the earlier corseted clothing produced a bride with the figure of a harem lily on a slightly curved stem. What a contrast to the newer high-waisted dress with a straight skirt broadening at the hemline by insets on the side, or a small train cut along an oblique line and embroidered with pearls to give weight so the train would trail behind.

Other distinctive features of early twentieth century bridalwear included tight-fitting sleeves with button fastenings and a veil of tulle and lace. By 1913, drapery had become the basic element of wedding dress, using soft fabrics such as silk or chiffon in off-white colors of ivory or light silver grey, often with additions of pearl embroidery and detachable trains that fell either from the waist or the shoulder (Figure 10.1). This refined, subtle, ethereal image of a bride in long dress disappeared at the outbreak of the First World War in 1914 and the demise of the Belle Epoque.

Russia and England: The First World War

World War 1 totally disrupted social life in Europe. Russians contended not only with the war but with the October Revolution of 1917 and the Civil War of 1918. These conditions paralyzed numerous Russian cottage industries. Clothing became more practical; women's skirts, for instance, became shorter as each year passed. During the war, wedding dresses virtually disappeared in both England and Russia. Fashion magazines concentrated upon mourning apparel and appealed to readers not to forget their appearance in wartime

Figure 10.1 Models of wedding dresses (1916) of muslin and marquisette. Waistline is raised, like that of dresses of Empire style, the sleeves are long and narrow. Trimmings out of lace, embroidery, flowers of mirta and fleur-d'orange. Veil out of marquisette and Swiss batiste. Illustration: Irina Safronova.

conditions. Shorter skirts gave women more freedom of movement and allowed them to assume work previously done by men. The new clothing styles that emerged, derived from the avant-garde art movement Constructivism (or Functionalism), could be seen in the 1920s in both England and Russia.

Wedding dresses in both countries became shorter, hemlines rose to the ankles by 1915. A wedding dress typically consisted of a loosely fitted bodice with a high waistline, a "V" shaped neckline, and a narrow, mainly tiered, skirt with scalloped hemline. Sleeves were either long or short, narrow or full with flounces, frills, and ruches combined with lace and open-work insertions. Details such as embroidery, large wax or silk flowers, ribbons, bows and scalloped necklines provided notable variation. The preferred color was cream, including cream silk stockings worn with satin or leather shoes with pointed toes and Louis heels. Long gloves typically appeared when the dresses had short sleeves. Veils were the most notable variation between the two countries, those in England were of trailing silk tulle while those in Russia had embroidered marquisette or Swiss batiste.

The conclusion of World War I allowed the people of England to return to a normal, peaceful existence while the Russian people had to endure further political events which radically changed future developments. Despite the extremely difficult situation in the country during the first years of Soviet power, the modern clothing industry emerged as did a new attitude towards dress. In 1918–19, a group of artists headed by Nadezhda Lamanova, Vera Mukhina, and Alexandra Ekster initiated a reform of existing clothing in response to the radical reconstruction of society and the emergence of mass consumerism. Although the three artists had different approaches to creativity, they shared a common understanding of the main direction in the development of Soviet dress design with its thrust towards functional clothing for working people. All the arts in the Soviet Union went through intense ideological struggle and dress served as the touchstone for some of the most intense debates. Alexander Rodchenko and Varvava Stepanova, both noted clothing designers, actively spoke out for new forms of Soviet dress, damning pre-revolution clothing as an example of bourgeois aesthetics with a disrespectful attitude towards labor and a non-aesthetic aspect of material-industrial activity. Rodchenko and Stepanova strove to replace the older types of dress with new ones designated "professional costumes" (Prozodezhda) or, as they called it, "costume of today." They noted proper sport attire as an example of this new direction for clothing. During the Russian Civil War and for several years afterwards, however, clothing factories concentrated on producing clothing for the army.

Soviet Union: The 1920s

Only after 1921 and the adoption of the New Economic Policy did civilian clothing receive attention and the Soviet Union re-establish modest ties to the Paris fashion world. Soviet fashion magazines published between 1922 and 1924 featured elaborate wedding dresses called "dresses for newlyweds" and not "wedding dress" (*podvenechnye*, literally "a dress for a bride to be led to the altar"), as they were called before the Revolution. Dresses for bridesmaids significantly disappeared from Soviet fashion magazines in the 1920s.

Wedding dresses in the Soviet Union and England, following trends in European fashion, nonetheless continued to have much in common. This included such features as the soft lines of a straight-shoulder, low waist, hip-length full-front bodice, and ankle-length skirt. A low draped sash emphasized narrow hips. The neckline varied between round or V-shaped. The veil was often longer than the dress and formed a train. Sometimes the train started at the waistline, or, a wide draped sash extended into the train. The veil fell low over the forehead to the eyebrow and tightly covered the head, although it allowed the curls of short hair to show.

Despite similarities in the compositional approaches and designs of wedding dresses in the Soviet Union and England, the 1920s saw a divergence in approach between the two countries regarding bridal attire. This new image gave a mystique to the Soviet bride. Whatever decorative elements appeared, such as embroidery or ornamental insertions, they did not override the constructive statement of the dress. Asymmetric draperies of the bodice and skirt enlivened the flat, straight form of the dress and introduced effects of light and shade. Fabrics which draped well, such as satin or crêpe-de-chine, were preferred. Lace or pleated insertions and floating panels, whose ends were embroidered with pearls or beads and decorated with bunches of myrtle and orange blossom, complimented the fabric. The hemline of bride's dresses continued to rise although their proportions had changed. The picturesque play of draperies soon disappeared, however, and wedding dresses became duller and eventually disappeared from fashion magazines.

England: The 1920s

Descriptions of wedding dresses in English literature and, over the past century and a half, the production of photographs, demonstrate great interest in this most important garment. Museums of costume at Bath, Manchester, and Bethnal Green preserve and often exhibit wedding dresses. Such descriptions, photographs, and actual examples document concern for knowledge of wedding attire. In 1922, English brides were given another notable model to follow when *The Times* published details of Princess Mary's wedding, including minute descriptions of her dress, embroidery, veil, trimmings, and the colors of the materials. Only the royal family and members of court previously had this information. Thousands of potential brides suddenly knew what the princess wore. Sharing details of this wedding attire went from newspapers to illustrated books of royal weddings and quickly became the ideal model in the fashion world. (The 1922 royal wedding dress may be seen at the Bethnal Green Museum).

In the 1920s, wedding dresses in England were either ankle or mid-calf length (Figure 10.2). White and pastels such as blue, peach, rose pink and ivory competed with cream as the most popular colors. Draping qualities of silk satin, crêpe georgette, and silk chiffon, made them the preferred fabrics. The

Figure 10.2 Dresses for brides (1924). The bodice is easy-fitting; waistline is lowered. The sleeves are long and narrow. The fabrics are: atlas, crêpe-de-chine, lace, Alanson and malignie. Trimmings: insets out of lace, flowers or mirta. Illustration: Irina Safronova.

long veil of silk tulle lost ground to a felt or straw hat with or without a wide brim decorated with silk roses or wax flowers. In the second half of the decade the proportions of the dress changed drastically as the hemline rose to the knee. Skirts were short, gathered, or pleated at the hipline and scalloped along the hem. Some skirts were knee length in the front but lower in the back. The frivolity of such a hemline was more than compensated by long trains falling from the shoulders or by a long rectangular or oblong veil. The same soft and well-draping silks, such as crêpe-de-chine and georgette, continued to be popular, particularly in light cream shades combined with rose pink.

Pearls, whose subtle shades blend with the various pastel fabric colors and bride's complexion, found extensive incorporation in wedding attire. Embroidery using pearls decorated all parts of the dress, head covering, and shoes. Use of pearls on shoes combined tiny silk and wax flowers, crystals and embroidery in the form of stylized flowers and leaves, lace trimmings and scroll. Pearls, however, have always been a favourite decoration of English wedding dress and thus represent a continuation of tradition.

Soviet Union: The 1930s

During the 1930s, the ideas of Constructivism dominated all types of art in Russia. The clarity of design, localism of form, simplicity, expedience, and functionality became synonyms for beauty. The founding of the House of Fashion in Moscow in 1934 established an agency designated as the design centre for the country. The House of Fashion primarily worked to design strictly functional sporting clothes intended for mass production. These designs needed to be simple, unpretentious, convenient for work and inexpensive. The earlier image of a woman resembling a boy changed to the image of a more mature, subtle, and refined person. The narrow, long, flexible silhouette, moderately wide at the bottom, came to be called "Woman-Line." Characteristics of the style included bias cut dresses with narrow sleeves and often asymmetric hemlines, embroidery and artificial flowers used as ornament and crêpe-georgette and crêpe-de-chine fabrics which gave fluidity to form and created plays of light and shadow. Accessories included shoes with pointed toes and low heels and small coquettish hats with small brims pulled low over the forehead.

In 1934 the shoulder line became broader, first due to detailing that emphasised the shoulders and later due to rigid lining. Russian fashion magazines portrayed young women wearing clothes with complex composition including fine detailing such as little pleats, tucks, cuts, flounces and draperies. The light dresses they wore also presumably served as their wedding attire (Figure 10.3).

Figure 10.3 Festive dresses (1939) of dense white silk, fi-de-chine, light taffeta,
crêpe-satin. The bodice is fitted. Padded shoulders. The skirt is
widened at bottom. Illustration: Irina Safronova.

Fashion magazines contained casual sport and professional wear but no mention
of wedding dress.

The exclusion of brides in distinctive dresses in fashion journals lasted from
the late 1920s until 1950. Several factors may account for this notable omission.
First, the country had endured the revolutionary events of 1905, the World
War of 1914–18, the October Revolution in 1917, and the Civil War and
Intervention of 1918. All these military activities paralyzed the economy and
markedly lowered the standard of living. Second, the Bolshevik victory in 1917
brought to power an elite that condemned wealth and luxury as narrow-
minded survivals of an earlier society. Former standard attire such as suit, tie,
and hat for men or dresses with ruches and flounces for women quickly became

condemned as bourgeois and unacceptable. Third, young girls who came of age in the post-Revolution age wished to follow these new ideals. In contrast to brides in England at that time, young Russian women considered themselves builders of a new society and did not wish to appear as princesses on their wedding day. Fourth, although the House of Fashion concentrated on designing functional clothing, fashion magazines during the 1930s devoted extensive coverage to extravagant stage costumes that not only had complex designs but were extremely refined and luxurious. Such media attention reflected the attitude that the theatre provided cultural entertainment for the masses. Fashion magazines of the era indicate private events such as weddings simply did not attract the attention of Russian designers. Fifth, with a communist government in power weddings took place in an entirely new venue. Prior to communism, the bride married in a church. The high vaulted ceilings with their elaborate decoration, gilded icons and paintings, the priests' sacerdotal robes, the music of the choir all created an atmosphere of solemn elation and exclusiveness. Such a setting demanded a corresponding sumptuous bridal dress. After the separation of church and state in 1917, followed by the subsequent closing of churches, marriages came under the acts of civil registration and took place in municipal registry offices. An elaborate wedding dress in such poor, often shabby, premises was entirely inappropriate. Finally, the state intervened in people's lifestyle and behavior; dressing in an ostentatious manner for a wedding, particularly in the severely depressed economy, simply was not done. The situation only began to change in the late 1960s when palaces of wedding ceremonies began to appear.

England: The 1930s

After the stock market crash of 1929, unemployment in England reached three million. While wealthy women continued to buy their wedding dresses from couturiers, those less well off resorted to homemade ones. Fashion magazines responded to this situation by showing not only simple styles of wedding wear but by also including patterns for making them. In a paradox, however, poverty only increased the desire to have a wedding similar to that of a princess. Marriages of film stars also received widespread interest.

Wedding dresses returned to floor length with a concentration upon the gown's magnificence. The bodice was narrow and semi-fitted with either a high or low waistline. Necklines were either round, boat-shaped, or sweetheart. Inset sleeves were fitted with points over the hands and had tiny self-covered buttons from wrist to elbow. By 1931, the top part of such Gigôt sleeves had gathers and tucks that visibly increased and broadened the shoulder line.

Two years later, in 1933, dresses also had padded shoulders, in contrast to the earlier extended shoulder line. The dress silhouette seemed narrower and slimmer and occasionally had asymmetric lines with a long train diagonally crossing it. A narrow, lithe shape could be created only from soft fluid fabric, such as crêpe-de-chine. Mass-producing dresses to fulfil this need could not be done. Wedding dresses were worn with chiffon or tulle veils, or a straw hat, and shoes with almond-shaped toes and high heels. In the early 1930s, English brides wore long, garden party dresses made of chiffon or silk in floral patterns. These dresses were worn with jackets with padded shoulders or short capes while a wide-brimmed hat replaced the veil.

After 1933, white replaced cream or ivory as the preferred color choice for wedding dresses. White satin, simply called "bridal satin," often with a tiny floral pattern, became extremely popular. Use of white, after fifty years of preference for cream or ivory, limited the use of wedding dresses for other accessories and brought a return to the concept of a special garment worn only once. Even in the midst of the Depression, brides wanted to make a statement about the importance of their wedding day.

Soviet Union and England: World War II

In contrast to England, there is far less evidence of bridal attire in the Soviet Union during the war. Fashion magazines disappeared during the war years; only surviving photographs and interviews of wartime brides provide what documentation we have. World War II put fashion on hold as the people of both England and the Soviet Union struggled to survive. The remaining clothing industry produced primarily for the military. Brides dressed in severe, simple clothing with many masculine characteristics. Not only did the dresses acquire square shoulders, looking much like a military uniform, but they also featured epaulets and brass buttons, although very modest and feminine. Images concentrated on young, athletic-looking women with small waists, narrow hips, and very feminine hairstyles.

By 1941, cloth prices in England had almost doubled after the introduction of a purchase tax the previous year. The Utility Scheme, the government coupon system, insured standard prices and equal distribution that prevented overspending. Regulations limited the amount of fabric one could buy and dictated the construction of every garment. In the difficult war conditions not all women could afford these utility clothes. In response, the government launched the "Make Do and Mend" campaign, which for brides meant borrowing and altering existing wedding dresses.

Couples in war-torn England and the Soviet Union still married and had children, but the times produced many young widows. In such conditions her bridal dress was sometimes a woman's only dress. A light-colored dress usually served as the wedding garment, made in the fashion of the time from fabric bought with clothing coupons. It typically had broad shoulders, a closely fitted bodice, a natural waistline, and a hem 12–14 inches (30–35 cm) from the floor. A straight skirt might have a less fitted, gentle bodice bloused with a belt. In contrast, a flared skirt featured a more fitted bodice that emphasized the bust, and a small waist. Low necklines simply did not exist; stand-up collars demonstrated the more modest times. Puff sleeves were popular or, if long, they were narrow with gathers at the top or cuffs. Darts shaped the dress and served also as decoration and trimming elements. A draped bodice and a short bolero jacket complimented the dress. Popular fabrics included georgette, silk, crêpe-sateen, light wool and taffeta. A combined dress served as one way of making one dress from two old ones.

Despite severe wartime conditions, many English brides wanted a special dress for their wedding. Some borrowed dresses and veils from friends and relatives who married in the 1930s. If new, veils only went to the shoulders. The wedding dresses were kept simple in style: narrow hip-length bodice; broadened shoulder line; small shoulder pads; long narrow sleeves; rather narrow long skirts; high round, square, or sweetheart necklines. Those so inclined and with the resources emulated royal wedding dresses with narrow hip-length bodices with a shaped seam under the bust; asymmetric or diagonal trimmings, ruches, lace, embroidery with pearls and full gathered skirts with a number of flounces. Sleeves could be puffed, Gigôt, three-quarter length, or inset and fitted either cuffed or with round points over the hand. Necklines decorated with wax or silk flowers, pearls, or lace completed the design element. White continued as the preferred color although soft shades of blue, rose, or ivory could be found. Fabrics changed to silk-crêpe, tulle, satin, chiffon, or even parachute silk. Accessories included headdresses of silk flowers and pearls attached to a silk or tulle veil, or a tiny felt or straw hat with wax flowers and a silk shoulder-length veil; cotton or silk gloves; and white or cream shoes, often with ankle straps and high heels. Brides who did not have a wedding dress wore a clean casual suit that consisted of a straight skirt and jacket with a bunch of flowers pinned to the jacket lapel. A tiny hat coquettishly pulled over an eye with a short veil completed the outfit. During the war years in England, bridesmaids in special dresses declined in popularity.

The conclusion of the war in 1945 saw a flourishing of weddings in England but wedding dresses were much the same as in 1941, simple and slender in shape. The veil served as the chief variation from the earlier period, re-emerging after its disappearance during the war and then disappearing again the 1950s.

Figure 10.4 Festive dresses (1941) out of crêpe-maroken, dense silk, crêpe-satin. The bodice is close-fitting and draped. Padded shoulders. The jacket is short and fitted. Illustration: Irina Safronova.

Soviet Union: The 1950s

Just after the war, dressmakers working from their homes became extremely popular in both England and the Soviet Union since it was cheaper to purchase fabric with a clothing coupon and have a dress made than it was to buy ready-made clothing. Many brides, or their mothers, made their dresses themselves. This period also witnessed the introduction of hired wedding dresses in England, a phenomenon that did not emerge in Russia until almost fifty years later.

Bridal dresses with broad shoulders existed in the Soviet Union until the late 1940s. Three new fashion directions then emerged: a straight silhouette with broadened shoulders and inset sleeves; an unfitted bodice with kimono sleeves and closely fitted hips; and an X-shaped silhouette with wide sleeves, full hips, tightened waist, and rounded shoulder line. As the end of the 1940s approached, Soviet women wanted to look beautiful in their wedding dress and to give a definite feminine impression. Women's clothing gradually lengthened and widened reflecting the ideals of the post-war period. Two silhouettes dominated fashion. The first, a reaction to the small fitted bodice, featured a wide skirt made of straight panels with pliable folds at the waist and usually with a bodice with small drapes. The second had a narrow skirt, loose panels, and a more gentle form of bodice with a smooth shoulder line and inset, raglan, or one-piece sleeves. Dress length varied from knee length to long or very long, depending upon the scale of the wedding celebrations. Fabrics varied greatly among chiffon satin, all kinds of crêpe, taffeta, moiré and guipure lace, and white or light pastel shades of satin. If a veil was worn, it barely reached the shoulders and often a tulle scarf worn over the head or shoulders replaced it. Such scarves resembled veils and corresponded to the romantic style of wedding dress of the period. Light and open-pointed toe pumps with medium-high, thin heels, sometimes made of the same fabric as the dress, completed the outfit.

The Moscow House of Fashion magazine remained sensitive to the modest means of its readers and stated it would not make any pretentious and extravagant bridal dresses that could never be worn again. A dress made of well-starched pique (cotton) or tulle with lining nicely served these goals. The publication concentrated advice on how to modify trimmings and other details so the dress could be worn again for other special occasions.

In 1954, reflecting the better financial situation, new houses of fashion opened in various Soviet cities. People once again indulged in current styles, competitions began to appear, and production of mass-consumer goods surged. Wedding dresses, long missing from magazines, reappeared. The prevailing taste remained fairly constant through the decade until 1958, when such items as straight one-piece shirt-dresses with minimal silhouettes, seven-eighths inset sleeves or sleeveless became fashionable. These dresses had straight short jackets or light coats made of the same fabric.

England: After World War II

With the war over, the English people expected an end to austerity and rationing, but this did not happen. Returning soldiers exacerbated the situation and shortages became even more severe than during the war years. With a war debt and an almost bankrupt economy, Britain did not end rationing until 1952. The enforced Utility Scheme provided a stable, ready-to-wear structure with improved methods and standards of manufacture, and better conditions of work control.

After the abolition of the Utility Scheme in 1952, England witnessed an increase in optimism, growth of a consumer society, development of industry, and interest in fashion. Advertising came into its own and the media projected an idealized lifestyle in this new consumer society. Paris couture set the trends and copying the custom-made dresses of film stars and leaders of society grew in England. New stores opened which specialized in wedding dresses to meet this demand and numerous new magazines often featured advice to the bride about her wedding, along with all the latest current trends. A confusing number of basic dress lines (A, Y, H, and the Sack), each with many compositional variants, emerged from fashion houses. Overall, however, wedding dresses remained romantic in style and rather conservative in design. Their basic principles included fitted bodices (sometimes boned), fitted sleeves, narrow waists, wide skirts (either long, low, or calf-length), with no train and a short veil.

The boned fitted bodice, sometimes princess line which emphasised the bust, was often hip-length and had a pointed waistline which gave the appearance of an even narrower waist when worn with a full gathered skirt and petticoats. Other features included inset full-length sleeves ending in points over the hands; a round, wide V-shaped (almost off the shoulder), or boat-shaped neckline; and the stand or shawl collar which became very popular in the mid 1950s. It even became fashionable to wear a sleeveless wedding dress with a short bust-length Bolero jacket. Suits, consisting of a short jacket and a narrow mid-calf skirt with a slit, along with a Breton hat with a large flower and upturned brim, were primarily worn for registry office wedding ceremonies.

Conclusion

Throughout the half-century examined in this study, it has become apparent that wedding dress in England and the Soviet Union depended on the conditions, culture, and political situation in which the bride found herself. Comparing wedding dress in England and the Soviet Union shows numerous similarities. The aesthetic ideas of the late-Czarist and Soviet society after the Revolution of 1917 were different from those of England, mainly because Communist ideology did not allow glorification of the individual. Indeed, no wedding dresses were to be found in Soviet fashion magazines from 1926 until the 1950s. In contrast, the class-conscious English society showed a bolstering of individual status through clothes, particularly on the wedding day when a bride wore the most expensive dress she could afford.

Only after the 1950s did Soviet brides once again begin to look elegant, thanks to the new freedoms in the country. Since then, the similarities of wedding dresses in England and the Soviet Union have followed general European fashion trends, yet they continue to reflect differences in national and historic sensibilities as well as in the economic condition of each country.

Analysis of the current status of wedding dress in the two countries shows that in England there exists a highly developed wedding industry, a rich tradition of bridalwear design, unlimited choice, and excellent quality in the application of technologies. In the Soviet Union, there is also a high aesthetic and technical input into the manufacture of bridalwear, unlimited choice, a large variety of fabrics and trimmings, and satisfactory quality control, but much higher prices.

References

Arch, N. and Marschner, J. (1990), *The Royal Wedding Dress 1740–1970*, London: Sidgwick and Jackson.

Baker, M. (1977), *Wedding Customs and Folklore*, Totowa, NJ: Rowman and Littlefield.

Clark, R. (1987), *Hatches, Matches and Dispatches: Christening, Bridal and Mourning Fashions*, Melbourne: National Gallery of Victoria.

Cunnington, P. E. and Luean, C. (1972), *Costume for Births, Deaths, and Marriages*, London: A. and C. Black.

Ginsburg, M. (1981), *Wedding Dress 1740–1970*, London: William Collins Sons.

—— (1984), *Four Hundred Years of Fashion*, London: William Collins Sons.

Kirsanova, R. (1986), "Uroki Russkogo Narodnogo Kostyuma," *Dekorativnoe Iskusstvo SSSR*, no.7, Moscow: Sovetskii Khudozhnik.

Lansdell, A. (1983), *Wedding Fashions 1860–1980*, Dyfed: Shire Publications

Levitt, S. (1986), *Victorians Unbuttoned*, London: George Allen and Unwin.

Maslova, G. S. (1984), *Narodnaya Odezhda v Vostochnoslavyanskikh Traditsionnykh Obychayakhi I Obryadakh*, Moscow: Nauka.

McBride-Mellinger, M. (1993), *The Wedding Dress*, London: Little, Brown.

Mertsalova, M. N. (1975), *Poeziya Narodnogo Kostyuma*, Moscow: Molodaya Gvardiya.

Probert, C. (1984), *Brides in Vogue*, London: Thames and Hudson.

Stirzhenova, T. (1972), *Iz Istoril Sovetskogo Kostyuma*, Moscow: Sovetskly Khudoxhnik.

11

He Gave Her Sandals and She Gave Him a Tunic: Cloth and Weddings in the Andes

Lynn A. Meisch

Andean societies continue to be among the most textile-oriented cultures in the world. This was evident in pre-Hispanic societies when no life cycle ritual was complete without the exchange or sacrifice of cloth (Murra, 1989 [1962]): 279–81). In this essay I examine the use of cloth and clothing in Andean matrimonies in highland Ecuador, Peru and Bolivia, which formed part of the pre-Hispanic Inca empire. I discuss the traditional Andean emphasis on exchanges and uses of cloth and clothing to mark ritual events, as well as the symbolism of such textiles. I also analyze the changes in the dress worn by the bride and groom resulting from the Spanish conquest, including the conversion of native Andeans to Christianity and subsequent acculturation. My analysis is based on written sources and my own ethnographic fieldwork in Ecuador, Peru and Bolivia over the past twenty-eight years, which involved participation in a half-dozen weddings in Ecuador and Peru.

Anthropologists have despaired of finding a universal definition of marriage, traditionally seen in Euro-American society as the union of a male and female for the purposes of production (work) and reproduction, with certain rights, obligations and benefits incurred by each party, and the children of the union considered the legitimate offspring of both partners.[1] I will use this definition, with exceptions as noted, because I am discussing a part of the world heavily influenced by Christianity since the Spanish conquest that began in AD1532.

Weddings in Inca Times

The Inca empire, that extended along the Pacific coast and Andean highlands from northern Argentina and Chile to the southern edge of Colombia, was composed of a multitude of polities and ethnic groups. Our knowledge of Inca customs, including matrimonies, comes primarily from Spanish chronicles, colonial written accounts of the Andean world, which must be read with the knowledge that the descriptions of Inca life were filtered through the eyes of men intent on political control, economic exploitation, and religious conversion. With the above caveat in mind, these accounts still offer valuable glimpses into late-sixteenth- and early seventeenth-century Andean life.

Origin myths are a fruitful source of information about how people conceptualize the universe. One of the early Spanish chroniclers, Juan de Betanzos, interviewed descendants of the Inca rulers in their native language Quechua. One Inca origin myth he recorded tells how the earth opened (near Cuzco, Peru) and formed a cave called the house of origin from which emerged four men and their four wives. These people wore complete traditional dress, which Betanzos discussed in some detail, woven of the highest quality camelid fiber (llama, alpaca for commoners, or vicuña for the highest ranking nobility) mixed with gold (Betanzos, 1996 [1557]: 13–14).

From a combination of sources including the chronicles and archaeological textiles, we know Inca males wore a tunic, cloak, sandals, and a headband. Noble males carried a coca leaf bag over their shoulder and wore large silver or gold earplugs, which led the Spanish to call them "*orejones*" (big ears). Women wore a rectangular body wrap held shut at the waist with a belt and fastened over the shoulders with two stick pins. They also wore a headcloth, a shoulder wrap also closed with a stick pin, and sometimes sandals (Figure 11.1).

Clothing was handspun from camelid fiber or cotton and woven by either men or women on stick looms. All garments were made to size on the loom and were four-selvedge. The Incas mandated that the different ethnic groups they conquered retain their traditional hairstyle and headdress as a way to identify them (Cobo, 1979 [1653]: 190). The details of dress, therefore, varied greatly among ethnic groups; for example, the color combinations, the use of stripes, weaving techniques, and motifs differed, and cotton was more common on the coast.

Two features of the Inca origin myth are important. The first is the appearance of the first humans as man-woman and woman-man married pairs, indicating the complementarity and parallelism that still form the basis for indigenous Andean understandings of gender. The male-female pair is considered an essential unit, and an unmarried adult is called one of something without its pair. A one-eyed person is *chulla*, as is one sandal. The sun god was male, the moon female; together they formed a matched pair. Each was necessary and each had its cult attended by persons of its same gender.

The second significant mythic feature is that these first humans emerged clothed in ethnic dress, which signified to the Incas and to contemporary

Figure 11.1 The church marriage of the Inca Sayri Topa and his sister Beatris in Cuzco, Peru, 1558. They are dressed in the finest traditional clothing of the Inca nobility. Drawing by Felipe Guaman Poma de Ayala c. 1615.

indigenous Andeans their status as civilized people. In Peru today, a person who does not wear indigenous dress is considered naked, uncultured or uncivilized (Mannheim, 1991: 19). In parts of Ecuador, young men who walk publicly in the parish without their poncho and hat are said to be naked or skinned (Weismantel, 1988: 7). The first Incas were both mythic ancestors and bearers of civilization.

Because the couples in the cave myth emerged already married, the story says nothing about the nature of Inca wedding ceremonies, but again we can turn to the chronicles for details. Polygymy was practiced in the Inca empire, but it was an honor and privilege awarded a man in return for services rendered to the Inca, to the government, or to honor someone of high rank, exceptional ability, or intelligence. The women given as wives were taken by the Inca from among chosen women, who were selected as young girls and sent to centers where they spun, wove, cooked, made corn beer in service to the Inca state and the Sun, the official state religion. Some remained virgins, some were given as wives, and some occasionally were sacrificed. Only the principal wife was married in a special ceremony (Cobo, 1990 [1653]: 204–5). The others, regarded as lesser wives, were not married with a special ritual. The offspring of all the wives were considered legitimate in the Euro-American sense. Unlike nobility, common men were permitted only one wife.

Weddings of indigenous nobility were elaborate affairs, and it appears the Inca nobility wore their finest clothes. The wedding of the Inca Pachacuti Yupanqui involved ten days of fasting and sacrifices. Then his bride was brought to him "dressed in garments finely woven with gold and silver." She wore four gold stick pins, which Betanzos says weighed four pounds each.[2] On her head she wore a gold ribbon the width of one thumb. She wore a belt woven of the finest camelid fiber and gold with elaborate motifs, a mantle also of camelid and gold with woven patterning, and gold sandals (Betanzos, 1996 [1557]: 78).

Although Betanzos says nothing of Inca male dress, a colonial illustration by Guaman Poma de Ayala (1980 [ca. 1615]: 442) of the marriage of the Inca Sayri Topa and his sister Beatris in Cuzco, Peru, shows both the Inca and his bride in elegant traditional dress decorated with elaborate woven motifs, which indicated nobility (Figure 11.1). As with Egyptian rulers, it was customary for the supreme Inca to marry his sister, and the author and illustrator, Guaman Poma, noted this was done with the blessing of the archbishop (also seen in Figure 11.1).

Representatives of the Inca visited the communities outside the capital, Cuzco, once a year and formally married common men and women. Before or after this ritual, local customs prevailed. In some areas, the bride and groom exchanged gifts of clothing after the ceremony performed by the Inca's representatives. The relatives of both parties attended the state ceremony. Then the groom and his kin went to the bride's home where her father or nearest relative formally agreed upon the union (which was *fait accompli*). The groom put a sandal of camelid fiber on the bride's foot if she was a virgin, one of a bunch grass if she was not. The groom took her by the hand and led the wedding party to his home. There the new wife took out from under her clothes a fine camelid

fiber tunic, a headband, and a flat metal ornament which her husband immediately wore. Older relatives of the bride took her aside and the groom's
relatives took him aside and each received lectures on the proper behavior of
a spouse. The relatives also gave the couple gifts before feasting and drinking.
"The Incas called this solemn ceremony a wedding . . ." (Cobo, 1990 [1653]:
205–6). The reciprocal exchange of clothing is a practice still followed. For
the Collao provinces, encompassing the area around Lake Titicaca, and the
altiplano (high plain) in modern Bolivia, a predominantly Aymara-speaking
region, we have one tidbit of information: the prospective groom gave a coca
leaf bag to his future mother-in-law (Cobo, 1990 [1653]: 206).

The Inca himself married couples from the communities close to Cuzco by
calling the single, young people to assemble in the city. He placed himself in
the middle of the contracting parties, took the hand of the bride and groom,
united them in marriage, and delivered them to their parents (de la Vega, 1966
[1612]: 205). Again, gifts of clothing were involved. The Inca ordered clothes
brought from state warehouses and gave both the bride and groom two sets.
He also gave each a carrying cloth of *"cabuya"* (*Furcraea andina*, a plant
similar to the *Agave* cactus) to use during work in the fields and on construction
projects so they would not destroy their good clothes (Betanzos, 1996 [1557]:
58). Another chronicler added the existence of the sandal ceremony (Cobo,
1990 [1653]: 206). In none of the descriptions of pre-Hispanic matrimonies
is there any mention of a specific color being associated with weddings. Rather,
discussion centers on the exchange of cloth itself and the use of cloth appropriate to a person's social status and ethnic group.

There are several levels of meaning to these Inca matrimonial rituals. In the
Inca empire, communities paid a labor rather than a monetary tax to the Inca
state. One such labor obligation included spinning, dyeing, and weaving
clothing, which was then stored for the state's use. Such activities are gendered,
but the division of labor varies by community throughout the Andes. For
example, women usually spin and ply using the hand-held stick spindle, but
in some instances males will spin in public or private or ply yarn (for example,
Isla Amantaní, Peru; Cañar Province, Ecuador). Dyeing may be done by either
or both sexes. Weaving similarly, may be a female or male task or done by both
depending on community custom, the technology used, and the kind of cloth
made. The variable, gendered nature of textile production accounts in part for
the local variations in cloth exchanges at Andean weddings. Such gifts embody
the reciprocity that has long been identified as a core Andean value. During
courtship and matrimonies, cloth represents the wealth, literal and potential,
the parties bring to the union, a recognition of the complementary nature of
their skills. For example, in communities where females spin and ply yarn and
males weave cloth, each spouse needs the other for the production of a finished
textile.

The Inca's gifts of clothing to local people embodied reciprocity as well as the wealth of the Inca state. When the Inca himself performed the wedding ceremony he invested it with a high degree of seriousness, and his gifts of equal amounts of clothing to the bride and groom emphasized gender complementarity and parallelism, as well as their new status as a social unit and as full adult members of Inca society. Although gender parallelism forms a core value in Andean societies, in the Inca empire there was not complete equality between the sexes; the male was considered superior to female. The Inca overall was the wife-giver who "claimed the right to allocate in marriage all the women of his empire" (Gose, 2000: 89). Reciprocity functioned within hierarchy. But if we accept Mary Douglas's theory that the human body "is a model which can stand for any bounded system" (1966: 115), it is possible to see the parallels between the union and reconciliation of opposites (male and female bodies) in matrimony, and the union of rulers and ruled in the Inca empire. This union was expressed in exchanges of cloth which covered the body and bound those bodies into a unit, of which both parts were essential for the functioning of society.

Weddings During Spanish Colonial Rule

During the colonial era the bride and groom wore their finest garments when possible, but exactly what these consisted of had changed, at least for upper-class indigenous people. In a drawing showing a priest conducting a "forced wedding," the groom and bride are shown wearing ordinary versions of pre-Hispanic Andean dress and the woman is barefoot (Guaman Poma de Ayala, 1980 [ca. 1615]: 573). In another drawing (Figure 11.2), titled "The Sacrament of Matrimony" (p. 617), the same author shows the groom wearing a mixture of pre-Hispanic and colonial fashions. His cloak appears pre-Hispanic as does his tunic, but the tunic has decorations that are not found on pre-Hispanic ones. He wears colonial pumpkin breeches, stockings and shoes. His bride, on the other hand, only wears pre-Hispanic-style garments except, perhaps, for her footwear. In addition, her mantle, belt and body wrap have Inca-style motifs suggesting her upper-class status.

Guamon Poma de Ayala wrote of such weddings that many times the couple "dressed if they were able in gold, silver, silk" (p. 618, my translation). The Spanish introduced silk to the Andes but only the upper-class could afford this luxury fiber. The groom's dress fits a pattern seen shortly after the conquest in which some indigenous males adopted features of Spanish dress while the women's dress remained more conservative. Such changes were not always voluntary. At various times in the colonial era, particularly after the indigenous

SACRAMEИTODEL·MÁ

6s7

Figure 11.2 The sacrament of matrimony in the early colonial era, with the groom's dress showing considerable Spanish influence. Drawing by Felipe Guaman Poma de Ayala c.1615.

revolts against Spanish rule in 1780–82, the Spanish outlawed the Inca-style garments including mantles, tunics and headbands for males (Areche, 1836 [1781]: 50).

While I have no data on exchanges of cloth during colonial weddings, given the pre-Hispanic and contemporary pan-Andean practice of this custom it is reasonable to assume it was continued in the colonial and republican eras. In addition, researchers have collected or identified textiles in Bolivia from the colonial period through the end of the nineteenth century, many of them heirloom pieces still worn by indigenous people on ritual occasions. Some of these garments were identified as "matrimonial," including women's mantles and rectangular body wraps (Adelson and Tracht, 1983: 87).

Twentieth and Twenty-First Century Weddings

Weddings in parts of the Andes still involve either an exchange of cloth, special dress for the bride and groom and some participants, or both. Wedding dress may include survivals, meaning the continuity of an older trait through a period of change into a new era (Tylor, 1920 I, 71), or it may involve wearing the dress of the dominant society (for example, long white dresses in the Euro-American mode or the clothing of another ethnic group). Survivals in Andean dress include the daily or fiesta clothing of an earlier era now worn only for such special occasions as weddings.

Ecuador

Although in Euro-American societies we tend to think of weddings as an opportunity for the woman to shine, in areas such as Otavalo, Province of Imbabura, the groom may wear unusual and colorful clothing. Here, as in Peru, cloth plays a vital role in courtship and marriage. Through the 1960s and perhaps a bit later, indigenous couples in the Otavalo Valley signaled their intent to marry by an exchange or theft of clothing. For example, a young man tried to steal a young woman's rectangular shawl (*rebozo*) and she had to fight him for it (Parsons, 1945: 50). Older Otavalo indígenas told me that the man could try to steal his intended's headcloth or shoulder wrap instead of her *rebozo*. A respectable young woman put up a fight, but if she liked the young man she eventually let him take the garment. He and his family later returned it, accompanied by a go-between and relatives bearing gifts of food and asked for her hand in marriage.

In the 1940s, wedding dress among Otavalo indígenas showed the fashion influence of dominant groups. In contrast to the early colonial era, the man's wedding dress was more conservative with survivals of earlier dress, and the woman's dress was more heavily influenced by outsiders. In an Otavalo church wedding, "The men (groom and godfather) wear blue-and-white check ponchos, their hair, excepting the top braid, is flowing, a rosary of red and brass beads around the neck" (Parsons, 1945: 57). The ponchos mentioned are *ikat*, a technique in which warp yarns are tie-dyed in a resist technique before the garment is woven. *Ikat* was gradually disappearing in the Otavalo area even as Elsie Crews Parsons wrote. Today, no *ikat* ponchos are made, and grooms wishing to wear the blue-and-white check cotton wedding ponchos must rent them from the few families who still own them.

The attendants at the 1940s wedding wore their finest traditional dress, but "bride and godmother are arrayed in full Chola skirt and blouse, with Indian backcloths of pink or white cotton. . . . [O]ver the head lies a piece of white net, coarse and shabby. To my eyes they look very unattractive" (Parsons, 1945: 57). *Chola* or *cholo* in northern Ecuador in the 1940s referred to an intermediate group between indigenous people and *mestizos* (people of mixed indigenous and European heritage) with *blancos* (whites) at the top of the social hierarchy. *Chola/o* designated an indigenous person who had changed her or his dress in an attempt to discard indigenous identity. These terms marked social, rather than racial categories, as someone's classification was based more on such cultural features as language and dress than phenotype. As clothing styles among *cholos*, *mestizos*, and whites became similar throughout the 1970s and 1980s, the boundaries between the categories became blurred until sometime in the 1980s the word "*cholo*" dropped out of use in Imbabura.

At the time Parsons wrote, indigenous women's dress in Otavalo conformed closely to that of Inca women's dress (see Figures 11.1 and 11.2) except that some women wore a tailored blouse with ruffles at the neck and sleeves, two rectangular wrap skirts rather than a full-length wrap, and a handmade felt hat over the headcloth. *Chola* dress consisted of a gathered skirt, blouse, shawl (sometimes fringed) and a fedora or straw hat. Footgear varied. Parsons observed "the bride and godmother putting on the straw hats that go with their *chola* costume. The whole *chola* outfit has been hired from a Chola *estanquera* [tavern]. (*Chola* wedding, hence *chola* dress – the complex borrowed as a whole)" (Parsons, 1945: 57). *Chola* dress consisted of a colored gathered skirt, blouse, shawl (sometimes fringed) and a fedora or straw hat. Footgear varied.

Figure 11.3, a photo by an unknown photographer titled "Indigenous Wedding 1935 Otavalo – Ecuador" [my translation], shows the bride and groom wearing dress virtually identical to that described by Parsons. The groom is dressed in a checked poncho with ornaments around his neck, although it is impossible to distinguish a rosary. The bride, to his right, is wearing a *chola*-style white, embroidered, fringed shawl over two other shawls and a light-colored fedora, as opposed to the traditional indigenous hat worn by the other women in the photo. She wears indigenous necklaces and earrings, and her rosary is clearly visible around her neck. Her skirt is not visible in the photo, but she may have been wearing a gathered *chola* skirt if her dress fit the model described by Parsons.

Clothing styles are never static, although the rate of change may vary. In the colonial-era drawing by Guaman Poma, the groom's clothing showed the

Figure 11.3 An Otavalo wedding in 1935 with the bride in *chola* dress and the groom wearing a checked *ikat* poncho. Photograph: unknown Ecuadorian photographer. Bought in Otavalo, Ecuador, bookstore 2000.

greater Spanish influence. In the 1935 Otavalo wedding, it was the bride's. Note that she was not wearing all-white clothing; this custom appeared later. The process of acculturation in Otavalo is most evident with the hats in Figure 11.3. The then-traditional hat was a white, tan, or reddish-brown handfelted *sombrero* with a broad brim and low crown, worn by the musician in the lower right and by the three women to the bride's right. The more modern style was the dark fedora, worn by the bride, groom, and most of the other men in the photo.

I attended my first Otavalo wedding in 1985. For the church ceremony the groom wore the fedora, blue poncho and spotless white pants, shirts, and sandals that constituted traditional dress. The bride wore a rented Euro-American-style long, white, wedding dress and veil. This was a continuation of the custom described by Parsons where the bride wears the dress of the dominant culture. The use of white for the bride's dress was relatively new, as Otavalo women who married in the 1960s wore dark wrap skirts. The long, white dress was an adoption of the local white-mestizo custom wherein white signifies the virginity and purity of the bride.

Virginity, particularly at the time of the church wedding, is not as important to indígenas as it is to those of Spanish culture. According to Ecuadorian law, couples must first get married at the civil registry. Indígenas usually wear ordinary dress for this and regard it as a bureaucratic necessity, if not an obstacle. The church wedding may take place the next day or several years after the civil ceremony. Some young couples start a family after the civil ceremony and save their money for a big church wedding and fiesta, which occurs years and several children later. Wearing white at the church ceremony is simply "the custom."

By the time my indigenous godchildren were marrying in the 1990s, ethnic dress for both daily and fiesta use had undergone another shift. Young men began to wear their long hair unbraided and pulled back in a ponytail after the style of a popular Otavalo music group. They also began abandoning the poncho, white pants, shirt and sandals for everyday use and wearing Euro-American style clothing instead (e.g. blue jeans, various shirts and t-shirts, and running shoes). Some even stopped wearing fedoras.

During the 1990s, for many young men the old-style dress became a survival worn only on special occasions including their wedding day (Figure 11.4). The *ikat* poncho, worn by some grooms, is also a survival. Brides, meanwhile, continued to wear white, but no longer selected Euro-American-style dresses. Instead they wore traditional Otavalo women's dress, but all-white. This included the white blouse with white embroidery, a white belt with white supplementary-warp motifs, two white, rectangular wrap skirts instead of a navy blue or black skirt over a white one, and men's white sandals. The one Euro-American feature they adopted was the veil (Figure 11.4). The young bride in this illustration, Luz Quizhpe, sewed sequins on her wrap skirt and sandals, and had a ten-foot veil.

In many communities throughout the Andes, an older couple (sometimes two, one set for the bride and one set for the groom) is chosen to be the god-parents of the bridal couple. The godparents stand up for the couple during the ceremony, and offer them advice and help throughout their lives. As Parsons pointed out the godparents sometimes wear special dress. In 1993, a friend and I were asked to be the godparents for an Otavalo indigenous wedding. Because we were foreigners we wore our own best dress but gifts of cloth were involved. When I asked Otavalos what gifts were appropriate for the couple they said that ideally the godparents should buy the groom a white shirt and pair of pants, and the bride a white blouse and wrap skirt. (This young couple dressed like the bride and groom in Figure 11.4.)

If we return to Douglas's point that the human body can represent any bounded entity, then one important function of Otavalo wedding dress is to reaffirm Otavalo ethnic identity. The union of the bride and groom literally

Figure 11.4 Luz Quizhpe and Jaime de la Torre at their wedding reception in
Ilumán (Otavalo valley), Imbabura, Ecuador, June 1998. Their dress is
typical of contemporary Otavalo weddings. Photograph: Lynn A.
Meisch.

embodies the reproduction of the Otavalo ethnic group as well as the reproduction of the couple. Indigenous wedding guests also don their best traditional
dress, adding to the sense of the wedding as an ethnic event. One of my Otavalo
indigenous godsons, who wears the latest hip hop fashions daily (but like all
Otavalo males, keeps his long hair), said that when he and the other Otavalos
wore their traditional dress at such events as weddings, he felt *"mas alzado"*
(more unified).

Peru

In an area the size of the Andes that encompasses several countries and numerous ethnic groups, there obviously are variations in the kinds and meanings
of dress worn at weddings. At an indigenous wedding I attended in 1984 on

Isla Amantaní, Peru (an island in Lake Titicaca), the bride's dress reminded me of Parsons's description of the 1940s Otavalo wedding. Instead of wearing her traditional Amantaní dress, the young woman wore the clothing of the Aymara women of the Peruvian and Bolivian *altiplano*, including the famous bowler hat, an elaborately embroidered, triangular, fringed, white shawl, turquoise sweater, and several voluminous, gathered, wool skirts (worn by both Aymaras and the women of Amantaní). Males on Amantaní wear Euro-American-style dress so the groom wore his best clothing but with flowers in his fedora.

In Chillihuani, Department of Cuzco, young people often court while herding in high pastures above human settlement. If a young man and woman are attracted and want to marry, they exchange articles of clothing. The young man takes the woman's shoulder wrap (*lliklla*) and she takes his small carrying cloth (*unkuña*). "The group affirms that an exchange of clothing or other personal items is a custom from long ago. It is a firm commitment . . . At this time they promise not to be with any other partner" (Bolin, 1998: 104). This custom of exchanging clothing has obvious parallels to the Inca one, which is not surprising given that Chillihuani is located in the Inca heartland. As I. Bolin notes with respect to courtship, "Exchanges of cloth are socially significant rituals of reciprocity that symbolize equality and further solidify the relationship" (116). Before the wedding, the young woman wove "an exquisite poncho covered with significant geometric designs for her husband, a green jacket and plain black pants" (128).

Cloth and clothing were also salient during the Chillihuani wedding ceremony. The young couple and both sets of godparents wore their finest handwoven, traditional dress, which included garments with elaborate woven motifs. The bride's shoulder wrap and full, gathered skirt had unusual designs resembling flowers with four petals around a center, similar to those in an old painting of the wife of the first Inca, Manco Capac. An unusual feature of the modern bride's and groom's dress was leather boots, rather than the usual truck-tire sandals. These boots are worn only during weddings and are lent to anyone who marries. As in Otavalo, there were dress survivals in the Chillihuani wedding in the form of a flat hat with a large brim which "is worn only during special festivities and has been handed down through generations." Families who do not own such hats borrow them (128–30).

Chillihuani weddings involve two sets of godparents who represent vertical and horizontal axes, male and female respectively. Such symbolism is found in textiles in Chillihuani and in many parts of the Andes, with vertical stripes predominating on such male garments as ponchos, and horizontal stripes predominating on such female garments as skirts and shoulder wraps. Each axis alone is missing its pair, but together they form a unit (woman-man), a cross.

Bolivia

Many features of this Pan-Andean wedding complex are also found in Bolivia. Around Oruro, in central Bolivia, gender complementarity is expressed in textile exchanges before marriage: "Weaving is still the critical measure of material worth: a boy weaves a belt for a girl before proposing to her; she weaves a coca bag for him in consent" (Goodell, 1969: 51).

In Calcha, Department of Potosí, a young woman's proficiency in spinning and weaving is considered essential for marriage. Residence is virilocal and, before her own marriage, a young woman should weave a shoulder wrap for the bride when her brothers marry, a way of welcoming the new woman into the family's lineage. Although a bride does not have a dowry, she takes all the cloths she has woven before marriage to her husband's house, and these are considered her property. She weaves a blanket with woven designs, but does not use it until after her marriage. Her husband owns only those textiles his other kin and his wife weave for him. In the first year of marriage the new bride customarily weaves her husband a poncho (Medlin, 1986: 278–81). In Kaata, northeast of Lake Titicaca, weaving signifies wealth, and when a Kaatan girl marries she presents a "dowry" of handwoven cloth to her husband (Bastien, 1985 [1978]: xvii). Friends of the groom's family who were asked to be one set of godparents for one couple's wedding contributed mantles (the woman's shoulder wrap) as well as food and a band of flute players. As in Chillihuani, Peru, the ritual involved both vertical and horizontal godparents.

According to Bastien, the bride was dressed in layers of skirts and mantles woven with curlicue snail motifs. Snails have magical powers because they live on both land and water and carry their homes (shells) with them. Altogether the bride wore three skirts and seven mantles over a pinafore-like dress; each skirt represented a pregnancy. The mantles were fastened shut with stick pins made from engraved silver spoons. The bride's head was covered with a canopy of black lace, completely hiding her face. "Her wedding dress expressed that her lineage was giving to Marcelino's [the groom] patrilineage layers of cloth, or fertility to his land and patriliny." The groom also wore clothing with snail motifs, including a poncho, medicine bag, and coca leaf pouch. In addition, he wore a multicolored knit stocking cap under a white felt hat, and black pants over longer white ones (Bastien, 1985 [1978]: 10, 122).

Because the bride and groom come from communities at different altitudes, Kaatan weddings make visible the male's vertical claim to land and the female's horizontal claim to cloth and children. "These two pairs become a complete set within the ritual" (Bastien, 1985: 125). The parallels to the Chillihuani, Peru, wedding are striking: both include gifts of cloth, the use of traditional dress with finely woven motifs at the wedding, two sets of godparents, and the association of horizontal with females and vertical with males, with their union making them a matched pair.

Summary

Since pre-Hispanic times in the Andes, cloth, especially handwoven clothing, has been given or exchanged during courtship and at weddings. These exchanges embody core cultural values that vary in their salience among communities but which form part of a Pan-Andean textile complex. At a very basic level, the exchange of homemade textiles by the courting pair provides evidence of the textile skills or access to fiber resources of each prospective partner which are essential to their survival as a new household. Gifts of gendered clothing appropriate to each sex emphasize gender complementarity and parallelism, and when a man and woman exchange textiles or receive textiles as a couple at their wedding, such gifts recognize their new status as a complete, fully adult unit. The young man and woman are no longer solitary but part of a matched pair.

Gifts or exchanges of handwoven textiles that are distinctive of the bride's and groom's ethnic group symbolize the couple's ability to reproduce not only as a couple, but as members of a specific ethnic community. This emphasis on ethnicity can also be seen in the use of traditional dress, including survivals, by the bride, groom, godparents, and wedding guests. The exact motifs, colors, symbolism, and composition of ethnic cloth and the kinds of garments exchanged and worn during courtship and at weddings vary by community and have changed through time, but their essential meaning and the messages they convey have a surprising historical and geographical consistency.

Notes

1. Some societies, however, recognize homosexual unions; others recognize the union of multiple spouses (polygymy or polyandry), or same-sex non-sexual unions, as in parts of Africa.

2. This is hard to believe because the *tupus* would have been very heavy.

References

Adelson, L. and Tracht, A. (1983), *Aymara Weavings: Ceremonial Textiles of Colonial and 19th Century Bolivia*, Washington, D. C.: Smithsonian Institution Traveling Exhibition Service.

Areche, D. J. de (1836 [1781]), "Sentencia Pronunciada en el Cuzco por el Visitador D. José Antonio de Areche, contra José Gabriel Tupac-Amaru, su Muger, Hijos, y Demas Reos Principales de la Sublevación," in *Documentos para la Historia de la Sublevación de José Gabriel de Tupac-Amaru, Cacique de la Provincia de Tinta, en el Perú*, Buenos- Aires: Imprenta del Estado, 44–52.

Bastien, J. (1985 [1978]), *The Mountain of the Condor: Metaphor and Ritual in an Andean Ayllu*, Prospect Heights, Illinois: Waveland Press.

Betanzos, J. (1996 [1557]), *Narrative of the Incas*, R. Hamilton and D. Buchanan (trans. and ed.), Austin: University of Texas Press.

Bolin, I. (1998), *Rituals of Respect: The Secret of Survival in the High Peruvian Andes*, Austin: University of Texas Press.

Cobo, B. (1979 [1653]), *History of the Inca Empire*, R. Hamilton (trans. and ed.), Austin: University of Texas Press.

—— 1990 [1653], *Inca Religion and Customs*, R. Hamilton (trans. and ed.), Austin: University of Texas Press.

de la Vega, G. (1966 [1612]), *Royal Commentaries of the Incas and General History of Peru*, Part One, H. Livermore (trans.), Austin: University of Texas Press.

Douglas, M. (1966), "External Boundaries," in *Purity and Danger: An Analysis of Concepts of Pollution and Taboo*, New York: Praeger Publishers.

Goodell, G. (1969), "The Cloth of the Quechuas," *Natural History* LXXVIII (10): 48–55, 64–5.

Gose, P. (2000), "The State as a Chosen Woman: Brideservice and the Feeding of Tributaries in the Inca Empire," *American Anthropologist* 102: 1, 84–97.

Guaman Poma de Ayala, F. (1980 [ca.1615]), *El Primer Corónica y Buen Gobierno* (three vols), J. L. Urioste (trans.), J. Murra and R. Adorno (eds), Mexico, D.F.: Siglo Veintiuno.

Mannheim, B. (1991), *The Language of the Inka since the European Invasion*. Austin: University of Texas Press.

Medlin, M. (1986), "Learning to Weave in Calcha, Bolivia," *The Junius B. Bird Conference on Andean Textiles*, A. P. Rowe (ed.), Washington, D.C.: The Textile Museum, pp. 275–87.

Murra, J. (1989 [1962]), "Cloth and Its Function in the Inca State," in J. Weiner and J. Schneider (eds), *Cloth and Human Experience*, Washington, D.C.: Smithsonian Institution Press, pp. 275–302.

Parsons, E. C. (1945), *Peguche: A Study of Andean Indians*, Chicago: University of Chicago Press.

Tylor, E. (1920), *Primitive Cultures: Researches in the Development of Mythology, Philosophy, Religion, Language, Art and Custom* (two Vols), New York: G. P. Putnam's Sons.

Weismantel, M. (1988), *Food, Gender and Poverty in the Ecuadorian Andes*, Philadelphia: University of Pennsylvania Press.

12

Slavic Wedding Customs on Two Continents

Patricia Williams

This essay explores wedding clothing and customs originating in the Slavic areas of Europe with emphasis on western Czechs, Poles and Slovaks.[1] It also analyzes an American custom, based on European tradition, that has been practiced for more than one-hundred years in the Chicago area by the descendants of immigrant Slavic women. An examination of the historical development of clothing in agrarian societies reveals the basis for both the European and American customs and chronicles the strength of tradition on two continents.

Among the western Slavs in Europe the name of the most important wedding ritual translates as "capping the bride" but Chicagoans call it "aproning the bride" or "the apron thing." In transmigration, the focus of the ritual evolved from European headwear to an American kitchen apron. The author observed the custom at European folk festivals, participated in the Americanized adaptation in Chicago, and conducted interviews with other American participants. When asked why it is done, Americans usually answer that it was always part of family weddings. It is, they state, a matter of "tradition" because they believe that their ancestors performed the same ceremony in Europe.

Slavic Ethnic Groups in Europe

The Slavic people have three broad divisions: the eastern, the southern, and the western, primarily composed of Czechs (Bohemians and Moravians), Poles, and Slovaks. Problems often arise when discussing the Slavic people since ethnographic, historic and political boundaries do not always correspond, the result of centuries of prolonged political conflict and the domination of various powers in Eastern Europe. A basic similarity pervades the folk customs surrounding the use of dress and ritual among all Slavs although differences in religion exist. Eastern Slavs are generally Orthodox, as are many southern and some western Slavs, while other western Slavs are Protestant or Catholic. This study concentrates on the predominantly Catholic western area.

Historical Development of European Folk Dress

Ecclesiastical Decrees and Sumptuary Laws

A Czech Catholic ecclesiastical decree of AD1279 prohibited European women of eighteen years and older from appearing in public with uncovered heads. Many, however, ignored it. Then, in 1355, a more restrictive decree ordered all women veiled (Sronkova, 1954: 32). Such decrees had a long history reaching back to ancient times but it is apparent that changes were occurring in Europe since, at this time, women ignored them. Veiling reflected a patriarchal society that viewed woman as private property together with issues of sexuality, moral conduct and class distinction.

Relative to this, "Many European feudal cities mandated that prostitutes were to remain unveiled, so they could be distinguished from 'respectable women' who covered their heads in public" (Kaiser, 1990: 389). Such practices were nothing new; similar laws existed in ancient or classical Greece and Rome. In ancient Assyria a prostitute caught wearing a veil was flogged, had her clothes confiscated and pitch poured over her head. The veil thus served to distinguish which woman was public and which was private property (Schmidt, 1989: 132). Officials in the early Christian church issued many such decrees but they slowly ceased as Europe moved from an agrarian to an urban economy. A. J. Schmidt states that as the concept of property became more abstract men began to view their wives in terms of human relationships rather than as property (1989: 137).

Sumptuary laws were periodically enacted to deal with "extravagant fashion." These laws dealt primarily with the maintenance of class differences in dress. Thus, by the fifteenth century, the dress of the European court and townspeople diverged from each other and also from that of the peasantry. The following centuries also saw the rise of regional distinctions in the dress of European peasants that still maintained its conservative nature.

Regional Differences in Dress

Differences in Czech peasant dress originally developed in the seventeenth century when each parish belonged to one estate and landlords identified their male peasants by the color of the lapels on their greatcoats (Bogatyrev, 1971: 55). By the early nineteenth century, however, the abolition of serfdom in

Europe increased prosperity in the agrarian sector. At this time, peasants added elaborate detail to their holiday dress, some adopting features from upper-class fashions of earlier times. The resulting variations reflected increased regional pride and allegiance to a specific village (Williams, 1996: 36).

Regional styles in Europe announced the locale, religion, social, and marital status of the wearer. For example, twenty-eight distinct costume types developed during the nineteenth century in Moravian Slovakia, a fifty-square-mile area between the present Czech Republic and Slovakia, with approximately sixty additional types added in Slovakia proper. Further, each area contained local variations (Zidlicky et al., 1979). Industrialization occurred early in the western part of the Czech lands, thus Bohemia lost many of its regional differences before this time. Research, however, determined that at the end of the eighteenth century seventeen style regions existed there (Stankova, 1987: 10).

Head Coverings

Village women in conservative parts of Slavic Europe, Slovakia, Belarus, and Moldavia (a region within the Russian sphere), to cite a few locations, continued to wear enveloping medieval-style veils and wimples well into the nineteenth and even the twentieth century (Felberova et al., 1990; Romanyuk, 1981; Zelenchyek, 1985). It appears, however, that in other parts of the Slavic world, head covering evolved into a variety of separate shawl and kerchief elements with a cap underneath becoming more prominent.

Most Slavic women wore a kerchief daily; underneath it, married women wore a cap, called a *cepec*. White linen, lace or net fitted tightly to the head and covering all or most of the hair composed the main part of the cap. Such caps, which survive today in Mennonite groups, were once customary in many parts of Europe and America. Some styles included a wooden support that was tied to the head and covered by the cap; others had a separate forehead band. Side strings or ribbons, when present, were not usually tied under the chin, but left hanging loose. Caps worn for festive occasions, weddings for example, might be covered with embroidery or beads.

In spite of the disappearance of serfdom and the accompanying prosperity it created among some peasants, no woman below the middle class, regardless of her wealth, would exceed existing social boundaries by wearing a fashionable hat. She continued to wear the mark of the rural woman: the veil or kerchief and cap. The hat, in European society, symbolized membership in the "privileged classes." The male peasant took off his cap "to those dressed like gentlefolk" whether he knew them or not and conducted himself with "inherited respect" toward them that could be friendly or "colored with distrust" (Balch, 1910: 42). Thus, with a conservative agrarian environment that viewed change in a negative light and a social system that encouraged visible class differentiation, urban and upper-class fashions influenced rural women very little. Change within these traditions occurred, but slowly.

Ceremonial Shawls

Tradition required both married and unmarried Czech and Slovak rural women to wear a linen shawl, called in Czech, a *plachta*, for ceremonial occasions. Villagers considered it an essential wedding garment for the bride and her bridesmaids well into the twentieth century. Shawls from the 1700s to the present document a consistent form: a line of embroidery or lace binds two narrow lengths of linen together and additional embroidery decorates the ends. The shawl was folded lengthwise in three sections and worn with the central embroidered section running horizontally around the outside of the body. Embroidery on the oldest shawls is usually red; on late-nineteenth- and early-twentieth-century examples it is often polychrome and more densely decorated. The shawls contain a variety of motifs identified as protective and fertility-giving symbols (Václavik and Orel, 40).

The shawl, like the cap, played an essential part in village life, particularly in marriage and childbirth rites (Williams, 1999: 137). Links, and at times entanglements, frequently existed between these two items. Both appear related to ancient concepts of protection from evil and fertility. Czech bridesmaids in the early twentieth century wore the shawl in hopes of a future marriage (Václavik, 40), presumably with a fertile outcome. In Bohemia during the late nineteenth century, H. N. Hutchinson told of a variation on *plachta* use: ". . . the groomsman places the bride's mantle on the bridegroom's back . . . this curious little custom is evidently of ancient origin, for the act is performed for superstitious motives: it is to prevent a 'marriage-devil' from creeping in and dividing [the couple]" (1974 [1897]: 236).

In southwestern Slovakia, the chief bridesmaid received the bride's shawl from the best man before the ceremony and carried it to the church. There, the godmother either wrapped the bride in it from head to foot or threw it over her. A priest then performed a "marriage churching," leading the covered girl around the altar three times and sprinkling her with holy water. After the shawl was pulled down to the bride's shoulders, she entered "the order of women" (Václavik, 40–1). Depending on locale, the "churching" or purification ritual, a vestige of ancient fertility rites, occurred either before or after the wedding. Some elderly village women who participated as brides remember the custom today (H. Cincebeaux, personal interview, Cedar Rapids, Iowa, October 1993).

Additional Bridal Dress

Czech and Slovak bridal attire included the chemise or blouse, vest, skirt and apron in addition to a shawl (*plachta*). An apron or apron-like garment once functioned as a spiritual-magical protection of the wearer's reproductive system, and as a ritual symbol, originated in the Neolithic period (Gimbutas, 1991: 278). Most European folk dress ensembles still include an apron or apron-like garment. Embroidered motifs on all ceremonial clothing once symbolized fertility and protection from evil, since brides were thought particularly vulnerable to demons and the effects of the "evil eye" (Williams, 1999: 152).

The bride and bridesmaids wore green or floral head wreaths in some villages, while in others the bride wore an elaborate crown-like headdress. Slovak crown (*purta*) makers still construct bridal headwear for those who wish a traditional wedding ceremony or for use in folk festival settings (Williams, 1996: 43). This headdress is removed, at some point during the wedding festivities, and replaced with a matron's cap. In the introduction to an extensive regional listing of Slovak cap styles, A. Gazdikova noted that in the nineteenth and twentieth centuries ". . . the (cap) . . . was of considerable significance . . . evidenced by the fact that (capping) a bride became a part of the traditional wedding ritual . . . among Slavs in general" (1991: 113).

Capping Ceremonies

Marriage ceremonies in early times secured the fertility of the union rather than solemnizing it. Though encouraged, the validation of a Christian marriage did not require an ecclesiastical act until the Council of Trent mandated it in 1563. A Christian ceremony was not, however, sufficient sanction among Slavs. An attachment to early agrarian beliefs required the performance of a ritual more important than the church ceremony. Not until after the bride was "capped," an event that usually ended the week-long celebration, could the bridal couple have sexual relations.

Slavic capping ceremonies have basic similarities, whether they originate in the eighteenth century or present-day Bohemia, Poland or elsewhere: the bride or bridesmaids sing melancholy songs, mourning the loss of girlhood, while an older married woman removes the bridal headdress and places a matron's cap on the bride's head (Figures 12.1 and 12.2). Village matrons then accept her into the ranks of married women with songs of welcome. The removal of the bridal headdress symbolizes the impending loss of virginity, as alluded to in all forms of the ritual. After the wreath is removed, it is sometimes thrown into a river where it floats away, lost forever, as is the bride's virginity.

Figure 12.1 Removing the bride's floral headdress, 1992 Folk festival, Myava, Slovakia. Photograph: the author.

In view of the almost universal association of hair with sexual potency and fertility, the cap not only identified the married woman, but also symbolized the protection of her fertility and, ultimately, assured the continued existence of the group. By the nineteenth century, however, a strong association of the cap with the loss of virginity caused matrons in some villages in Moravian Slovakia to forcibly "cap" unwed mothers (Bogatyrev, 1971: 72). Thus the cap marked the fertile woman, married or not (Williams, 1999: 139). The medieval relationship between head covering and modesty resurfaced in full force,

Figure 12.2 Village matrons "capping" the bride, 1992. Folk festival, Myava, Slovakia. Photograph: the author.

making the appearance of a married woman in public without a cap equal to "appearing on the street naked" (Linder, 1993: 11) due, in all probability, to issues related to sex.

The capping ceremony once held a prominent place in upper-class wedding ritual although it was usually linked to agrarian culture. The Countess Françoise Kransinska 1759 account of a wedding among the nobles of Poland describes her sister's capping ceremony which followed the same form as the peasant ritual:

> At midnight the music stopped, and the cap ceremony was begun. A stool was placed in the middle of the room, the bride sat down, and the bridesmaids began to undo her hair, singing in plaintive voices the old song, "Ah we are losing you Basia." Then my honored mother removed the rosemary wreath and the Woivodine Malachowska (Mistress of Ceremonies) put in its place a big lace cap . . . the cap is very becoming to her, which they say is a sign that her husband will love her very much (Balch, 1910: 146n).

A special eighteenth-century "capping chair" kept in the castle library at Krivoklat in Bohemia for use at weddings on the estate, further highlights the importance of the ceremony (Williams, 1999: n.3).

In Radom, Poland, it was customary for the bride to run away when it was time for the capping ceremony and to be brought back, kicking and screaming, by the groomsmen. They sat her down on a dough box covered with a sheepskin coat (sheepskin being a sign of fertility and abundance) and the village matrons finally capped her. Other folk customs disappeared but ceremonial capping is still present in conservative areas of Poland (Knab, 1993: 210) and in the Czech and Slovak Republics when a couple wishes to have a traditional wedding celebration. Capping ceremonies also exist as re-enactments of old customs in folk festivals. Sponsors of government festivals during the Communist era in Czechoslovakia permitted it because they did not consider capping a religious ceremony (Williams, 1996: 39–40).

Czech writer Milan Kundera described the ceremony in his novel *The Joke* along with the emotions created by the symbolic loss of virginity. The setting is in Moravia (Czech Republic) during the post World War II era:

> My friends staged a real Moravian (folk) wedding for me . . . late in the evening, the bridesmaids removed the garland of rosemary from Vlasta's head and ceremonially handed it to me. They made a pigtail of her loose hair and wound it round her head. Then they clapped a bonnet over it. This rite symbolized the transition from virginity to womanhood. Vlasta had long since lost her virginity. She wasn't strictly entitled to the symbol of the garland. But I didn't consider that important. At a higher and more binding level, she didn't lose it until the very moment when (the) bridesmaids placed her wreath in my hands . . . the women sang songs about the garland floating off, across the water and . . . it made me want to weep . . . I saw the garland go, never to return. No return (1993: 128–9).

The hairstyles of Slavic brides varied from region to region but the association with sexual potency and fertility made hair and head rituals important at the time of marriage in most agrarian societies. Some brides wore one braid, some wore two and still others left their hair flowing. In parts of Poland and Russia the bride had her long hair cut at the time of receiving the matron's headdress. This bride uttered regrets in simple songs expressing sorrow at the loss of her "curls" and "fair golden hair" that symbolized her virginity (Chambers, 721). The bride's hair was cut off by the groom in some regions of Poland and by her mother, older brother, or matrons of the village in other areas (Knab, 1993: 211–12). It appears that feigned resistance and/or sorrow accompanied haircutting as well as capping in most cases.

Hidden Meanings

Rituals that include concealment with cloth, purification, welcoming into a group and/or haircutting present the possibility that what became marriage rites had originated from now-forgotten puberty initiation rituals that signaled availability for marriage and protected the fertile young female as she entered adulthood. A. van Gennep viewed veiling and purification as rites of separation applied to either marriage or adulthood (1960: 20–130). In many cases, such rituals became hopelessly entangled as they passed through the generations. Concealment also protects from the "evil eye," a well-documented belief among the Slavs (Roberts, 1976; Stein, 1976: 193). An incident during a 1948 Slovak wedding illustrates the persistence of this belief: attendants held a feather tree, said to be a symbol of male fertility, and a *plachta* (shawl) over the bride and groom "to keep off the evil eye" (Z. Zilkova, personal interview, Jakubany, Slovakia, 30 June 1995).

Immigrant Dress in the United States

Between 1750 and 1850, the European population doubled and although there was some increase in the prosperity of agrarian people, limited village acreage could no longer support the population. The standard of living, minimal at best for most peasants, deteriorated further; thus, one answer to reduced economic status in the community was emigration. During the thirty-year period from 1880 to 1909, seventeen-million immigrants came to the United States, over one-fifth of whom came from the Slavic regions of Europe, primarily from the agricultural classes. Population data indicate the city of Chicago attracted large numbers of these Slavic immigrants. It was the leading Czech-American metropolis in the 1860s; and by 1900, after Prague and Vienna, was the third largest Czech urban center in the world. Chicago also attracted Poles and received the title "the American Warsaw" in the mid-1880s. Of the Slavic immigrant groups in the United States, only the Poles outnumbered the Slovaks.

One of the immediate cultural barriers faced by immigrants concerned clothing. The use of folk dress in Europe was in decline but women who lived in rural areas still wore clothing significantly different from the western fashionable dress of urban women. Those intending to emigrate often purchased European urban fashions as preparation for the journey. Few who wore folk dress at home arrived in it at Ellis Island. Friends in America advised them to leave their village dress behind since wearing it subjected newcomers to ridicule (Williams, 1994). A short story of the times, *Aunt Betsey's Best Bonnet*, illustrates that ethnic dress was the subject of mockery. The author, comparing Aunt Betsey's ignorance of fashion to that of a new immigrant, described her bonnet as having trim "which greatly resembled the cap-border of a newly-landed emigrant" (Fairfield, 1860: 23).

Social commentators in the United States and Europe wrote of the "displays of finery" seen in both urban and rural America and frowned upon the absence of class distinction in dress (Banner, 1983: 17, 21). As with the old European sumptuary laws, "extravagant dress," and "displays of finery" were not the true causes of criticism; it was instead, the daring of the lower classes to wear clothing similar to upper-class fashion. In paradox, it was expected that "ethnic Americans" should assimilate along the lines of an "Anglo-American proto-type" leaving any consciousness of ethnicity behind (Alba, 1990: 2).

Wedding Clothing and Custom Adaptations in America

A flowing white veil, symbol of the fashionable bride, moved into the popular stratum of society during the same time period as concentrated Slavic settle-ment occurred in the United States. Prior to 1900, only the wealthy wore a wedding veil and white gown. Working class and immigrant brides adopted the white veil but paired it with a colored "best dress" to which they often added white ribbons and other trim in order to imbue it with a celebratory air. Budget constraints (white was impractical) and custom (lack of color was a mourning sign in some European folk societies) are possible reasons for their choice. Another influence may have originated with widely circulated photo-graphs of Queen Victoria wearing a black dress with her white lace bridal veil (Williams, 1993: 101).

Numerous examples of ancestral "dark brides" found in photograph albums often puzzle their contemporary descendants. One gentleman anxiously inquired if the dark wedding dress his immigrant grandmother wore "meant that she was not a virgin." Visible relief appeared on his face when he learned the probable circumstances surrounding her choice. He did not wish to "think of Grandma that way."

Although such wedding wear created a satisfactory compromise for festive folk dress, there was no American equivalent in headwear to use for the capping ceremony. Colonial era matron's caps were long out of style in the United States, surviving only among Mennonite groups and in vestigial form as headwear for female servants and nurses. The concern of urban-based immigrants with having a fashionable "American" appearance led both married and unmarried women to wear a hat as a sign of their rise in social position (Balch, 1910: 372). Headwear no longer distinguished marital status. It is easy to see, in view of the social conditions, why immigrants chose a new sign of the married woman to use at wedding ceremonies. Thus, tying a kitchen apron around the bride's waist replaced capping and signaled her status change to Chicago's Slavic-American community and, since aprons were familiar items of dress included in European festive folk wear, they were already associated with ritual. Not all Slavic families in Chicago perpetuated the custom. The drive to be "American" and be accepted by the Anglo-American community led many to distance themselves from their roots and abandon all signs of ethnicity.

Those descendants who perpetuated the custom related that "aproning the bride" was part of family wedding tradition from the time of their earliest immigrant ancestors. They were unaware of the original capping ritual and assumed the ceremony as practiced in America was the same as that practiced in Europe. The American adaptation of the capping ceremony affirms D. Yoder's findings on folk culture and change. He observed European rural populations adapted factory-made clothing "in ways that still express folk cultural needs," marking changes "selectively to their own ideas" (1993, 302–4). The immigrants who developed the Americanized form of capping expressed cultural needs in their desire to assimilate yet keep tradition alive in their new country.

Through loss of contact with their agrarian heritage and its concern with fertility symbolism, emphasis in America shifted from the sexual aspects of the matron's cap to the kitchen apron and its association with the new responsibilities of marriage. It is this latter idea that American informants cited as the purpose of the apron ceremony. American love songs usually replaced melancholy European songs; however, elderly family members told some informants that a proper ceremony should be bittersweet in feeling. Descendants interpreted this as meaning that, although it was a happy occasion, the parents of the wedding couple felt sadness because they were losing their children. No one cited the loss of the bride's virginity as a reason for the note of melancholy sounded in the European custom.

A second generation Czech–American, born in Chicago in 1904, gave an account of the American ritual. Her earliest memory of the ceremony was as a child at the wedding of her uncle: bridesmaids removed the veil of the seated bride, they tied an apron around her waist and a peasant-style kerchief on her head. Wedding guests formed a circle and sang songs. Another woman gave a similar description from the same time period in Kewaunee County, Wisconsin, but all other reports of "aproning" came from the Chicago area. Local historians knew of no tradition for capping or any modification of the ritual in Portage County, Wisconsin, site of the largest concentration of rural Polish–Americans in the United States. Likewise, in Cedar Rapids, Iowa, no information was found in its sizable Czech–American community.

Some Slavic-American wedding festivities incorporated the groom, usually in a humorous way; after the bride was aproned, the groom received a symbol of responsibility. They presented him with a baby doll while the bride vigorously waved a wooden spoon or broom or the groom might receive the broom. Observers declared such antics implied the groom was now a "hen-pecked husband" expected to help with the housework and childrearing. In fact, the tradition arrived from agrarian Europe, where bawdiness ruled at wedding festivities and the idea of "being responsible" had a different twist. A folk group presented wedding traditions including the original Czech "baby and wooden spoon" custom at the 1995 Straznice Folk Festival in Moravia, Czech Republic. In it, "the other woman" appeared at the wedding with her "baby" and placed it in the groom's arms. The bride then showered the two-timing groom with blows from a wooden spoon. Decreasing language proficiency and misunderstanding nuances of the "mother tongue" among the American descendants of the immigrants may account for the altered interpretation of this and other customs.

More Changes in Ritual

A variety of delicate satin and lace aprons decorated with ribbons and wedding rings and made specifically for the occasion replaced the use of American utility aprons in the late 1940s and 1950s. The bride could not make her own apron in some families as it was considered bad luck. This was the responsibility of the godmother and parallels European custom where the godmother provided a wedding cap for the bride. Items given to the groom after the bride's aproning now also varied; he might receive a drain plunger or other household tool instead of a broom.

The ancient idea of fertility returned overtly to the ceremony during the "Baby Boom" era, when small dolls, representing future children decorated the apron (Figures 12.3 and 12.4). One informant's family determined the number of dolls to be added by the number of ribbons broken while unwrapping gifts at the bridal shower. In some families, an aproning ceremony evolved for the groom, with miniature tools embellishing his utility-type apron. After the removal of her veil, the bride might take the groom's boutonniere and place it in her hair as a unity symbol. Informants related many differences in the details.

During the 1960s and 1970s, when friends asked the prospective bride if she planned to "do the apron thing" at her wedding reception, her answer might be "yes," accompanied by a self-conscious smile or a resounding, "No. I wouldn't be caught dead doing it." In a climate of challenge to the traditional roles of women and men, many young women expressed distaste at the idea of an apron ceremony, linking it to an implication of subservience and male domination. When the bride's family explained the ritual to one particular groom who was unfamiliar with the custom, he insisted on also wearing the bride's apron. This gesture of equality and sharing "caused eyes to roll" in the

Figure 12.3 Bridesmaid removing the bride's veil, 1964, Chicago area.
Photograph: courtesy of Karen Barger.

bride's family and they decided against doing it at the wedding. Details change, but this was apparently too much change.

The strength of family and ethnic ties remain influential in the Chicago area in spite of changes in society. At the Fifth Czechoslovak Genealogical/ Cultural Conference in the Chicago suburb of Countryside in 1995, attendees contributed memories of the ritual and stated they still apron the bride at family weddings. Further, through mixed ethnic marriages and friendships, some brides of non-Slavic background now also include "aproning" in their wedding celebrations.

The *House of Brides,* a Chicago-area wedding salon, carries basic white and ivory satin aprons, sold to brides whose families no longer sew. A personal choice of trimming can then be added to "customize" the apron. When questioned about the custom, a bridal consultant responded that those of Polish descent seemed to place more importance on the ceremony than other ethnic groups, but Hispanic brides also did it. Along with garter and bouquet throwing, aproning, she said, was just "one of those cute things they do at weddings" and had no ethnic reference.

Figure 12.4 Tying the apron, 1964, Chicago area. Note the baby dolls on the apron and the groom's boutonnière in the bride's hair. Photograph: courtesy of Karen Barger.

Hypothesis

One can understand, with the help of research into the attitudes toward dress in Europe and in America and with information on the original custom in Europe, how the custom of aproning probably evolved. Why the veil and apron custom developed in Chicago and not in other Slavic–American settlements has not, however, been conclusively determined. Informants with a strong family tradition of aproning who moved from the Chicago area reported that the custom was unknown in their new location, even among Slavic–Americans. This surprised them because they assumed everyone did it.

From the time of their initial arrival in America around 1900, Slovaks continued the original custom in some settlements, bringing family wedding caps with them. Elizabeth Borovicka Cappozi, an informant in Broome County, New York, was capped with a family heirloom at her wedding reception in 1970. As the fourth generation of brides to wear the cap, she wished to help other Slovak–Americans to keep their heritage alive and has since constructed over a thousand replicas of ancestral village caps for ceremonies in the United States.

Emily Greene Balch, who worked with immigrants, reported in 1910 that "the cap ceremony still takes place at Polish weddings in America" (1910: 146n). Balch did not further elaborate on the ceremony, nor did she specifically state the location in America, so it is not known to what degree the ritual followed its European antecedent or how long it continued. Both Slovaks and Poles in Chicago, however, followed the American aproning tradition along with the Czechs rather than "capping the bride" in the European tradition.

Czechs and Poles outside of Chicago emigrated to small town and rural areas and settled permanently; as landowners, they continued an agricultural way of life. It was possible for them to abandon ritual at some point in the assimilation process and still know who they were as a group. In small towns and rural areas use of the native language was retained longer than in urban areas. Slovaks in mining communities did not own land; many, in fact, planned to return to Europe. They experienced an insular non-urban lifestyle and, cut from their agrarian roots, they sought comfort in keeping rituals brought from Europe.

Slavs who came to Chicago experienced stronger pressures to assimilate. The majority were rural in origin and settling in urban America separated them from an agrarian or small-town lifestyle. The large Slavic community, surrounded by earlier arrivals from other countries who had already assimilated, became "Americanized" in order to compete economically. This combination of factors may account for the retention of the wedding ritual in its Americanized form among Chicagoans.

Author's Postscript

As I researched this subject, I recalled memories of gossip between my mother and her relatives. They always referred to a woman who actively pursued a man as one who had "set her cap" for him. Although I understood, even as a child, the implications of the phrase, it never made sense. How could that phrase, "set her cap," apply to a woman who wished to be married? Maybe they were mistaken and the phrase really was "setting a trap" for the man. Or did she "set her cap gun" in an effort to scare him into marriage? The women explained that this was "just a saying" and did not need to make sense since everyone understood the meaning. During research I discovered a folk song from the Styrian region of Austria that used the phrase "girls set their caps for boys" and the phrase finally made sense. It arrived in the United States along with the emigrants as a survival of European clothing customs. The matron's cap was "set out" or ready to be worn when the right man came along.

Notes

1. I extend my thanks to the following individuals and the many participants at the Fifth Czechoslovak Genealogical/ Cultural Conference who provided information on the apron customs of their families and friends: Kathleen Anderson, Karen Barger, Elizabeth Borovicka Capozzi, Lillian Endriz, Edna Fligel, Sylvia Jakubiec, Dennis Kolinski, Dorothy Kurtz, Nancy Lewandowski, Debbie Nelson, Josephine Prochaska, Carol Palmer, Marianne Polli, Florence Renc, Donna Rossow, Betty Slabenak, Marie Slabenak, Florence Vodicka, Marianne Winters.

References

Alba, R. D. (1990), *Ethnic Identity: the Transformation of White America*, New Haven: Yale University Press.

Balch, E.G. (1910), *Our Slavic Fellow Citizens*, New York: Charities Publication Committee.

Banner, L.W. (1983), *American Beauty*, Chicago: University of Chicago Press.

Bogatyrev, P. (1971), *The Functions of Folk Costume in Moravian Slovakia*, R.G. Crum, (trans.) The Hague: Mouton.

Chambers, R. (ed.), (1926?) *The Book of Days, v.1. "Marriage Superstitions and Customs,"* London: Chambers.

Fairfield, C. E. (July 1860), "Aunt Betsey's Best Bonnet," *Peterson's Magazine* 38: 1, 23.

Felberova, M., Fabianova, V. and Olejnik, J. (1990), *L'udovy odev na Spisi* [Folk Dress from Spis], Spisskej Novej Vsi: Okresny Norodny Vybor.

Gazdikova, A. (1991), *Zenske cepce v l' udovom odeve* [Women's Caps in Folk Dress], P. Tkac, (trans.), Martin: Vydavatelstvo Osveta.

Gimbutas, M. (1991), *The Civilization of the Goddess*, San Francisco: Harper.

Hutchinson, H. N. (1897), *Marriage Customs in Many Lands*, London: Seeley. Republished, Detroit: Gale, 1974.

Kaiser, S. (1990), *The Social Psychology of Clothing: Symbolic Appearances in Context*, 2nd edition, New York: Macmillan.

Knab, S. (1993), *Polish Customs, Traditions and Folklore*, New York: Hippocrene.

Kundera, M. (1993), *The Joke*, New York: Harper & Row.

Linder, V. (1993), *Slovak Heritage Live*, Vol. 1 (3).

Roberts, J. (1976), "Belief in the Evil Eye in World Perspective," in C. Maloney, (ed.), *The Evil Eye*, New York: Columbia University Press, pp. 223–78.

Romanyuk, M. (1981), *Byelorussian National Dress*, Minsk: Vidabyotsba.

Schmidt, A. J. (1989), *Veiled and Silenced: How Culture Shaped Sexist Theory*, Macon: Mercer University Press.

Sronkova, O. (1954), *Gothic Women's Fashion*, Greta Hort, (trans.), Prague: Artia.

Stankova, J. (1987), *Lidova Umeni z Cech, Moravy a Slezska* [Folk Art in Bohemia, Moravia and Silesia], Prague: Panorama.

Stein, H. F. (1976), "Envy and the Evil Eye," in C. Maloney (ed.), *The Evil Eye*, New York: Columbia University Press, pp. 193–222.

Vaclavik, A. and Orel, J. (n.d.), *Textile Folk Art*, H. Kaczerova (trans.), London: Spring.

Van Gennep, A. (1960 [1908]), *The Rites of Passage*, M. B. Vizedom and G. L. Caffee (trans.), Chicago: University of Chicago Press.

Williams, P. (1993), "From Folk to Fashion", in P. Cunningham and S. V. Lab (eds), *Dress in American Culture*, Bowling Green, KY: Bowling Green State University Popular Press, pp. 95–108.

—— (1994), "'Glory of Glories . . . She Wears a Hat' – Dress, the Immigrant and Social Equality in America," Presentation to the Fifth Congress of the International Association for Semiotic Studies, *Synthesis in Diversity*, San Francisco, CA.

—— (1996), "Festival, Folk Dress, Government and Tradition in Twentieth Century Czechoslovakia," *Dress, Journal of the Costume Society of America* 23: 35–46.

—— (1999), "Protection from Harm: the Shawl and Cap in Czech and Slovak Wedding, Birthing and Funerary Rites," in L. Welters (ed.), *Folk Dress in Europe and Anatolia*, Oxford: Berg, pp. 135–54.

Yoder, D. (1993), "Folk Costume," in R. M. Dorson (ed.), *Folklore and Folklife*, Chicago: University of Chicago Press, pp. 295–323.

Zelenchyek, V.S. (1985), *Moldavian National Costume*. Kishinev: Timpyel.

Zidlicky, V., Orel, J. and Rehanek, F. (1979), *Lidove Kroje na Hodoninsku* [Folk Dress in Hodon], Martin: Neografica.

13

Always Remembering the Motherland: Tai Dam Wedding Textiles and Dress

Elyse Demaray and Melody Keim-Shenk

Historical and Ethnographic Data

In 1975, approximately 2,000 Tai Dam, or Black Tai, immigrated to Des Moines, Iowa, from refugee camps in Thailand. Before the Tai Dam fled to Thailand, they migrated from southern China to current-day northwest Vietnam in the seventh century AD, from northwest Vietnam to Laos in 1954, to Thailand, and subsequently to Des Moines in the mid-1970s. With each migration, the Tai Dam have had to negotiate their expression of ethnic identity in relation to the cultures where they lived.[1]

One way people mark ethnic boundaries and create community is through distinctive forms of dress and use of textiles (Eicher and Sumberg, 1995; Graburn, 1979). Few scholars have focused on Tai Dam wedding textiles and dress; no one has looked at their forms and uses in the United States or considered how they have changed over time. This study examines the Tai Dam currently living in Des Moines, Iowa, through three generations, each of which grew up and married in a different geographical and cultural setting: the older generation (OG) in northwest Vietnam (now ages 65–87), the middle generation (MG) in Laos (ages 45–64), and the younger generation (YG) in Iowa (up to age 39). Using ethnographic field methods, we collected data on wedding textiles and dress for each generation through structured interviews, photo-documentation, and participant observation.[2] Identifying the changes that have taken place in the use of textiles and dress in wedding rituals, we show how the Tai Dam have negotiated their expression of ethnicity during different time periods and in the various geographical locations.

When the oldest generation of our participants lived in northwest Vietnam, textiles established social relationships in many aspects of Tai Dam life, particularly those related to three primary ritual occasions: weddings, funerals, and New Year's celebrations. In their various ways, these rites of passage affirmed the specific Tai Dam way of viewing the world and structuring their lives within it. As in many other cultures, coming of age for the Tai Dam manifested itself through marriage and the formation of a new family unit. Matrimony also assured the continuance of accepted gender roles and the social hierarchy between generations. The production of textiles as well as how they are worn and used symbolizes the processes inherent in betrothal and marriage: a separation from parents, transition into a new life, and incorporation into a new role within the family and community (Van Gennep, 1960).

From the time she was very young, a Tai Dam girl began to weave and embroider cloth, and spent many years preparing a dowry for her future as a wife. The ability to process and successfully weave silk or cotton signaled the transformation of a Tai Dam girl into a woman and established her ability to transform social relations through marriage (Gittinger and Lefferts, 1992). The quality of a girl's weaving and embroidery, therefore, served as an indicator of her value as a potential spouse. As one of our older generation interviewees stated succinctly, "When young and falling in love, a girl must know how to weave" (OG1).[3]

While changes in the forms and uses of wedding textiles and dress have taken place, many aspects of the dress women wore in northwest Vietnam remain the same, or similar enough that the Des Moines Tai Dam community sees them as a continuance of historical forms established in northwest Vietnam. Tai Dam culture crystallized in northwest Vietnam, as the people adopted a set of cultural traits and material goods that synthesized those they brought with them from China with those they encountered in Vietnam. The fact that Tai Dam women in Des Moines continue to wear wedding apparel that looks very similar to that worn in northwest Vietnam serves as a visual reminder of a shared, historical homeland, the area of northwest Vietnam still referred to as "Tai Dam" or "back home." In this way, the Tai Dam "always remember the motherland," a gesture that enables them to maintain a cohesive ethnic identity, despite disruptive changes over time.

Ethnicity: a Key Issue in Tai Dam Acculturation

A common definition of an ethnic community is a group of people who have one or more cultural characteristics in common and, to some degree, work together in harmony (Hutchinson and Smith, 1996). More specifically, common language, territory, religion, and dress serve as essential cultural markers in definitions of ethnicity and related terms such as "ethnic identity" and "ethnic community." Some of the most important cultural markers for the Tai Dam include the written and spoken language called Tai Dam, the identification of northwest Vietnam as their homeland, a belief in ancestor worship, and their distinctive forms of dress.

Ethnic dress acts as a basic form of social organization through both inclusion and exclusion. Visually similar clothing expresses a group's shared history and unifies individuals through group cohesiveness. Conversely dress may also maintain a group's cultural distinctiveness by differentiating it from other groups, just as a common language and common customs do. The distinctive dress that Tai Dam women wore in northwest Vietnam continues to act as a clear cultural marker for the community. We refer to this particular form of dress as the "traditional" Tai Dam wedding attire: a shiny black skirt, long-sleeved blouse with butterfly buttons sewn on a strip of black cloth, a green sash around the waist, and one or more silver chains hanging from the waist.[4] (Figure 13.1)

TAI DAM "traditional" dress

Piav or Scarf

Seua Koom or Blouse
Mga Paem or Butterfly Buttons

Saay Aev or Belt

Saay Tang or Silver chains

Sin or skirt

Figure 13.1 Components of "traditional" Tai Dam women's dress in Northwest Vietnam prior to 1954. Illustration: Melody Keim-Shenk.

Social markers are susceptible to change, however. When social situations alter, pre-existing patterns of social action may also be modified, precipitating either consciously or unconsciously, a "reassessment of the appropriateness of the functions of ethnic group identities" (Keyes, 1981: 15). When the Tai Dam moved to Laos in 1954 and then to the United States in 1975, they had to reassess their culture and customs vis-à-vis the people of Laos and the United States, which resulted in re-examining the cultural markers that signified their ethnic identity, including their distinctive dress. While changes have taken place in wedding dress and textiles as the Tai Dam came in contact with other groups of people, their ethnic identity persisted, a common tendency among ethnic groups (Barth, 1969). To better understand Tai Dam ethnicity, we examine how and why the cultural markers of wedding textiles and dress changed while Tai Dam ethnic boundaries remained in tact.

Questioning the concept of tradition as a fixed set of cultural markers can lend some insight. Many scholars who study the longevity of cultural markers view tradition as dynamic, not static, as a symbolic act that relies on the past but changes to serve individuals' needs in the present. Edward Shils, for example, believes that "tradition is a sequence of variations on received and transmitted themes . . . [that] change in the process of transmission" (1981: 13). R. Handler and J. Linnekin's (1984) perspective furthers Shils' ideas by examining how and why changes take place in tradition. They see tradition as a symbolic act that carries on the *meanings* of tradition for people in the present. The actual form of material goods, behaviors, or beliefs from the past can change yet still reinforce their historical meanings in the present. "Tradition," they state, "is a model of the past and is inseparable from the interpretation of tradition in the present . . . [it is] a symbolic process that both presupposes past symbolisms and creatively reinterprets them" (1984: 276). If we view tradition as a symbolic act that enables people to transmit meanings from the past through an ever-changing set of cultural markers, such as dress, we can see how ethnic boundaries could stay intact despite material changes over time and across geographical boundaries. The historical meanings of Tai Dam wedding textiles and dress, therefore, could persist, despite actual differences in fabric content or embroidered designs.

Graburn's Typology of Change

While a definition of tradition as dynamic and symbolic can account for changes in the traditional forms of Tai Dam wedding textiles and dress as well as a continuity in Tai Dam ethnic identity, these concepts do not indicate or predict specific ways that traditions are likely to change. N. H. Graburn's (1979) typology acts as a starting place for viewing specific Tai Dam expressions of ethnic identity in wedding textiles and dress. Graburn asserts that when two societies are at different economic and development levels, the long-term exchange in materials and/or ideas can result in significant modifications to the less-developed society. Most often, change occurs when the non-dominant group takes on the identity of the dominant group to achieve enhanced status. Because the Tai Dam have held a non-dominant social status within the stratified societies of Vietnam, Laos, and the United States, they are, therefore, likely to have changed their form of dress to conform to the more dominant societies in which they have lived. By identifying what transformations occurred in wedding textiles and dress over three generations, we may come to understand the Tai Dam reassessment of tradition.

Transformations in art forms can take many different directions, according to Graburn. We apply the relevant modifications to Tai Dam wedding textiles and dress to discuss what has occurred and what may occur in the future:

1. "Traditional" or functional textiles and dress could continue with subtle changes that do not alter their symbolic meanings.
2. The introduction of new materials or techniques, new ideas, or a change in cultural aesthetics could lead to "reintegrated" dress and textiles. Reintegrated dress occurs when cultural interaction between dominant and non-dominant groups leads to new forms of dress that have roots in both the past and the present.
3. Assimilated textiles and dress could emerge, i.e. the Tai Dam could use only the textiles and dress of the dominant group in the United States.
4. Tai Dam textiles and dress could disappear or become extinct altogether.

Using Graburn's typology of change, a definition of tradition as dynamic rather than static and the belief that wedding textiles and dress play an important role in the expression of ethnic identity, we made several hypotheses. First, Tai Dam reassessments of ethnic identity would lead to changes in traditional wedding textiles and dress, yet wedding textiles and dress would continue to play an important role in the expression of both the evolving ethnic identity and the meeting of old and new ways for the Tai Dam in the United States. Second, this expression, moreover, would shift with the generations from traditional forms to reintegrated forms and to assimilated dress based on exposure to first Laotian and then United States culture. Finally, the continued use of traditional textiles and dress at weddings would depend on the variables Graburn identifies: the availability of the materials needed to make wedding apparel and special textile forms, the continuance of the Tai Dam cultural aesthetic, and the continuing role of textiles and clothing in support of Tai Dam ethnic identity.

Tradition and Transformation across the Generations

Because Tai Dam wedding textiles and dress from different geographical locations and time periods have not been discussed in relation to each other, we begin with a descriptive summary of their weddings in Northwest Vietnam, Laos, and Des Moines, Iowa. We then discuss their differences and analyze the significance of these changes in relation to Tai Dam ethnic identity. Our descriptions provide necessarily composite pictures typical for each time and place.

Weddings "Back Home" in Vietnam, 1935–1954

Textiles played a central role in shaping Tai Dam family and social relations in northwest Vietnam and ritual occasions such as weddings brought the meanings and values attached to textile production and dress into relief. Events surrounding the actual wedding ceremonies also highlighted their social significance. For example, courtship rituals during New Year's celebrations included "dragon tails" (*maa koon*) constructed with fabric strips and small pillow-shaped squares attached to a long string (Figure 13.2). The game gave young

Figure 13.2 Sisters Sack and Chap Baccam with a "dragon tail" or *maa koon* at a New Year's celebration in Des Moines, Iowa, January 2001. Photograph: Elyse Demaray.

people a chance to interact, become acquainted, and establish relationships that might develop into a future union. A line of young men would throw the long "dragon tails" to a group of young women; whoever dropped or failed to catch the dragon tail became indebted to the other for a small gift.

For both the engagement and wedding rituals, the bride would wear a long black shiny skirt (*sin*), a black and white striped or solid colored blouse (*seua koom*) with silver butterfly buttons (*maa paem*) and a green belt (*saay aev*). On top of these, she wore a long black robe with a surplice front opening, frog closures, and a mandarin collar: a formal garment that showed deep respect for the elders. The young woman wove the fabric for her garments from cotton, since northwest Vietnam did not have ideal conditions for cultivating silk worms. Then, she might embroider flower designs on the hem of her skirt or robe with brightly colored silk threads.

The oldest man we interviewed in this generation (eighty-five years old) wore the loose white cotton trousers with a tied waist and a long black shirt for his wedding in Vietnam that were also the everyday clothes men wore. Tai Dam men's clothing, however, rapidly changed to more Western styles, even throughout the lifetimes of this older generation. By the time the younger men in this generation (now 65–75 years old) married, they wore more structured Western trousers with a black Chinese-styled jacket for their engagement and wedding, all made by their mothers and perhaps sisters.

For the Tai Dam wedding ritual, known as *su faa*, three separate ceremonies took place, all centered on textiles or components of dress, such as jewelry. First, the groom came to the bride's house with jewelry for her, most of it in pairs as a symbol of their imminent union: two gold rings, a pair of silver bracelets, a pair of silver earrings and a silver hairpin. Second, before the sun came up, the ceremony of the bed took place, a symbol of their new life as a couple. The bride and groom each brought a mattress, a pillow and a blanket which were put together with a special wedding blanket (*faa*) on top (Figure 13.3). The center of the wedding blanket consisted of two intricately woven pieces of cotton, usually red with supplementary weft designs, sewn together. Several borders constructed from strips of white and colored cotton surrounded the centerpiece to create a finished textile measuring approximately 62.5 × 23.5 inches (1.6 × 0.6 meters) (Gittinger et al., 1995/96). As a sign of their wealth, the couple might bring two or even four of each item.

When the bed was made, friends helped the bride move her hair from a bun at the nape of her neck to a bun on top of her head. The repositioning of her bun signaled the bride's transformation from a single to a married woman. While the family members of the bride and groom looked on, four women brought the groom into the bedroom, led the couple under the black mosquito netting that covered the bed and put the couple's hands together. Then they

Figure 13.3 A wedding blanket or *faa* made in the United States using fabric from Laos for the center panel. Photograph: Melody Keim-Shenk.

would wish the couple long life and many children. Black symbolized privacy, and the black netting as well as the black in the man's and woman's clothing carried this meaning. The couple could not touch the bed until they got into it together that night. A large party followed, as friends from the community joined the couple's families at the bride's house.

Finally, in the third ceremony, the couple traveled to the groom's house where he presented the bride to her new in-laws. The trip to his home could take place a day, a month, or even a year after the wedding party. The bride made a packet for each member of the groom's family and knelt down three times as she presented each of her gifts, a sign of homage to the older members of her new family. For her new father-in-law, she made long pants and shirts; for her mother-in-law, a long black skirt and short blouse. If the bride were wealthy she also presented similar packets of clothing to the groom's aunts, uncles, brothers, and sisters.

Most important, the bride gave her mother-in-law and other female relatives black cotton scarves (*piav*) (Figure 13.4), the exact number dictated by the

Figure 13.4 An example of the embroidered black scarf or *piav* made by the bride and given to her mother-in-law and other female relatives. Photograph: Melody Keim-Shenk.

specific request of the mother-in-law. In one case, a future mother-in-law required the future bride to make ninety of these scarves – a request that took the girl two years to fulfill (OG2). Embroidered with designs in bright colors on a black plain-woven ground material, the scarves typically measured approximately 52 × 14 inches (1.35 × 0.36 meters) and were used to protect a woman's face from the sun, to carry a baby, or to be used as a shawl (Gittinger et al., 1995/96). Brightly colored paired lines of embroidery ran both parallel and perpendicular to the selvedge, creating a rectangular space for additional embroidery, often completed with branch-like motifs. The paired lines of embroidery represented the stilts of a house, while the whole scarf symbolized the young woman's ability to be a good wife and daughter-in-law. In addition, four, six, or eight "coins" made of different colors of embroidery threads decorated the borders and indicated the economic status of the family according to the number of coins the bride attached.

Other gifts from the bride might include a robe made with strips of bright colors ending in a large red hem for the wife or wives of her father-in-law, long black robes like the one the bride had worn for her wedding, and long shirts. A big party followed the gift-giving with plenty of food, sake, music and dancing. Afterwards, if the couple decided to live with the man's family, his parents would give their daughter-in-law her own loom.

Marriage in Laos (1954–1975)

In Laos, a Tai Dam wedding closely resembled the "traditional" wedding in northwest Vietnam. For example, a young woman's ability to weave and embroider became less important than her ethnicity. Men wanted a "pure Tai Dam" woman, a desire generated perhaps by the large-scale changes the Tai Dam experienced in their move to Laos. Women's traditional apparel remained a constant for the older generation, but younger women wore it only for ceremonial occasions, such as weddings. Tai Dam women bought the necessary shiny black fabric needed for skirts in the market rather than weaving it at home, but they continued to hand-sew their garments nonetheless.

During the engagement and wedding rituals, the dress of the man included either the traditional black cotton surplice closed jacket with light colored western-style pants or western dress of a shirt, pants and tie. The bride's dress remained firmly rooted in tradition. As one of our interviewees said, "I was dressed just like my mother" (MG3). The change in fabrics from hand-woven and dyed cotton or silk to "whatever material we could find at the market as long as it was black and pretty," did not constitute a significant difference in the minds of the women we interviewed in the middle generation. The ability to weave, which had been of prime importance in the courtship and marriage of their mothers and grandmothers, held little meaning for them. The style of "traditional" dress and use of embroidery, however, continued as a showcase for a young woman's abilities as a deft needle worker.

At the same time, an animist ceremony called *sukhuan* appeared during the bedroom ceremony in Tai Dam weddings in Laos. *Sukhuan* consisted of family members tying a string around each wrist of the bride and groom as a way of tying their souls to their bodies. Generally, the Tai Dam used black strings rather than white because the Tai Dam view black as more auspicious (Connors, 1996). The couple could not remove the strings for at least three days. For some couples, this was performed while they sat on the bed, but others did not touch the bed until after the party. Wedding *sukhuan* ceremonies fostered good luck, wealth, and many children (Zolvinski, 1993; Naenna, 1990). Interviewees in the older generation viewed *sukhuan* as a replacement of the traditional gift of two silver bracelets; however, individuals in the middle generation did not know how the ceremony began and did not associate the *sukhuan* with silver bracelets.

Marriage in the US (1975–2000)

While Tai Dam weddings in Vietnam and Laos remained relatively similar, Tai Dam weddings in the United States have taken on new dimensions reflective of American culture. At New Year's celebrations, the dragon tail (*maa koon*) no longer plays a role in the courtship of young men and women. Instead, the game has become a light-hearted event between the middle and older generations of women or between these women and small children. Of significance, the ability to weave or embroider is no longer a criteria for a good wife.

The biggest differences, however, appear in the wedding rituals. While the youngest generation still has a traditional Tai Dam wedding, either before or after the Tai Dam ceremony, most couples also have what they refer to as "an American wedding" where the bride wears a long white dress and the groom wears a dark suit or a tuxedo (YG 5). The "American wedding" ceremony we attended lasted no longer than ten minutes, and most of the couple's relatives do not attend – evidence that the "American wedding" does not hold as much importance for the Tai Dam in Des Moines as their traditional ceremony. The traditional Tai Dam wedding ceremonies clearly hold the most meaning for the couple and their families. After the Tai Dam ceremonies, the Des Moines Tai Dam community views the couple as legitimately married, even though the marriage is not legally binding in the state of Iowa.

The younger generation of women we interviewed described their Tai Dam ceremonies and the style of their wedding clothes as "the same" as their mothers. While the current generation of brides does wear the traditional style of long black shiny skirt, colorful blouse with butterfly buttons, green sash and silver chain, some differences do exist. The skirt, blouse, and sash are now most often made of silk, and the butterfly buttons come from Vietnam or a local silversmith. Fabric is purchased, and the mothers of the brides make their daughters' garments, since most young Tai Dam women do not know how to sew or embroider. In addition, the couple exchanges different types of jewelry. Rather than two gold rings, the bride now receives a diamond engagement ring and then a wedding band at her American marriage ceremony. In addition, the bride's family might give their son-in-law a gold necklace and/or a bracelet.

Activities similar to those in Vietnamese or Laotian Tai Dam weddings also continue to take place, however. The bride puts her hair up in a bun before the ceremony of the bed to indicate her new status, and the wedding blanket, black scarves, and fabrics still hold prominent positions. The youngest generation, however, now depends on its mothers to make or to buy these textile items. The mothers make the blankets from specially woven fabric with traditional Tai Dam designs that they import from Laos or Vietnam and then add shiny polyester purchased at local fabric stores in Des Moines. The handwoven cotton fabric serves as the centerpiece and bright pink or red, white and green strips of polyester surround it. Individuals in the younger generation consistently referred to the blankets their mothers made for them as "exactly the same" as those used in their mothers' and grandmothers' weddings, and they described the blanket as having "the red border."

One reception at a local hall serves as the celebration for both the Tai Dam and American ceremonies. The bride generally will not wear "traditional" Tai Dam dress for the reception, although her clothing likely will be made of Laotian or Asian cloth. The bride may wear her western-style wedding dress if the civil or church ceremony happens just prior to the reception. The bride's mother will wear "traditional" Tai Dam dress at some point during the evening, but both the bride and her mother typically change outfits several times during the reception. One of our interviewees referred to her reception as a "Laotian reception" because she wore a skirt and blouse made from Laotian fabrics during the first part (YG6). Most Tai Dam couples in the United States do not live with the bride's family at any point in the courtship or marriage process.

Always Remembering the Motherland

We hypothesized that traditional dress would continue in the oldest generation and our data support that prediction. In the United States, the oldest generation continues to wear "traditional" dress every day. We expected to find "reintegrated" dress for weddings within the middle generation. Instead, we found the use of traditional dress, although the brides no longer wove the fabrics for their wedding clothes and textiles. In the United States, the middle generation reserves traditional dress for special events and rites of passage and wears western-style dress on a daily basis. This dual direction most probably stems from the fact that many Tai Dam women in the middle generation worked outside the home in Laos and continue to work outside the home in the United States. The oldest generation, however, tends to stay home and care for the grandchildren, a situation that at least contributes to this change across generations.

The youngest generation of Tai Dam women, like the middle generation, wear mainstream American clothes on a daily basis and reserve the traditional Tai Dam dress for special occasions. The weddings of the youngest generation, however, have moved in two directions, a dynamic that Graburn does not identify. While younger Tai Dam women don western wear for everyday, a clear assimilation of dominant forms of dress, they wear both "traditional" style Tai Dam clothing and western-style clothing for weddings. They have not incorporated western styles into traditional Tai Dam dress to create rein-tegrated forms; neither have they abandoned traditional dress. Rather, the young women have *added* a western-style wedding and wedding dress. By wearing "traditional" dress in the United States, a Tai Dam bride deliberately expresses herself as a member of the Tai Dam community, an important gesture for the younger generation who have no memories of Vietnam and few, if any, memories of Laos. At the same time, the adoption of western-style wedding attire expresses young women's identification with the dominant culture of the United States where most have grown up.

Because Graburn's discussion of change does not provide an adequate view of what has happened for the Tai Dam, we propose an additional category, what we call "segregated" dress. Segregated dress refers to the use of two or more separate styles of dress by individuals in the same generation, worn for the same purpose. Looking at the relationship between these two forms is essential for understanding how the Tai Dam have redefined their tradition within the American setting. By adding western wedding dress outside of the context of the Tai Dam wedding ceremonies, the younger generation draw a distinct line between Tai Dam and American styles. This clear separation enables them to maintain their ethnic identity as Tai Dam while, at the same time, aligning themselves with the dominant culture around them.

Because the middle and younger generations of Tai Dam women made and wore traditional styles constructed from materials purchased in a Laotian market or a Des Moines fabric store, we might assign them the label of "rein-tegrated" forms. In Graburn's scheme, however, reintegrated forms signal a degree of assimilation that moves toward replacement and, ultimately, to the disappearance of older art and craft forms. The middle and younger gener-ations of interviewees consistently perceived their wedding textiles and dress as "the same" as those of their parents and even grandparents. They defined their items as "traditional," not as a hybrid form of past and present. More-over, the wedding textiles and dress symbolized traditional Tai Dam values and beliefs. As a symbolic act, therefore, the Tai Dam understanding of tradition today remains essentially the same, despite some alterations in the materials and technologies used to produce current textiles and clothing.

The cultural aesthetics of the Tai Dam also have remained intact through their immigrations to Laos, Thailand, and the United States. The color and style in the women's dress remain the same: a consistent use of the long, straight black shiny skirt (*sin*), a colorful solid colored blouse (*seua koom*) with silver butterfly buttons (*maa paem*), a green sash (*saay aev*), and the silver chain (*sooy tang*). The importance of using a shiny black material for the skirt, green for the sash and a black cloth for mounting the butterfly buttons continues despite the use of changing materials.

The current generation of Tai Dam women have adopted both Tai Dam and United States wedding ceremonies with their corresponding textiles and attire, but will Tai Dam traditional dress and textiles eventually disappear? Based on Graburn's premise for the continuance of traditional arts, the outlook for Tai Dam wedding dress appears optimistic. Materials are readily available, either locally or from Asia, for producing the "traditional" wedding dress. Family members buy the silver butterfly buttons in Vietnam and pass them along to other family members. The continued use of the special wedding blanket (*faa*) and the black scarf the bride gives to her mother-in-law and other female relatives (*piav*) seems less likely, however. Although the older generation and some of the middle generation still make the wedding blanket and the black scarves, the younger generation seldom participates in their creation. Moreover, not all young women give their female relatives the black scarf as a part of the traditional Tai Dam ceremony in the United States.

Despite the cultural pressures of the world around them, or perhaps in response to them, women's traditional wedding textiles and dress still symbolize Tai Dam ethnic identity and community. A Tai Dam bride in Des Moines wearing the shiny black skirt (*sin*), the long sleeved blouse (*seua koom*) with silver butterfly buttons (*maa paem*) backed by black cloth, and the green belt (*saay aev*) with silver chains (*sooy tang*) hanging from her waist continues to express a collective image of a people always remembering the motherland.

Notes

1. The Tai Dam are part of the Tai or Tai Kadai language group. Special thanks to Siang Bachti for giving us access to the Tai Dam Cultural Center in Des Moines, guiding us through the collections and providing Tai Dam names for wedding textiles and ceremonies.

2. Interviews were conducted in keeping with Iowa State University's Human Subjects Committee standards. General interviews initially were conducted, followed by structured interviews with participants from the three generational groups. Participants were selected through snowballing. This research was funded by a Professional Advancement Grant at Iowa State University administered by the Graduate Student Senate.

Special thanks to Kamkieb Baccam for his untiring efforts at helping us set up interviews and for translating during the interviews from both Tai Dam to English and English to Tai Dam.

3. Interview data is coded according to the generation and participant number throughout the manuscript, i.e., OG = older generation.

4. In Vietnam, the women obtained the sheen of the black cotton skirt by using a combination of dye, soybean paste and beating the fabric.

References

Barth, F. (1969), *Ethnic Groups and Boundaries: The Social Organization of Cultural Difference*, Boston: Little Brown.

Connors, M. F. (1996), *Lao Textiles and Traditions*, Oxford, Singapore, New York: Oxford University Press.

Eicher, J. B. and Sumberg, B. (1995), "World Fashion, Ethnic, and National Dress," in J.B. Eicher (ed.), *Dress and Ethnicity; Change Across Space and Time*, Washington, D.C.: Berg Publishers.

Graburn, N. H. H. (ed.) (1979), *Ethnic and Tourist Arts; Cultural Expressions from the Fourth World*, Berkeley: University of California Press.

Gittinger, M., Chungyampin, K. A. and Saiyalard, C. (1995/6), "Textiles and Textile Customs of the Tai Dam, Tai Daeng, and their Neighbors in Northern Laos," *Textile Museum Journal* 34–5: 92–112.

Gittinger, M. and Lefferts, H. L. (1992), *Textiles and the Tai experience in Southeast Asia*, Washington, D.C.: The Textile Museum.

Handler, R. and Linnekin, J. (1984), "Tradition, Genuine or Spurious," *Journal of American Folklore* 97: 385, 273–90.

Hutchinson, J., and Smith, A. D. (eds) (1996), *Ethnicity*, Oxford & New York: Oxford University Press.

Keyes, C. (ed.) (1981), *Ethnic Change*, Seattle: University of Washington Press.

Naenna, P. (1990), *Costume and Culture: Vanishing Textiles of Some of the Tai Groups in Laos P.D.R.*, Chiang Mai, Thailand: Studio Naenna Co. Ltd.

Shils, E. (1981), *Tradition*, Chicago: University of Chicago Press.

Tai Studies Center (1988), *The Tai Dam: Nowhere to Stay* (copyrighted manuscript for slide set), Des Moines, Iowa: Tai Studies Center.

Van Gennep, A. (1960), *The Rites of Passage*, Chicago: University of Chicago Press.

Zolvinski, S. P. (1993), *Continuity and Change in Family Systems of the Central Iowa Tai Dam*, unpublished Master's thesis, Ames, Iowa State University.

14

The American Groom Wore a Celtic Kilt: Theme Weddings as Carnivalesque Events

Theresa M. Winge and Joanne B. Eicher

Bagpipes screamed, piercing the afternoon silence, until the melody became recognizable as a march. The groom in a tam, tartan kilt, black long-sleeved shirt with loose ruffles down the front and on the cuffs, walked hand-in-hand with the bride down the castle's steps, across the lawn, to the altar. She wore a full-length tartan skirt, matching shawl and brilliant white blouse with lace collar and cuffs. Guests lined the aisle, many wearing plaid clothing. They swayed to and fro and cheered when the Wiccan priestess bound the couple's hands with a colorful ribbon.[1] Is this a handfasting wedding ceremony in Scotland at the turn of the century?[2] No, it is a modern theme wedding in the United States.

According to recently published articles and internet web sites, theme weddings appear to be gaining in popularity, replacing traditional or "white weddings" for some couples in the United States.[3] For example, Gail Stirler, owner of Chivalry Sports in Tucson, Arizona, claims she "has watched the theme wedding market grow from a relatively closed group to a much wider one" (Stuart, 1999: 24). Our attendance at and knowledge of weddings that we categorize as theme weddings illustrate this observation. We present an analysis of theme weddings based on reviewing seventeen periodical articles, fifty-two internet web sites, eleven television programs and attending nineteen weddings.[4]

We define a theme wedding, sometimes referred to as a "concept wedding," as a non-traditional, Western marriage ceremony where the bride and groom designate a theme that is marked by the dress of its participants, particularly the bride and groom. Instead of the bride wearing a white gown and the groom a suit or tuxedo, the wedding couple select a theme for their ceremony that includes their own dress that often extends to the invitations, decorations and food. Guests and the official performing the ceremony may even wear dress as determined by the couple's theme for the wedding. According to Dennis Stuart, a writer for *Costume*, "Theme weddings are on the rise and costume professionals are cashing in on the business of turning romantic dreams into profitable realities" (23–4).

Traditional Wedding Dress

Since ancient times, weddings have existed as social practices, performed in public and often as religious ceremonies. The wedding typically resonates with the characteristics and customs representative of the couple's social stratum. The material culture displayed during a wedding ceremony, especially that of the wedding party's clothing, represents the cultural practices of couples and their families.

By the late 1800s, a traditional wedding clothing ensemble in the United States consisted of a white or off-white formal gown for the bride, commonly referred to as a wedding gown, and a dark suit or tuxedo for the groom. The white gown represented the all-important virginal status of the bride, and dates back to the nineteenth century when, in 1840, Queen Victoria, dressed in a white wedding gown, married Prince Albert (McBride-Mellenger, 1993: 180). As queen, Victoria set the fashion standard at court and the popularity of the white wedding dress soon came to the United States (Tortora and Eubank, 1994: 211). Grooms commonly wore formal attire for their weddings until about the mid-twentieth century when dinner jackets and less formal dress became more acceptable (Tortora and Eubank, 1994: 366–8). Wedding ensembles historically communicated a great deal of information about the couple, such as their culture, ethnicity, religion and social standing.[5]

Dress plays an important role in all weddings in distinguishing the wedding couple from their attendants and guests.[6] Guests, for example, quickly identify the bride from her bridesmaids. The bridesmaids typically dress alike in the same style and color of gown, with the bride dressing distinctly from, and often more ornately than, her bridesmaids. The groom often dresses similarly to his groom's men; the distinction is often less clear than between the bride and bridesmaids.

The contemporary role of dress in a theme wedding also plays a significant and distinct role for the couple. Theme wedding dress creates a space in which both the bride and groom have more individuality, freedom, and play than allowed the bride and groom who dress in a formal white gown and somber suit or tuxedo.

Theme Weddings

A theme wedding that we both attended on 13 October 2000 prompted us to examine this new development in American weddings. For their handfasting wedding ceremony, held outdoors during a full moon, the bride and groom chose dress inspired by ancient Celtic (Scottish or Irish) and Bohemian (Gypsy) garb. The honor attendants wore crudely fashioned leather garments and a wide variety of tartan fabrics, while the couple's parents dressed in homemade Celtic costumes. Over half of the guests dressed in various versions of ancient Celtic and Gypsy costumes, some homemade and some rented.

Using the October 2000 wedding as inspiration, we additionally examined similar, recent weddings using Mikhail Bakhtin's theoretical framework of "carnivalesque" and our interpretation of the role dress plays within these weddings. We give specific examples of such weddings and wedding ensembles to discuss the carnivalesque characteristics present. We analyze our combined first-hand knowledge of nineteen theme weddings, which took place from 1985 through 2002.

We constructed a chart for comparison and analysis of each of the wedding themes. We looked at the year and location of the wedding and the bride's and groom's dress. From our knowledge of the couples involved, we conclude that the primary inspirations for their theme weddings involve several factors. These include the couple's ethnicity, alternative religions, budget concerns, group affiliations (such as Gothic subculture membership or being a Civil War re-enactor), or influences on the couple, like movies, holidays (such as Valentines Day, Halloween, Christmas, and New Years), literature, hobbies, and other special interests.[7] In the case of the Oneida wedding, the bride wanted the theme because she was a Pow-Wow dancer and the groom had some American Indian heritage. Their wedding on the reservation was their image of an Oneida wedding and had no historical base, but was chosen for its inexpensive cost and tie to the background of the couple.

Our chart illustrates that the dress of the bride and groom determined the theme chosen for their wedding. These theme wedding ensembles were acquired in various ways. For the brides, six rented most of their ensemble, seven had custom-made garments especially for them, two made their own garments, and four purchased ready-to-wear ensembles. For the grooms six rented most of their ensemble, three had garments custom-made for them, one made his own ensemble, and nine purchased ready-to-wear ensembles. These figures indicate that both bride and groom chose to rent their ensembles for six of the theme weddings (rented ensembles are indicated in the chart), two brides and only one groom made their own wedding ensembles, three more brides than grooms had custom-made garments, and five more grooms than brides wore ready-to-wear ensembles. Of the nineteen weddings, we found that at least one of the couples chose the theme, nine brides choose the theme, four grooms, and both chose the remaining six themes.

Twelve of the wedding couples specifically selected locations which would reflect their wedding themes. Because we live in the mid-western United States, the majority of the weddings we observed or know about were in mid-western locations. Reading about theme weddings in published articles and viewing numerous television programs that included theme weddings, however, leads us to suggest that the phenomenon is not a regional phenomenon.

Year	Theme	Bride's Dress	Groom's Dress	Location
1985	Scandinavian	White dress with rosemaling beadwork	Black tuxedo with white shirt	Lutheran Church Fridley, Minnesota
1993	Renaissance	Tailored white satin dress	Tailored white tunic and tights	Renaissance Palace, Milwaukee, Wisconsin
1995	Picnic	Ivory, sleeveless, knee-length sundress	Khaki pants and white shirt	Cliffside Amphitheater, Denver, Colorado
1995	American Western (e.g. Cowboy)	White square dance dress	Cowboy boots, black jeans and black tuxedo jacket	Lutheran Church Fridley, Minnesota
1996	Mountain Top Picnic	Purple, calf-length sundress	Shorts and polo shirt	High Cliff Park, High Cliff, Wisconsin
1997	Mexican	Mexican ethnic costume	Tuxedo, bolo tie and cowboy boots	St. Peter's Catholic Church, Oshkosh, Wisconsin
1998	Oneida Indian Wedding Dance	Red jingle dress with jingle shawl	Turtle dance (Pow Wow) costume	Pow-Wow Circle Oneida Indian Reservation, Wisconsin
1998	Outdoor Adventure	Outdoor hiking gear (rented)	Outdoor hiking gear (rented)	Olympia Rainforest Olympia, Washington
1998	American Western (e.g. Cowboy)	White dress with ruffles	Western-style tuxedo, cowboy boots and bolo tie	Yosemite Park, Yosemite, California
1999	Irish	Celtic knot quilted gown, trimmed in burgundy velvet	1930s black tuxedo and top hat	Horticulture Domes Milwaukee, Wisconsin

Year	Theme	Bride's Dress	Groom's Dress	Location
2000	Irish	Emerald green satin gown	Black tuxedo with plaid bow tie and cummerbund	Universal Church Oshkosh, Wisconsin
2000	Irish Handfasting	Ivory lace gown	Waist-length black jacket and kilt	South Park, Oshkosh, Wisconsin
2000	Celtic/Bohemian Handfasting	Mesh shawl, black bustier, blue wrapped skirt	Black shirt with ruffles at the cuffs and plaid kilt	Neenah Park Neenah, Wisconsin
2000	Renaissance	Red Renaissance-style gown (rented)	Black tunic and tights (rented)	Walker Sculpture Gardens Minneapolis, Minnesota
2000	Halloween Masquerade	Little Red Riding Hood costume (rented)	Big Bad Wolf costume (rented)	VFW (Veterans of Foreign Wars) Hall Oshkosh, Wisconsin
2000	Golden Age of Hollywood	Marilyn Monroe: Pink, strapless, satin gown, with long gloves (rented)	Clark Gable: black tuxedo (rented), pencil mustache	Heights Theatre Minneapolis, Minnesota
2001	1920s Gangster	Flapper dress with long string of pearls (rented)	1920s style tuxedo and violin case (rented)	Velvet Lounge Chicago, Illinois
2002	Scottish Handfasting	Antique white, Celtic quilted gown (rented)	White shirt, black jacket and plaid kilt (rented)	Melrose Abbey Melrose, Scotland
2002	Dark Fairy Princess & Prince Charming	Small top hat, black velvet top, and long, full satin skirt with overskirt of black tulle with glass crystals	Black suit with silver and black vest and tie and white shirt	Napa Wine Train/ St. Helena Park Gazebo Napa Valley, California

Theme Weddings and the Carnivalesque

According to a reader's poll conducted by *Renaissance Magazine*, couples reported three primary reasons for choosing a Renaissance theme:[8]

1. Inspiration from attending Renaissance Faires (sic.) (35%)

2. Romantic notions about the time period from reading books or viewing films (35%)
3. A desire to be different or to express their individuality (25%) (Perrett, 2001: 22).

With the possible exception of ethnicity and alternative religions, we argue that theme weddings express what Bakhtin describes as "folk humor" or carnival-esque elements (Bakhtin, 1968: 5). He states that carnivalesque:

> . . . is the people's second life, organized on the basis of laughter, [and] [i]t has a universal spirit: it has a special condition of the entire world, of the world's revival and renewal. . . . Such is the essence of carnival, vividly felt by all of its participants (7–8).

Thus, the idea of carnivalesque or carnival metaphorically applies to the ephemeral structure and nature of those events and activities that invert conventional or traditional relationships, subvert power, and celebrate a "fantastic" canon of the body. At the same time, the carnival atmosphere does not negate nor parody its subject. Bakhtin stresses "that the carnival is far distant from the negative and formal parody of modern times" (11). We interpret Bakhtin to mean that carnivalesque can be a serious matter; therefore, the choice of theme weddings should not be seen as a trivial or insignificant choice.

Ephemeral Nature of Carnival and Weddings

Bakhtin states the carnival celebrates a temporary release from expected and established order, most notably there is a "suspension of all hierarchical rank, privileges, norms and prohibitions" (10). During a theme wedding, although finding themselves in an ephemeral space and time, participants and guests revel in the opportunity to play at being royalty or knights or even fictitious characters for the duration of the celebration.

Many people say one's wedding is a once in a lifetime event. The ephemeral nature of the wedding itself has the carnivalesque elements that appear to reflect and even exaggerate the fleeting nature of any wedding. This temporary space occupied by weddings becomes a commonality between both traditional and theme weddings. One couple whose favorite holiday is Halloween, decided to marry on 31 October 2000 in Oshkosh, Wisconsin, and have a Halloween-Masquerade wedding. Using "Little Red Riding Hood" as the theme, the bride dressed as Little Red Riding Hood, and the groom dressed as the Big Bad Wolf. Nearly every guest dressed in costume, presenting themselves as knights and princesses, super-heroes and villains and witches and warlocks. The couple's wedding officiate dressed as a mad scientist. After the service, he toasted the newlyweds with a vial of green liquid.

Freedom of Choice and Individuality

Two significant elements of carnivalesque – freedom and individuality – assume equally important roles in the theme wedding. Exploring the roles these elements take on in the theme wedding sets the stage for the importance of dress during this occasion.

Bakhtin declared, "During carnival time life is subject only to its laws, that is, the law of its own freedom" (1968: 7). Couples similarly find freedom in planning a theme wedding in contrast to adhering to the expectations typically found in traditional weddings. Many usual customs, which do not fit the theme from dress to setting, can be cast aside with no more explanation than "it doesn't fit with the theme."

Options in alternative dress available to those who choose a theme appeal to both brides and grooms. The bride no longer must wear a white hourglass-shaped gown, nor does the groom need to don a well-fitted suit or tuxedo. According to Stuart, "many full-figured brides wear early eighteenth century wedding gowns because such gowns create a more appealing silhouette than do those of contemporary styles" (1999: 26). For example at an Irish wedding (1999), the bride chose an empire-style gown with a scooped neckline and a long skirt that fell straight to the floor from just under her breasts. This style accented bodily features that the bride found appealing, while those with which she was not completely comfortable were disguised under the long skirt.

An older bride, remarrying or renewing her vows, may prefer a theme wedding in order to avoid wearing a white dress or to gain a wider choice in gown styles for a more mature body type. She perhaps may not want to wear a white wedding gown or perhaps cannot find a suitable dress because many stores or departments feature gowns designed for younger brides. A theme wedding permits the older bride to wear any color and style that flatters her figure. In our examples, this became evident in the planning of a Dark Fairy Princess and Prince Charming wedding scheduled to take place in spring 2002, in Napa Valley, California. The bride, in her mid-thirties, found the wedding gowns at retail shops and those available through on-line sources were primarily white or off-white, in styles designed for a younger, slimmer body type. She opted instead to have a theme wedding because she believed she could have more freedom in choosing a wedding dress style to suit her. She decided to dress as a "dark" fairy princess, an idea carried over from her childhood fantasies about a wedding combined with her contemporary lifestyle. The bride wore a custom-made ensemble: a skirt had a large full black tulle skirt with tiny glass crystals; a black velvet top with beaded neckline; and small black top hat, decorated with tulle similar to the overskirt. As a result, the groom dressed as "dark" Prince Charming.

Stuart asserts that examples of the theme weddings in which the groom benefits from his choice of attire usually relate to his special interests, such as hobbies or re-enactment groups (1999: 27). For example, a groom might wear a Klingon uniform if he is a *Star Trek* enthusiast, or a Union or Confederate uniform if he belongs to an American Civil War re-enactment group.

We found that individuality and play associated with theme wedding dress were significant motivators both for brides and grooms. For instance, some grooms expressed that they gladly wore kilts like those they saw in the 1995 movies *Braveheart* and *Rob Roy*, instead of being forced to wear an uncomfortable suit and tie. Still other grooms commented that they found period costumes, such as Renaissance garb, fun to wear because they were able to carry a sword and have mock sword fights with their friends.

Theme weddings provide opportunities for the bride and groom to express their individual identities. Even if more than one couple choose the same theme, the results differ and become individual in their expression, reinforcing Bakhtin's observation that "[t]he utopian ideal and the realistic merged in this carnival experience, unique of its kind" (1968: 10). As an example, we compare the dress of two Renaissance theme weddings, one held in 1993 and another in 2000. Each distinguished itself from the other, despite the similar theme. These two weddings proved to be especially individualistic in the dress chosen by members of the wedding parties.

The 1993 wedding, held indoors at the Renaissance Palace in Milwaukee, Wisconsin, featured a traditional Christian ceremony, followed by a formal Renaissance Ball reception. A period costume design studio, Hook and Eye, designed and constructed the bride's and groom's clothing. The groom wore a white velvet tunic with gold trim, white tights and white slippers. The bride wore a highly embellished burgandy velvet dress which fell from the shoulders to the floor, and a tiara on her long black hair.

The 2000 Renaissance wedding ceremony took place outdoors, in Minneapolis, Minnesota, at Walker Art Center's Sculpture Garden. The bride, groom, honor attendants, and immediate family rented costumes from a costume shop that provides the costumes for a Renaissance Festival held annually in Shakopee, Minnesota. The groom wore a plain black tunic with black tights and beret, and the bride wore a simple full-length crimson dress, with embellishments around the neckline.

Although the silhouettes of the two couples choosing Renaissance-theme weddings resembled each other, the details of each item of the clothing ensemble differed. The heavily embellished outfits of the couple married in 1993 fit their bodies precisely. The rental costumes of the other couple married in 2000, however, gave them little choice in the colors and the details of their garb, especially because their primary concern centered on properly fitting the one meter ninety centimeters (six foot five inch) tall groom. Still, both couples expressed their individuality while at the same time maintaining the emphasis of the Renaissance wedding theme. According to Bakhtin's theory of carnival, these two weddings each demonstrate the importance placed on individuality which separates the participants in the theme weddings from the outside world, as well as from other more traditional weddings (1968: 29).

Dress as a Boundary Setter

The theme of the wedding establishes the broad boundaries for the carnival-esque fantasy. As we have previously indicated, the dress of the participants most obviously delineates these boundaries. For example, if the wedding invitations indicate "Scottish Wedding," guests expect to see the groom wearing a tartan kilt, knee-high socks and a tam, whether or not the guests choose to wear kilts themselves.

The boundaries of the carnivalesque fantasy continue with the choice of setting, décor, food, music and location to reflect the designated theme. One such example involves a Scottish theme wedding for an American couple in a castle in Scotland decorated with yards of tartan material. The menu included authentic Scottish foods, such as tea, oatcakes, and haggis, and a group of bagpipers played Scottish pub tunes and American classics for the reception following the wedding.

Dress also visually establishes the mood and illusion for the wedding. Women wearing long flowing velvet gowns and men wearing velvet tunics and tights create the romantic and chivalrous mood necessary for (their interpretation of) a Renaissance theme wedding. Even if the dress is not accurately representative of the Renaissance period, there are enough elements that the bride, groom and guests can identify the time period to establish the atmosphere that makes the carnivalesque fantasy possible.

Through dress, the illusion of the theme continues throughout the wedding and reception. Moreover, dress acts as a constant reminder of the theme created and, therefore, the dress of participants potentially keeps them involved with the theme or fantasy. In fact, theme wedding planners suggest that brides and grooms explicitly state on their invitation the type of dress they encourage their guests to wear and they suggest a wedding web site to help guests find appropriate dress (Perrett, 2001: 26).

One couple even created their own theme wedding web site. The formal invitations encouraged guests to go on-line to view images of kilts and various Celtic knot patterns; in addition, guests were asked to use the list of provided resources to find costume shops or retailers that could supply appropriate clothing. A second couple, who adopted an Irish theme, sent out a wedding newsletter about one month before the wedding. This newsletter included details about the bride's emotions, assistance of various family members with activities, and suggestions for appropriate dress for guests willing to join in the Irish theme by wearing tartan kilts, shawls and lace. Yet a third couple, in 1998, chose a theme of an outdoor adventure in Olympia State Park, Washington. They stated clearly in their invitations that guests should wear clothing to the wedding in which they could hike and climb. A fourth couple, in 1985, chose to have invitations, programs and thank-you cards with the same Norwegian rosemaling designs the bride had beaded on to her wedding gown, and the food and music at their reception reflected the Scandinavian theme of their wedding.[9]

Dress as a Vehicle for Play

Donald Wood Winnicott, in his book *Playing and Reality*, states that play is key for group relations (1971: 41). Theme weddings allow adults to interact with other adults in a playful manner. Play is both a significant element of theme weddings and a characteristic of carnivalesque. The theme dress of both wedding participants and guests allows for the experiences of escapism and voyeurism, the same happenstance that occurs during a masquerade. Among adults, this escape from reality to fantasy encourages carnivalesque play. For instance, a wedding with a King-Arthur-in-Camelot theme permits grown men in tights to participate in pretend swordplay, while ladies-in-waiting wager dances for their champions, or, the bride and groom may cut the cake with a sword while horns blow (Kernan, 1999: 30–2; Seiden, 2001: 49–53). A Halloween theme wedding allows adults to become scary monsters who may grunt and growl instead of talking or to become superheroes who save the day.

One bride and groom emphasized the element of play in their Golden-Age-of-Hollywood wedding in September, 2000, in a rented movie theatre in Minneapolis, Minnesota. They encouraged guests to put on a director's beret and direct the video camera technician to film a mini-movie of the bride (dressed as Marilyn Monroe) and the groom (dressed as Clark Gable). In addition, the wedding favors included faux beauty marks and eyelashes, and faux pencil-line mustaches.

At the weddings where the grooms and male guests wore kilts a common question arose from other men, as well as women guests: "Are you wearing your kilt traditionally?" This is understood to mean: "Are you wearing under-wear under your kilt?" Wearing a kilt "traditionally" is apparently wearing one without underwear. It is difficult to determine where this idea came from. One possibility is from the battle scene in *Braveheart*, where the Scottish lift their kilts and expose their lack of undergarments beneath their kilts to the enemy before going into battle. The level of play at one wedding was so great that by the end of the evening about twenty men wearing kilts "traditionally" gave a "Scottish battle cry;" that is to say, the men bent over facing away from their audience, then lifted their kilts.

Conclusions

We observed that a theme wedding provides a creative approach to a traditional event. Theme weddings display numerous elements of carnivalesque: dress, setting, music and activities, which reflect the individuality and playfulness of the couple being married. Their dress conveys the mood, establishes the character(s) and creates an illusion. Theme dress furnishes the primary vehicle for the carnivalesque atmosphere which draws guests into the fantasy that the bride and groom want to create with their theme wedding. Just as traditional wedding dress communicates a great deal of information about the couple, so does the theme wedding ensemble.

Bakhtin recognized that during a period of carnival, the ideal or fantastic blended with reality to create a unique experience (1968: 10). In a similar manner, a theme wedding combines an idealistic fantasy with the reality of a contemporary wedding, marked as an extraordinary event not only for the bride and groom, but for their guests as well.

Notes

1. Wicca is a pagan tradition based on Celtic spirituality (McCoy, 1998: 316).

2. Handfasting is an ancient Celtic wedding ceremony during which the bride and groom are bound by a piece of cloth wrapped around their joined right hands (Buck-land, 1995: 97).

3. We use the term "traditional" when referring to wedding ensembles in the United States, not to suggest that wedding ensembles have remained static, without change. Instead we use this term because the brides and grooms have identified the white dress and dark suit or tuxedo as "traditional."

4. The television programs viewed were "A Wedding Story" (Discovery Channel), and various specials on Las Vegas weddings (E!). The internet sites viewed were chose from a search requesting articles on weddings with themes. The periodical articles were selected from *Renaissance Magazine, Costume! Business,* and *Smithsonian.*

5. We would like to thank Colleen Kahn for her help with this section in providing information about wedding ensembles for brides and grooms in the late nineteenth century and early twentieth century.

6. Dress is defined as an assemblage of any body modification and/or supplement, as well as a means of non-verbal communication (Eicher and Roach-Higgins, 1992).

7. Valentines Day, Halloween, Christmas and New Years were mentioned more than any others in wedding magazines and on television programs that focused on weddings. We speculate that this has to do with the fact that every year these holidays are on the same date. Thus, a couple could celebrate the holiday and their wedding anniversary on the same day every year.

8. The typical dress for Renaissance theme weddings is loosely based on the silhouettes and dress from Italy from the 1400s–1600s. Still, some dress is inspired from previous eras and called "Renaissance." The food is often buffet style with large round loaves of bread, wine and shanks of meat.

9. The word "rosemaling" is used to describe a form of decorative flower painting that originated in Norway in the 1700s. These graceful designs are derived from C and S strokes and are characterized by flowing lines and scroll with imaginative, fanciful flowers, and subtle colors.

References

Bakhtin, M. (1968), *Rabelais and His World,* Helene Iswolsky (trans.), Cambridge: Massachusetts Institute of Technology.

Buckland, R. (1995), *Buckland's Complete Book of Witchcraft,* St. Paul, Minnesota: Lewellyn Worldwide.

Eicher, Joanne Bubolz and Roach-Higgins, Mary Ellen (1992), "Definition and Classification of Dress: Implications for Analysis of Gender Roles," in R. Barnes and J. B. Eicher (eds), *Dress and Gender: Making and Meaning,* Oxford: Berg Publishers.

Kernan, M. (1999), "Finding a Knight in Shining Armor," *Smithsonian* 30: 7, 30–2.

McBride-Mellenger, M. (1993), *The Wedding Dress,* New York: Random House.

McCoy, Edain. (1998), *Celtic Women's Spirituality: Accessing the Cauldron of Life,* St. Paul, MN: Lewellyn Worldwide.

Mordecai, C. (1999), *Weddings: Dating and Love Customs of Cultures Worldwide,* Phoenix: Nittany Publishers.

Perrett, S. (2001), "Period Wedding Inspiration," *Renaissance Magazine* 6: 1, 22.

—— (2001), "Wedding Costuming Recommendations," *Renaissance Magazine* 6:1, 22.

Seiden, E. (2001), "44 Ways to Make History on Your Wedding Day," *Renaissance Magazine* 6: 1, 49–53.

Stuart, D. (1999), "Theme Weddings: Ladies in Waiting – Men in Tights," *Costume! Business* 2: 4, Jacksonville, Florida: Festivities Publications, Inc.

Tortora, P. and Eubank, K. (1994*), Survey of Historic Costume: A History of Western Dress,* New York: Fairchild Publications.

Winnicott, D. W. (1971) (reprinted 1980), *Playing and Reality*. London: J.W. Arrowsmith Ltd.

Index

Ait Khabbash (Berber), 105–20 *passim*
Alaska, 2, 23–38
Alberta, Canada, 3, 5–21
Andes, 157–72
  see also Bolivia, Colonial Spain, Ecuador,
    Inca, Peru
Apotropaic, protection
  aâbroq, 108
  amber, 112
  bags of herbs and incense, 110
  blue bead, 133–4, 139n15
  embroidered wool and silk, 175
  evil eye
    Ait Khabbash, Morocco, 2, 110,
      113–14, 118
    European folk, 177
    Greece, 133–4, 139n15
    Russia, 142
    Slavs, 181
  gloves, 2, 142
    see also bridalwear, gloves
  henna, 113–4
    see also make-up; footwear, bride and
     groom
  jnoun, 110, 114, 117
  marriage-devil, 176
  purity, 79
  scissors, 134
  shur, 118
  snail, 170
  talisman, 142
aproning the bride, 173, 182–186
arranged marriage, 40, 42, 53, 72
attendants' dress, 32–3, 55, 129–30, 146,
  176, 208

bed, 55
  bed ceremony, 128–9, 200

blanket, 129, 170, 201–2, 204
Berber (Ait Khabbash), 2, 105–21 *passim*
Bolivia, 2, 157–71 *passim*
bridesmaid, 55, 152, 176
  see also Attendants' dress
bridalwear
  apron, 94, 97, 104n6, 138–9n13, 173,
    177, 182–4, 186fig12.4
    see aproning the bride
  atikluk, 23, 28, 31–35, 37n7
  bags of herbs and incense, 110
  belt, 113, 120n10
    see fertility
  blouse
    Ecuador, 164, 167
    Gujarati, 86
    Rabari, 73
    Tai Dam, 193, 197, 201, 203
  borrowed, 143, 169
  chemise, 131, 177
  gloves, 2, 132–4, 142, 152, 211
  jacket, 54, 57 60, 62–3, 152, 154
  kimono, 42, 44–7, 49–50
  mantle, 160, 163, 176
    shoulder wrap, 170
  parka, 23, 27–9, 37n7
  robe, 54–6, 60–1, 197
    engagement, 63
  sari, *gharcholu* and *panetar*, 2, 85–92
  sash, 61, 63, 193, 201, 204
    obi, 49
  shawls, 165, 176
  skirt
    Ecuador, 167
    Greece, 138n13
    Korea, 54–5, 60–2
    Peru, 169
    Rabari, 73

Swazi, 97, 100
Tai Dam, 193, 197–8, 200–1, 203–4
theme wedding, 211
trousseau, 74–5
use after wedding
  stored, 19
  worn, 88, 92, 98
veilcloth, 72, 78
  see also veil
vest, 177, 211
see also headwear; footwear

candle, 134
  ceremony, 43, 48, 54
capping the bride, 173, 182–3, 186
carnivalesque
  see theme weddings
changes in wedding dress, 3
  Alberta, Canada, 10
  Andes 157, 162–9
  Gujarati, 85
  Iñupiaq, 32–6
  Korea, 63–5
  Tai Dam, 201–2
  Slavic, 173, 182–7
  Swazi, 95, 98–104
Chicago, Illinois, 3, 173, 181–7, 211
  see Czechs, Polish, Slavs, Slovak
childbearer
  see fertility
civil ceremony, 150, 167
colonialism
  England/British, 98
  France/French, 105
  Spain/Spanish/Hispanic, 157, 160–2,
    166–7, 170
color
  black
    auspicious, 200
    belt, and red, green, yellow, 113
    boots, 57
    canopy, lace, 170
    cloth, and yellow stripe, 111
    crown, sateen, 59
    feathers, 98
    hat, 57
    headband, 57
    jacket, 197

natural environment, symbol of, 111
privacy, symbol of, 198
robe, 197
skirt, 167
Tai Dam (or, Black Tai), 191
theme wedding costumes, 210–11
veil, and white with red trim, 142
blue
  Alberta, Canada, dress, 6
  blue bead, 133–4, 139n15, 143
    see Apotropaic, blue bead
  Ecuador, poncho, 164, 166
  England, bridal gown, 147
  Hindu, assoc. with Krishna, 87–8
  Iñupiaq, qupak, 33
  Korea
    jacket, 55
    robe, 58
    skirt, 54–5
  Soviet Union, bridal dress, 152
green
  auspicious, embroidery, 76
  belt, and red, green, yellow, 113
  cord, head, 100
  natural environment, symbol of, 111
  rainbow, symbol of, 120n8
  robe, 54, 56, 60–1, 64
  sari border, 87–89
  sash, 193, 201, 203–4
  theme wedding costume, 211
  wreath, head, 177
ivory,
  apron, 185
  bridal dress, 143, 147, 151–2
  suit, bridal, 6
orange,
  rainbow, symbol of, 120n8
  sari, 88
pink,
  auspicious, 76
  backcloth, 165
  bridal dress, 147
  jacket, 62
  skirt, 63
purple,
  auspicious, 120n8
  ribbons, hair, 59
  robe, 58

veil, 61
red
  auspicious, 76, 120n8
  blood, fertility, symbol of, 111
    see fertility
  belt, with green, yellow, black, 113
  face cloth, groom, 117
  fertility, symbol of, 111
  head cloth, 109, 111
  headdress, 142
  joy, symbol of, 142
  makeup, 62
  ochre, 95
  ribbons, hair, 59
  robe, 54, 56; queen's, 61
  sari, and white, 2, 86–7
  scarf, 105
  skirt, 60
  soil, for hair, 96
saffron, 87
turquoise, 6, 169
white
  atikluk, 33
  backcloth, with pink, 165
  blouse, 167, 197
  bridal dress
    Ait Khabbash, 105, 107
    Alberta, Canada, 6, 9–11
    Andes, 164
    Ecuador, 166–7
    England, 151
    Iñupiaq, 31
    Japan, 45
    Russia, 143
    Slavic, 182
  hat, groom, 170
  headband, 99, 102
  kimono, 45, 48
  pants, groom, 170
  poncho, and blue check, groom, 164
  purity, symbol of, 2, 13, 117, 142
  ribbons, on dress, 182
  sari, 86–7, 89
  shirt, groom, 29, 47
  shoes, bride, 133, 152
  socks, bride and groom, 62
  veil
    see veil

Victorian/Western, 2, 44, 164, 166–7,
    202–3, 207–8
  see also Western influence
  virginity, 182
commercial wedding
  clothing
    see ready-made
  hall, 42–3, 63
  hotel, 42–3
  "industrial complex," 11–13
  packaged wedding, 45–6
  reception, 42–3
  salon, 185
  shops, 126, 131, 138n9, 214–15
Constructivism (Functionalism), 144, 148
  see also Soviet Union
Czechs, 3, 173–80
  see Chicago, Polish, Slavs, Slovak

dowry,
  Bolivia, 170
  Greece, 128
  India, 3, 67–82
    brideprice, 73
    bridewealth, 70, 73
  Korea, 56
  Swaziland, 94–5, 98
  Tai Dam, 192

Ecuador, 2, 157, 159, 161, 163–8
engagement,
  ceremony
    Korea, 54
    Tai Dam, 200
    India, Rabari, 71–2
    Japan, 42
    Korea, 54, 63
  ring
    Greece, 124, 132
    Japan, 49
    Tai Dam, 201
  Tai Dam, 197, 200
England, 2, 141–8, 150–2, 154–6
  see also Colonialism, Soviet Union
ethnic (cultural) identity, wedding as, 1
  Ait Khabbash, 106
  Ecuador, 167
  Iñupiaq, 35

Tai Dam, 192–5, 203–4
evil eye
  see Apotropaic
exchanges of cloth and dress
  Bolivia, 170
  Gujarati, India, 94–5
  Inca, pre-Hispanic, 160–62
    Andes, 163
  Korea, 54, 63
  Peru, 169
  Rabari, dowry, 73
  Tai Dam, 198–200

fabric, wedding dress
  brocade, 16, 89
  camel, 113
  camelid (alpaca, llama, vicuña), 158, 160
  chiffon, 143, 147, 151, 154
  coca leaf, groom's pouch, 170
  cotton, 67, 89, 154 (pique), 165
  cowhide, 97
  cowtail, shredded, groom, 98
  crepe, 16, 154
  crepe-de-chine, 146, 148, 151
  gauze,
    bridal head covering, 60
    groom's fan, 58
  georgette, 147–8
  goatskin, 96, 100, 113
  gold, 160
  handwoven, 169–70, 197, 202
  linen, 176
  marquisette, 145
  moosehide, 33
  oxhide, 97
  ramie, 53, 62
  satin
    Alberta, Canada, 16
    Iñupiaq, 23, 31–3
    England/Soviet Union, 146–7
    theme wedding, 210–11
  sheepskin, 29 (mouton), 113
  silk
    England and Soviet Union, 143–4,
      147–8, 151–3
    Greece, 124, 132–3
    India, Gujarati, 86–90
    Korea, 52, 57, 61

Morocco, Ait Khabbash, 108–9, 117
  Swaziland, 101
  Tai Dam, 192, 194, 200–1
  Swiss batiste, 145
  synthetic, 73–4, 77–99, 102
    polyester, 101, 202
  taffeta, 132, 152
  terrycloth, 99–100
  tree bark, bridal headband, 96
  tulle, 151–2, 211, 214
  velvet, 16, 32, 211–14
  wool, 66, 73, 152, 169
    Ait Khabbash, 105, 113
    purity, symbol of, Rabari, 77–9
fertility, bride
  Ait Khabbash, 100–4, 106–7, 118–19
    headdress, fertility protection, 110
    red cloth, reproduction, 111
  Bolivia, 170–1
  childbearer, 2
  India, Rabari embroidery, 73
    see ornamentation
  Japan, 48
  Poland, 180–81
  symbol of fertility
    apron, Slavic, 177
    bat, Japan, 63
    belt, Ait Khabbash, 105, 113, 120n10
      see also bridalwear
    black wrist string, Tai Dam, 200
    hair
      length, Ait Khabbash, 107
      Slavic, 178–80
      see also hairstyle, bride
    horseshoe, England, 142–3
    orange blossom, England, 142
    rainbow, Ait Khabbash, 111, 120n8
    red, Ait Khabbash, 111
    shawl motifs, Slavic, 176–7
    skirt, Bolivia, 170–1
    wreath, removal of, Slovak, 177
  Tai Dam, 200
flower
  bouquet, bridal, 63, 133, 142
    throwing, 134, 143, 185
  boutonniere, groom, 131, 184
  flower girl, 32 myrtle, romance, 142, 146
  orange blossom, fertility, 142, 146

peony, wealth, 61
rose, red, passionate love, 142
rosemary wreath, 179
silk, 59, 152–3
wax, 136, 145, 148, 152
wrist corsage, 134
footwear, bride
  boots, 169
  henna, 113–14, 117–18
  kamiks (skin boots), 25, 33fig2.4
  pumps, 154
  sandals
    Inca
      pre-Hispanic, 158, 160 (grass), 161
        (ceremony)
      Ecuador, 167
      Peru, 169
    Swaziland, 98, 102
  shoes
    England/Soviet Union, 150, 154
    Greece, 133
    Korea, 44, 46, 62
    saved after wedding, 133
    Swaziland, 98, 102
    upturn toes, 62
  socks, 62
footwear, groom
  boots, 169
  henna and white cloth, 117–18
  kamiks (skin boots), 27, 33fig2.4
  needle in right shoe, 118
  shoes, yellow, 118
  socks, 215
  tights, 214–5

Greece, 2, 123–39
groom's wear
  atikluk, 23, 29, 31–3, 35–6, 37n7
  dark suit, 29, 129, 201, 207, 217
  dressing the groom, 114–18
  cape
    hooded, 28, 115
    shredded cow tails, 98
  fan, 58
  girdle, 58
  gown, hooded, 115
  head band, horsetail hair, 57
  jacket, 58, 169, 197, 211

kilt, 207, 216–17
poncho
  blue, 166
  blue-and-white check, 164
robe
  green, 56
  purple, 58
  red, 56
scarf, 72, 105–6
shoulder belt, 117
smock, 72, 82n5
sword, 72
tie, 129, 200
  bowtie, 211
trousers, 58, 72, 82n5, 197
tuxedo, 201, 207, 210–11, 217n3
uniform
  Chosun Dynasty official, 57–8
  warrior court, 72

hairstyle and additions, bride
  animal fat, 96
  beehive, 95, 99, 102
  bun, 197
  braids, 59, 107
  chignon, 59
  clay, 96
  extension, 47
  henna, 113–14
    see Apotropaic
  length, 107, 180
  middle part, 59
  perfumed herbs, 107
  pigtail, 180
  soil dust, brown and red, 96
  symbolic, 178–80
    see also fertility, hair
  Western style, Japan, 47
  wig, 45, 99
hairstyle, groom
  braid 164
  middle part and knot, 57–8
  ponytail, 167
handfasting
  see religion, Wicca
handmade wedding dress, 5–21, 150
  apron by godmother, 184
  bride makes, 153, 209

custom-made, 209
dressmaker, 20, 153
family makes, 33
mother makes, 153
seamstresses, 27, 29, 37, 131
Tai Dam, 200
headwear, bride
barrette, 96
canopy, black lace, 170
cap, 173, 177–80, 182–3, 186–7
cord, green with tassle, 110
crown, 54–5, 124–5, 135–7, 177
  with amber, coral, jade, pearls, 59
  saved after wedding, 136
gauze silk, 61
gilt birds, butterflies, 59
hairpin, 59, 96, 197
hat
  bowler, 169
  Breton, 155
  cotton, 45
  fedora, 165, 169
  felt, 148, 152
  flat, 169
  symbolic, European, 175, 182
  straw, 148, 151–2, 165
  top, 211
headband
  tree bark, 96
  white, 99
headdress, 45, 60, 108–11, 158
  aâbroq, 108–11
  pendant and silver chain, 109
kerchief, 175, 183
lace, black, 170
net, 175
pin, silver, 197
ribbon, decorated, 59 scarf, 105
shawl, 175
wig, 44
wreath, 136, 177, 179
  floral, 178
  removal, 177
    see fertility
  veil
    see veil
wimple, 175
headwear, groom

cap, knit stocking, 170
crowns, 124–5, 135–7
  stored after wedding, 136
face covering, 117
feathers, black, 98
hat
  bamboo, lacquered, 57
  fedora, 166, 169
  felt, white, 170
  horse hair, 57
  silk, stiff, side flaps, 57
  sombrero, 166, 210–11
  top, 210–1
headband, horsetail hair, 57
turban, 72, 82, 117

Inca, 2, 157–72 *passim*
India, 2–4, 67–84, 85–92
influences on wedding dress
  church/religion, 10
  community, 3–4
    Canada, Alberta, 8, 10, 14, 20
    Iñupiaq, 25
    Rabari
      dowry ban, 68–71
      honor, 77
    family, 9, 90
Iñupiaq (Inuit), 2, 23–36 *passim*
Iowa, Des Moines, 3, 191–204 *passim*
  see also Laos; Tai Dam; Vietnam

Japan, Osaka, 3–4, 39–51
jewelry, bride, 87
  amber,
    chocker, 112
    in crown, 59
  anklet, seed pods, 98
  borrowed, 133
  bracelets, 62
    bead, 97
    seed, 97
    silver, 112–13, 120n9, 197, 200
  coins, 139n13
  coral, in crown, 59
  cord, green, 109
  diamond, 49, 124, 132, 201
    see also engagement
  earplugs

gold, silver, 157
  wooden, 97
earrings, 62, 64n3, 102, 165
  diamond, 132
  silver, 197
fibulae, 112–13
  see Apotropaic
gold
  band, finger, 134
  chain, 203–4
  gilt birds, butterfiles, 59
  ring, 197
  stick pin, 160
ivory bangles, 78
jade, in crown, 59
necklace, 63, 102, 165
pearls, 211
  see also ornamentation on bridalwear
  in crown, 59
pendant, 63, 110
pin, 101
ring, 65, 124, 134–6, 139
  amber, 65
  bearer, 33
  borrowed, 133
  engagement, 49, 124, 201
  jade, 65
silver
  bracelets, 112–13, 120n9, 197, 200
  chain, 76, 101, 112, 192, 200–1, 203
    and pendant, 110
    waist, 193, 201, 203
  crown, 136
  earrings, 197
  hairpin, 197
  pin, stick, 170
  ring, 65
  wristwatch, 102
jewelry, groom
  gold
    bracelet, 58
    necklace, 58
    ring, 134–36, 139n16
    silver crown, 136

Kenya, 4
Korea, 2, 53–65

lace, bridalwear
  apron, 184
  atikluk, 23, 31–3
  collar, 207
  canopy, black, 170
  dress, 7, 211
  hair cover, 175
  Irish theme wedding, 216
  ornamentation, 79, 144, 147, 152, 154
  shawl, binding, 176
  veil, 182
Laos, 191–204 *passim*
  see also Iowa, Des Moines; Tai Dam

make-up, bride
  artist, 46, 49
  beeswax, 62
  clay and fat, 95
  eyelashes, fake, 47
  henna
    face, 105
    hands and feet, (and groom), 113–14, 117–18
  paper circle, red, 62
  powder, 62
  red ochre, 95
  rouge, circle of, 62
Minnesota, 4, 210–11, 214, 216
  see also theme wedding
Morocco, 2, 4, 105–21 *passim*
motherhood
  see fertility

ornamentation, on bridalwear
  beads, 146
    blue, 133–4
  bows, 145
  buttons, silver butterfly, 197, 203
  embroidery
    Ecuador, 167
    Greece, 138n13
    Gujarati, 88
    Korea, 52, 60
      cranes, 58
    Rabari, 67–82 *passim*
  flowers, silk or wax, 145
  gold-leaf imprints, 53–4, 59–60
  grass, 95

herbs and incense, bags of, 110
jari/zari (metallic braid), 78, 79, 86, 88
    see also Apotropaic; fertility
knot, 101–02
metallic braid
    see jari/zari, above
myrtle and orange blossom, 146
pearl beads, 59, 146–7, 151
    see also jewelry
ribbon, 145
seeds, 95
sequins,
    heddress, 110
    sandals, 166
    skirt, 166
silver, 79, 88, '97
    see also jewelry
tassel, green, 111
tie-dye (tie-and-dye), 73, 86–9, 91–2
water buffalo horn, groom, 58

Peru, 2, 157–71 *passim*
Polish/Poles, 172, 180, 183–4, 186, 188
    see Chicago, Czechs, Slavs, Slovak

Rabari, 67–84 *passim*
ready-made (ready-to-wear), 18, 136,
    209
    "factory-made", 183
reception, after wedding
    Greece, 125, 132, 134
    Iñupiaq, 32
    Japan, Osaka, 42–3, 50
    theme wedding, 202, 214–16
religion
    ancestor worship, 193
        cultural group
            Inca, 156
            Iñupiaq, Alaska, 26, 29, 32, 34–5
            Japan, Osaka, 43–4, 49
            Slavic, 174, 177
            Swaziland, 93, 99
            Wisconsin, 214
    Christian
        Denomination
            Catholic, 123, 174–8, 209
            Orthodox, 122–4, 134–8, 174
            Protestant, 123, 173, 210, 211

Confusianism, 64n3
        Hindu, 71, 74, 80, 82n2, 85–7, 90
        indigenous beliefs, 93
        Islam, 76, 106, 115, 118
        Jain, 85–7, 90
        Shinto, 39, 43–5, 48, 49
        Wicca, 217n1
            handfasting, 207, 209
rented (hired) dress
    Ecuador, 165
    England, 153
    Greece, 136
    Japan, Osaka, 44
    theme wedding, 209–10, 214
royalty
    England
        Princess Mary, 146
        Queen Victoria, 182
            see also Victorian influence
    Inca, 160
    Korea, 64
    Morocco, 120n11
    Swaziland, 98, 101

Slavs/Slavic, 173–89 *passim*
Slovak, 3, 175–88 *passim*
Soviet Union/Russia, 2, 141–56 *passim*
Swaziland/Swazi, 2, 93–104 *passim*

Tai Dam, 3, 191–205 *passim*
    see also Iowa, Des Moines; Laos;
        Thailand; Vietnam
Thailand, 191, 203
    see Tai Dam
theme wedding, 207–18
    carnivalesque, 207–9, 211–14, 215–17
    web site, 207, 216
tie-dye
    see ornamention

undergarment, bride
    drawers, 61
    petticoat, 47, 54, 62, 86, 100, 138n13
    slip, 100
United States
    Alaska, 23–38
    Euroamerican
        see Western influence on dress

immigration from
  Alberta, Canada, 8
immigration to
  Slavic, 173–89 *passim*; Tai Dam,
    191–205 *passim*
theme weddings, 207–18
wedding customs
  exported from, 124
  imported to, 181–7, 201–4

veil
  Ecuador, ten-foot, 167
  England/Soviet Union, compared, 143,
    145–6, 148, 150
  face not covered, 125, 131, 138n8
  groom's, 58
  Korea, use of Western, 63
  modesty, symbol of, 72–3, 77–8
  protection, symbol of, 2, 142
  Queen Victoria, 182
  silk gauze, purple, 61
  unveiled, 10, 173

veilcloth, 72
virginity, symbol of, 10, 182
Victorian influence, 2, 15, 142, 182, 208
  Osaka, Japan, 44, 49–50
  see also Western influence on dress
Vietnam, 3, 191–3, 195–6, 200–3, 205n3
  see also Iowa, Des Moines; Tai Dam

Western/American/Euroamerican influence
    on dress
  American or Euroamerican, 164, 166–7,
    207
  cultures influenced
    Alaska, Iñupiaq, 28–9, 34
    Japan, Osaka, 44, 49–50
    Korea, 54, 61, 63
    Slavic, 181
    Swaziland, 98–104
    Tai Dam, 197, 200, 202–3
    see also Victorian influence
Wisconsin, 183, 210–11, 214
  see also theme wedding